REVOLUTION AND DEFEAT

Revolution and Defeat

THE STORY OF THE GREEK COMMUNIST PARTY

D. GEORGE KOUSOULAS

With a Foreword by
C. M. WOODHOUSE

LONDON
OXFORD UNIVERSITY PRESS
NEW YORK TORONTO
1965

Oxford University Press, Amen House, London E.C.4

GLASGOW NEW YORK TORONTO MELBOURNE WELLINGTON
BOMBAY CALCUTTA MADRAS KARACHI LAHORE DACCA
CAPE TOWN SALISBURY NAIROBI IBADAN ACCRA
KUALA LUMPUR HONG KONG

*Printed in Great Britain by Richard Clay (The Chaucer Press), Ltd.,
Bungay, Suffolk*

Foreword

To be what we used to call a *koukoués*—a member of the KKE or Communist Party of Greece—requires attributes which are rare in a Greek. There have never been very many of them. Occasionally the patriot and the idealist may join the Party in times of crisis; so may the man who is 'fed up', in moments of frustration or despair. But these never stay long. To be a life-long Communist in Greece one must be either very naïve or very unscrupulous; and it does not require much insight to guess which of the two is likely to win and retain control of the Party's leadership. This is the sorry tale, with the same cycle of crisis and intrigue repeated again and again, which Professor Kousoulas unfolds in his authoritative and scholarly book.

I call it 'authoritative' with good reason. For a short but crucial period—from 1942 to 1945—I could claim to be an authority on the KKE myself. My knowledge of their character, intentions, and methods was derived from living cheek by jowl with them and with other Greeks of all kinds and classes during the German occupation. I recorded the results and impressions of personal experience in a book, *Apple of Discord*, upon which the sceptical reader will observe that Professor Kousoulas relies a good deal in Part III. But he does not do so uncritically. He supplements it with documentary evidence to which I could have had no access at the time; and the point that I want to make is that the evidence of different sources for those years dovetails into a coherent picture, which in its turn forms a consistent whole with the earlier picture displayed in Parts I and II, and with the final cataclysm of Part IV. Again and again, in reading this book, I have come upon information entirely new to me which exactly tallies with, or confirms, or explains more fully, things which I experienced or observed but failed to understand at the time. Nowhere have I come across a conclusion or an inference which has led me to say that either I or Professor Kousoulas must be totally wrong.

It is perhaps because the Greek Communists are so alien to Greece that I do not feel myself at a disadvantage, compared with a Greek, in understanding them. Why are they so alien?

They are required to be everything that a Greek is not. A Greek is patriotic, religious, emotional, loyal to his friends, hot-blooded but quick to forget a quarrel; he is loaded with *philó-timo*, for which 'self-respect' is a feeble translation; however poor, he has a strong sense of private property; and he is passionately devoted to democracy. Of all the doctrinaire follies which Communism has imposed on the KKE, none was more fatal than the 'national question', that is to say, the proposition that Greek Macedonia should be detached to form part of an independent Macedonia or a unit in a Slav federation. And of all the nonsense in Communist dogmatism, perhaps none seemed more ludicrous to the ordinary Greek than the notion that the Party is always, by definition, infallibly right. When a Greek disagrees with his political party, he leaves it, or breaks it up and forms a new one. When a Communist does so, he invites the Party to destroy him. The Greeks, naturally, have a word for this kind of thing: in fact, they have several.

A glance at the biographical notes at the end of this book will show the seemingly endless repetition of the pattern. Every name in the list has been 'denounced' by the Party sooner or later, including the arch-denunciator, Zachariades himself. The list could be greatly extended without adding a single name altogether immune from denunciation. Most of them were personally known to me in the 1940s. There was the brutal, dynamic, black-bearded Aris Velouchiotis, who used to say that he would rather execute ten innocent men than let one guilty one go free, and frequently proved that he meant it. There was the glib, smooth, lapsed bourgeois Karayiorgis; there was the 'Old Man', George Siantos, whom my American colleague, Major Gerald K. Wines, likened to a rural mail-carrier in the States; there was the wild-eyed fanatic Markos Vafiades, always living furiously on his nerves; and many others. All or most of them are dead, many of them at each other's hands.

Inevitably the question arises, as it arose about the leaders of Nazi Germany, how did such men ever impose themselves on their people at all? The answers are many and complex, and they will be found set out with scrupulous fairness by Professor Kousoulas. The German occupation, the short-sightedness of the political world of Athens, the inconsistent policies of the British and American governments, the ambitious machinations of Stalin and Tito (though at cross-purposes with each other)—all these carry their very different degrees of responsibility. Only the Greek people may be acquitted, except perhaps of failing to see the menace in time. For as Professor Kousoulas points out, most of the party history with which his story is concerned took place 'in the twilight', ignored by all but a minority of 'insiders'. Unfortunately, it was an energetic, determined, skilful, and unscrupulous minority; twice at least— in 1944 and 1948, and perhaps also in 1936—it came near to being an overwhelming minority.

The defeat of the Communist revolution was of course first and foremost the work of the Greek people. But they were not alone. The British and Americans made indispensable contributions, after living down earlier mistakes. The defection of Tito from the Soviet block was crucial at a decisive moment. Those of us who took part in the struggle, trying to achieve the dual aim of liberating Greece from Nazi occupation without surrendering her to Communism, would claim no special credit, because we were fighting for something of which we felt ourselves to be a part, not simply lending a hand from the outside. I knew this to be true of everyone who formed part of the military mission which I commanded in the Greek mountains, whatever their nationality: British, American, Greek, Polish, and many others. My proudest memory is of being called by my Greek subordinates *dhikós mas*: 'one of us'. Many of them I never met or even knew by name until after the war; many of them I have still never met, though I know all that I need to know about them. It has been a pleasure to learn from this book that among them was a young Greek—he can have been no more than a boy at the time—who is now an American professor, called Dimitrios George Kousoulas.

C. M. W.

Note to the Reader

The Greek Communist Party (KKE) enjoys the dubious distinction of having applied in the course of its history practically all forms of political and revolutionary warfare. From strikes and demonstrations to electoral coalitions, clandestine subversion, and guerrilla operations, the KKE's record in the inter-war period and the turbulent war and post-war years can provide the student of world affairs with a wealth of information and insight of more than mere historical significance.

Two major factors have played a formative role in the evolution of the Greek Communist Party: the fundamental organizational and ideological concepts which form the foundation of any Communist Party; and the Greek stage on which the KKE had to perform. These two factors were not always in harmony with each other. On the contrary, there was friction between them, affecting the attitudes of the party members and throwing the party again and again into spiralling crises.

The KKE has acted on a narrow stage—the microcosm of a small country perched at the southernmost promontory of the Balkan peninsula. But its internal spasms, its tactics, its drive for power, its aspirations, crises, victories, and defeats reflect the broader volcanic convulsions emanating from the centre of the Communist world.

Part I of this study, under the title 'The Early Years', deals with the formative period of the Greek Communist Party, its tortured relationship with the Comintern, the incessant quarrels of its leaders, its frustrated efforts to escape the isolation imposed by public indifference, and the stigma of its 'Macedonian' policies. As with the childhood of a human being, the record of the KKE's early years may not be as dramatic or absorbing as its story in the years of maturity. Yet it is an indispensable introduction to its later history.

Part II covers the efforts of its Comintern-installed leadership to expand the party's influence by exploiting the country's economic difficulties in the early thirties, its unsuccessful attempt to foment revolution when in the middle thirties the Greek people lost confidence in, and respect for, their parliamentary institutions, and then the disintegration of the KKE's organization under the effective measures of the Metaxas dictatorship.

Parts III and IV deal with the most dramatic period in the party's history, the years of the Occupation, the December Revolution, and then the guerrilla war of 1947–9, the collapse of the rebellion, and the years of frustration behind the Iron Curtain.

D. G. K.

Howard University
   Washington D.C.
    1964

Contents

Maps

Part I
THE EARLY YEARS

1. The Convulsions of Affiliation

The conference at the Piraeus Hotel

On the morning of 5 November 1918 small groups of shabbily-dressed men began to filter into the lobby of the Piraeus Hotel in Athens for the first nation-wide meeting of Greek Socialists. Unlike many other European countries, Greece did not have a Socialist party with deep roots and traditions. Being a small agricultural country, she lacked in the 1910s and even in the 1920s the 'class basis' for a viable Socialist organization. But under the overpowering impression of the Bolshevik revolution, the few Marxist groups felt it their duty to provide Greece with her own Socialist party.

The delegates who met at the Piraeus Hotel discussed a great number of topics and passed impressively-worded resolutions. For example, the resolution on foreign affairs dealt with an amazing variety of subjects and offered an equally amazing variety of solutions: abolition of secret diplomacy, the freedom of all seas and the opening of all straits, an international customs union and an international parliament as the economic and political foundation of the League of Nations. The conference further advocated the establishment of a Balkan Democratic Federation, and the transformation of the Greek state into 'a federation of autonomous vilayets [districts] organized democratically so that the nationalities of the East will achieve an autonomous status and thus enter the Balkan Federation'.[1]

The above statements represented the views of the majority; but in true democratic fashion a minority resolution was also

---

[1] *To KKE apo to 1918 eos to 1931*, Vol. I (Athens, 1947), pp. 3–8; hereinafter cited as *To KKE, 1918–1931*.

published in *Rizospastis*—the liberal newspaper, which by the time of the conference had become closely associated with Socialist circles. The minority resolution revealed strong nationalist tendencies, then rather unusual for Socialists. It dealt almost exclusively with the redistribution of territories in the Balkans and the Middle East. According to this resolution, Turkey would be reduced to a small state 'in the centre of Asia Minor, with the port of Alexandretta as a free outlet to the sea'.[2]

In the economic and social sector the conference demanded the following benefits for the 'working classes':

Complete freedom of assembly, association, etc.; complete freedom of the press, without any censorship or limitations; complete assurance of personal liberty, compensation for any person detained illegally, inviolability of the home; an eight-hour working day, protective measures for the workers, prohibition of night work for women and children, and the abolition of any law curbing the right to strike.[3]

The conference at the Piraeus Hotel established the Greek Socialist Labour Party (Sosialistikon Erghatikon Komma Ellados, SEK for short), and designated itself as the First Congress of the newly-founded party. The resolutions and the platform of the First Congress, as well as the Charter of the SEK, showed no trace of Leninist influence; the Charter, in particular, could have been that of any democratic party. The founders of the SEK were well-intentioned idealists with a commendable, albeit unrealistic, aspiration to rid the country of all social ills. In the following years the party they founded became, step by step, through crises, purges, and intrigues, the present-day Greek Communist Party.

Under the impact of the Third International

The success of the October Revolution in Russia had exerted a magnetic influence on the Greek Socialists even before the establishment of the SEK; yet, at the beginning, this influence was of a somewhat sentimental nature. The Greek Socialists had a rather vague and confused understanding of Leninism. Their source of wisdom was still the literature of the Second International.

The establishment of the Third International in March 1919,

---

[2] *To KKE, 1918–1931*, p. 7.   [3] Ibid., p. 7.

as the new centre of the international Marxist movement, had a dramatic effect on the young party which, through its association with the Socialist Federation of Salonika, had an inherited affiliation with the Second International. The party's international affiliation became a basic issue when the National Council of the SEK—a body meeting between the yearly Congresses—convened for the first time in May 1919. In spite of the heated arguments aired at the meetings, most participants had a rather vague and uncertain comprehension of the real issues involved. This was hardly surprising, since the Communist International had been formed only two months earlier, and the situation in Russia was still unsettled.

After a long and involved discussion the Council decided to sever all formal ties with the Second International but voted down a proposal to join the Third International immediately. The Central Committee of the party was merely instructed to 'prepare the ground' for the party's adherence to the new organization. At the same time the Council declared that such adherence 'should not prevent the Party from maintaining relations with those parties of the Second International which remain faithful to Socialist principles'.[4] Clearly, the Greek Socialists viewed affiliation with the Comintern as not being necessarily 'exclusive'.

When the deliberations of the Council came to an end two trends were clearly visible, gradually taking shape within the party. One group was for temporizing, uncertain as to where the party's allegiance should lie. The other was arguing strongly in favour of direct affiliation with the Communist International. Greece's young Socialist Party was already entering its first crisis.

A precipitous step to join the Comintern

Because of the controversy over the party's international affiliation, the Second Congress, which under party rules should have convened in the autumn of 1919, was tacitly postponed until the spring of 1920. During the winter months of 1920 the gradual consolidation of the Bolshevik régime in Russia strengthened the position of the pro-Comintern faction within the SEK. Those who opposed affiliation with the Comintern, having nothing positive to offer, were constantly losing ground.

---

[4] *To KKE, 1918–1931*, pp. 16–17.

When the Second Congress of the SEK finally convened on 5 April 1920 in Athens the question of formally joining the Third International held a prominent place on the agenda.

The discussion revealed that most of the delegates were rather confused about the nature of the Comintern. Even N. Dimitratos, the Secretary of the Central Committee, seriously argued that 'the Third International is not an organization but a concept'.[5] To be sure, the founders of the Comintern never thought of it as merely a 'concept'. This ignorance played into the hands of those determined to bring the Greek Socialist movement into the Comintern fold. Under their insistent pressure and adroit manoeuvring, the Congress almost unanimously voted in favour of 'organizational affiliation' with the Third International, and accepted 'all its principles and resolutions'.[6] With this decision, the embryonic party entered the road which was to bring it ultimately under the aegis of Moscow.

The Congress declared itself 'in favour of a centralized organization of the Party' and approved a new Charter in line with this decision. Under the new Charter the Central Committee became 'the high command and the executive body of the Party, possessing all party powers'.[7] The title of the party was significantly modified: the word *kommounistikon* was added in parenthesis. A May Day proclamation published a few days later in *Rizospastis* urged the 'proletarians of all Greece' to cheer the 'World Soviet Republic', and branded any absence from the May Day demonstrations as 'desertion from the struggle' and 'treason'.[8] In another proclamation the Central Committee declared that the party expected 'all its members to obey its rules in the way of united and disciplined soldiers, its main and essential aim being the final overthrow of the bourgeoisie by all possible means'.[9] With remarkable speed the party was adopting Communist phraseology.

The advocates of affiliation with the Comintern must have felt quite confident, even before the Congress, because one month earlier, in March 1920, they sent Dimosthenis Ligdopoulos, a young university student, to Moscow as the party representative to the forthcoming Second World Congress of the Comintern. Ligdopoulos was authorized by the Central Committee to request financial assistance from the Comintern,

[5] *To KKE, 1918–1931*, p. 64. [6] Ibid., p. 73.
[7] Ibid., p. 75. [8] Ibid., p. 83. [9] Ibid., pp. 83–84.

as the coffers of the fledgling party were practically empty. In October the Central Committee officially announced that 'at the meeting of 21 September, Zinoviev, the President of the Communist International, announced that the Communist Party of Greece has been unanimously accepted'.[10] The announcement had a triumphant air. For the first time the party was called the 'Greek Communist Party' (Kommounistikon Komma Ellados), although there had been no official action by any appropriate party organ to assume this title.

The willingness of the Greek party to line up with the Comintern was appreciated in Moscow. Ligdopoulos was given five thousand dollars in gold as the Comintern's first contribution to its Greek 'section'. Orion Alexakis, a Russian-born Greek, was appointed official representative of the Comintern to Greece. The two young Communists hired a caïque to cross the Black Sea from Odessa. They never reached the opposite coast alive. On the night of 20 October 1920 they were slain by the crew of the caïque and their bodies, together with the Communist literature Ligdopoulos was taking to Greece, were thrown overboard. The sailors kept the gold, but before long they were apprehended by the Soviet authorities of Novorosisk and were hanged.[11] The first contact of the Greek party with the Comintern had ended tragically; future missions had to be planned more carefully.

Affiliation causes more trouble

The decision of the Greek Socialists to join the Comintern was the product of a strange mixture of ignorance, naïve enthusiasm, and shrewd calculation. The party was small, its political influence negligible. It lacked tradition and deep roots among the people. Operating on its own, it appeared as a group of noisy but unknown politicians whose claim to power bordered on the ridiculous. By joining an international organization such as the Comintern, the Greek 'Socialists' expected to share in its prestige and power. The party could thus become the local projection of a mighty international force. Its inherent weaknesses would be offset by the strength borrowed from the international proletarian movement. Very few even among the

[10] *Ergatikos Agon*, 11 October 1920.
[11] El. A. Stavrides, *Ta Paraskinia tou KKE* (Athens, 1953), p. 42; also *Rizospastis*, 20 October 1945.

leaders of the party realized at the outset how heavy a burden affiliation with the Comintern would entail. All were willing to accept the benefits of association with the international Communist movement, but few were prepared to accept the regimentation which was the hallmark of the Leninist party. When its members learned about the Twenty-One Conditions of Admission which had been adopted by the Second World Congress of the Comintern, the small party was shaken to its roots. The Greek Socialists who had voted in April 1920 for the 'organizational' affiliation of their party with the Comintern could hardly have anticipated that three months later the Comintern would set up one of the most centralized international organizations ever created.[12]

All efforts to convene the Third Regular Congress for the purpose of 'weeding out all elements which continue to act in the spirit of the Second International', in accord with one of the Twenty-One Conditions, foundered on the opposition of many party members who were shocked by the brutal demands for subordination contained in those Conditions. On 8 August 1921 the Central Committee broke off relations with the owner of *Rizospastis*, and three weeks later they launched a fierce attack against the Independent Communist Youth of Athens for urging the youth organizations to leave the party. The SEK(k) was split wide open. The Third Regular Congress had to be postponed indefinitely. It materialized six years later, in March 1927. By then, the party was safely within the Comintern fold; most of the old leaders had been driven away, while a new crop of dedicated and ambitious Communists had taken hold of the reins of the party.

Nikolaos Zachariades, who in 1931 was appointed by Moscow to the leadership of the KKE, wrote in his booklet *Theses gia tin Istoria tou KKE* (Theses for the History of the KKE), with reference to the party's early years: 'The revolutionary ideology had at that time as its standard-bearers the petty-bourgeois intellectuals who were driven to the Left by the revolutionary wave of that time.'[13] Zachariades implied that the party leaders of the early years lacked the genuine Bolshevik mentality, an

---

[12] Cf. text of 'Twenty-One Conditions' in *Theses and Statutes of the Second World Congress* (Moscow, Publishing Office of the C.I., 1920), pp. 26–32; hereinafter cited as *Theses, Second World Congress*.

[13] N. Zachariades, *Theses gia tin Istoria tou KKE*. (Athens, Central Committee, KKE, 1945), p. 29; hereinafter cited as *Theses*.

indispensable quality which assured unquestioning submission to the dictates of Moscow. To a certain extent he was right. To the founders of Greek Socialism and the early leaders of the SEK(k), Bolshevism was something new and unfamiliar, while most of them cherished nationalistic and social concepts impressed upon them since childhood. N. Zachariades, a trainee of the Communist School of the KUTV, was particularly familiar with the essence of Leninism. He had been taught that a Communist party should achieve absolute control over its members through 'identification' and 'involvement'. The party was expected to be a 'militant' organization, an 'army of professional revolutionaries'. A party member ought to be emotionally dedicated, physically mobile, and fully prepared to sacrifice time, career, and life itself, faithfully following the directions given by the supreme hierarchy of the movement. Zachariades himself was not handicapped by so-called petty-bourgeois, nationalistic prejudices. Born in Asia Minor under the Ottoman rule, he had come to Greece as a young refugee. But unlike most other refugees from Asia Minor, he felt no patriotic attachment to Greece and none, of course, to the country of his birth. He was emotionally prepared to accept the creed of Leninism and become an unquestioning soldier in the 'great proletarian army'. In a brochure entitled *O Kommounistis, Laikos Agonistis, Melos tou KKE* (The Communist, People's Fighter, Member of the KKE), Zachariades defined the qualities of a party member in these words:

The member of the KKE and even more so the *stelekhi* belong totally and exclusively to the Party. This means that (a) the interest of the Party is the primary and highest consideration; (b) our personal life is organized in such a way that the Party and its struggle will benefit most; and (c) every action or word must be weighed on the scales of party interest.[14]

In the early twenties this identification of the individual with the party was foreign to most of the followers of the SEK(k). It was hard for them to accept total involvement in party affairs and the implied party control over non-political aspects of a member's life such as family ties, education, professional

---

[14] N. Zachariades, *O Kommounistis, Laikos Agonistis, Melos tou KKE* (Athens, Central Committee, KKE), p. 5. '*Stelekhi*' in party parlance are the party officials at all levels.

career, even recreation. Their reaction to the Twenty-One
Conditions should have surprised no one.

A move to regain independence

The Greek Communists, lacking any substantial popular
backing at home, expected to find inspiration and support in
the forward march of international Communism. Yet in 1921
the progress of the Communist movement was hardly a source
of encouragement. In Russia itself the Bolshevik régime was
facing a serious economic crisis, while on the international, or
more precisely on the European, scene the revolutionary agitation of 1918–19 was gradually ebbing under the impact of a
series of failures.

The Third World Congress of the Comintern which convened in Moscow on 22 June 1921 formally admitted that the
Communist movement had passed from the stage of 'imminent
revolution' to a period of 'defence and regrouping of forces'.
The poor prospects for revolution in Europe damped the enthusiasm and weakened the position of those among the Greek
Socialists who were in favour of binding the party to the
Comintern. In February 1922 a party conference went much
farther than the broadest interpretation of the Comintern
resolutions would warrant. In assessing the Greek political
scene the conference declared that 'the examination of the
present situation of the labour movement shows that after three
years . . . the reaction of the ruling class against the movement,
and in particular against our Party, has increased beyond the
point that our Party and the working class can endure'.[15] The
latter remark probably referred to the police measures taken by
the Greek Government in November 1921 against the Central
Committee of the party and the management of *Rizospastis* for
spreading defeatist slogans while the Greek Army was fighting
in Asia Minor. Those police measures were relatively mild; but
the Greek Communists had apparently assumed the revolutionary role in the secret hope that it would lead them to power,
not to jail. Discouraged by the reaction of the Greek Government to their revolutionary anti-war slogans, they found in the
resolutions of the Comintern Third World Congress a face-
saving escape. Interpreting those resolutions quite broadly, the

---

[15] *To KKE, 1918–1931*, p. 167.

conference adopted what became known in party history as the February thesis:

The Party, going through a period of organization and propaganda, *needs a long period of lawful existence.* Since Greece is a petty-bourgeois country, it is necessary to fight the spirit of petty-bourgeois compromise—shown by the devotion of the people to the democratic and parliamentary principles—not with negative and fruitless propaganda but with the *widest possible participation of the Party* in all the parliamentary struggles and organizations.

As an afterthought it was added: 'The Party is always fighting all the parties of the bourgeoisie.'[16]

Apart from the admission that the people were devoted to the democratic and parliamentary institutions, the most important statement was that the party needed 'a long period of lawful existence'. Later, Zachariades severely criticized this departure from the basic rule of Communist parties in non-Communist countries, namely the combination at all times of 'legal' with 'illegal' activity. In *Theses gia tin Istoria tou KKE*, Zachariades wrote:

The opportunists, who did not believe in the possibility of an independent proletarian policy and a solution of the crisis, left the political initiative to the 'progressive' bourgeois parties and tied the working class and the revolutionary movement to the tails of bourgeois democracy by advancing the theory that 'the party needs a long period of lawful existence', i.e. it must remain outside of the political life and activity of the country.[17]

In fact, the February Conference had decided in favour of an even more vigorous participation in the political life of the country; but it seems that for a seasoned Communist such as Zachariades the party's participation was inadequate without the addition of 'unlawful' activities.

In their effort to regain a measure of independence the leading group at the February Conference went even farther. The declaration that 'the Party according to the resolutions of its Second Congress remains unbreakably united with the Third International' seems to have been mere lip-service when compared to the following statement:

The party will in due course define its appropriate position towards the obligations imposed by the resolutions of the Second and Third

[16] *To KKE, 1918–1931*, pp. 170–1.   [17] Zachariades, *Theses*, pp. 30–31.

Congresses of the Third International, and declares that for the time being . . . it accepts all the resolutions of the Congresses of the Communist International up to this time *as documents of historical significance* which should enlighten the party in its course, according to the historical period the movement in Greece is going through.[18]

It was certainly quite a departure from the Twenty-One Conditions to declare formally that the resolutions of the Third International were merely 'documents of historical significance' without binding force on the 'sections' of the Comintern.

The Communists from the Asia Minor front

The drive for the communization of the party was uncertainly resumed in October 1922 at the 'Extraordinary' Congress.[19] It was assisted by the return to Greece of more than two hundred Communist veterans from Asia Minor, following the collapse of the front in August; yet the advocates of binding ties with the Comintern were checked by opposition at every turn. The Congress never touched the essential issues. It was bogged down by the secondary and superficial.

Given the internal power distribution, only one solution seemed feasible: to split the party, just as the French and the Italian Marxists had done. None of the opposing factions felt bold enough to take such a drastic step. They all realized that their party was too weak to withstand such surgery. The end product was a hodge-podge of compromises. The theory of the 'documents of historical significance' was discarded as the party again accepted the resolutions of the Comintern as 'obligatory'. At the same time, to quell the fears of those who opposed a slavish submission to a foreign organization, it was added that the Comintern decisions should be interpreted and applied 'according to the local conditions and the policies of the Party'.[20]

In the months following the Extraordinary Congress the position of the pro-Comintern faction was considerably strengthened by the arrival of new groups of Communist veterans from Asia Minor. Those Communists boasted that they had been 'instrumental' in spreading confusion and panic among the Greek troops during the critical days of August 1922 when

[18] *To KKE, 1918–1931*, pp. 177–8.

[19] An 'extraordinary' congress is one presumably called to discuss a specific question at a time when a regular congress is not provided for by the Charter.

[20] *To KKE, 1918–1931*, pp. 191–200.

the Turkish Army broke through the Greek lines. They had formed a 'Central Council of the Communist Soldiers of the Front Line' with the avowed objective of undermining the morale of the Greek forces, gaining hold of the system of military communications, expanding their numbers, through careful recruitment, and preparing to paralyse the front at the crucial moment. The inflammatory anti-war proclamations of the Council were carried from post to post by Communist muleteers. As army intelligence kept rather poor records, many Communists managed to be placed in field communication posts. They justified their actions by pointing out that the Soviet Government openly supported the régime of Mustapha Kemal under the terms of the Turco-Soviet Treaty of 1921. Although the effectiveness of the Communist agitators at the crucial moment should not be exaggerated, they did contribute to a further disruption of the front lines when the Turkish assault reached its peak.

The men who had directed and carried out the campaign of subversion in Asia Minor returned home after the collapse of the front carrying a strong revolutionary spirit which was to shape party policies in the following years. The undecided intellectuals, the confused Socialists, the reluctant petty-bourgeois 'Communists' were soon crowded out of the party ranks. After a short retreat at the conference of February 1922 the party resumed its course towards Communism under the leadership of the tough men from the front.

2. The Process of Bolshevization

Purging the ranks

On 16 September 1923 the party convened its second Extra-ordinary Congress to map out party strategy in the forthcoming parliamentary election—and also to weed out the remnants of the 'opportunist' faction. In its first communication the new Central Committee[1] elected by the Congress struck a strange note of moderation. 'In view of the internal dissensions,' it said, 'the Committee will follow a policy of impartiality, and will allow the expression of all trends of thought so that at the next regular congress, the struggle will be based on platforms and clear-cut trends, not on personal antagonisms.'[2] It is a long-established rule of Communist organization that the appearance of factions should be forestalled and suppressed. The seeming departure of the Central Committee from this rule had an ulterior motive which was unveiled in the following months. Like the 'hundred flowers' of the Chinese Communists many years later, its objective was to uncover dissenters or potential opponents and then weed them out of the party.

The defeat of the party candidates in the parliamentary election of 1923 set the purging process in motion. The demand for a 'workers' and peasants' government' had left the great majority of Greek voters totally unimpressed. The party's candidates received altogether less than 20,000 votes in a total of more than 800,000. For many party members who were not thoroughly familiar with the dialectics of Communist partici-pation in parliamentary elections, the electoral disaster of their party came as a stunning blow. Most attributed the party's poor showing to the extremist slogans which, they said, were unsuit-able to Greek social conditions. On 14 November 1923, in an article expressing the views of the Central Committee, *Rizo-spastis* denounced the 'people's democracy' slogan which had been advanced in Salonika by members who disagreed with the

---

[1] Eleutherios Stavrides, Serafim Maximos, Thomas Apostolides, and Christos Tzallas.

[2] *Rizospastis*, 25 September 1923.

Central Committee's extreme views. By the end of the Second World War 'people's democracy' had been accepted by international Communism as a necessary and useful stage 'on the road to Socialism and Communism'. In 1923, however, the Comintern favoured the 'workers' and peasants' government'. The departure of the KKE's provincial organizations from the Comintern line was only the opening act of a new party crisis. In the following months more deviationist movements developed in Piraeus and Salonika. By now a pattern had been set. After every failure the party went through a crisis.

To overcome the opposition, the Central Committee sought the support of the Comintern and its branch organization in the Balkans, the Balkan Communist Federation. The reply came in the form of a BCF resolution published in *Rizospastis* on 7 February 1924. In it the Presidium of the Federation declared:

The Communist Party of Greece with its organ *Rizospastis* is the section of the Balkan Communist Federation in Greece. The Presidium of the Balkan Communist Federation denounces every attempt to form other Communist organizations outside the Communist Party of Greece. All true Communists must join the ranks of the party and submit themselves to its discipline.

Armed with the unqualified endorsement of the BCF, the Central Committee convened a National Council in February 1924 with the stated purpose of purging the party of all the 'opportunist' and 'extremist' elements. The Council elected a new Central Committee[3] 'vested with dictatorial powers'.[4] The Committee were entrusted with the preparation of 'a clear-cut and concrete programme based on the resolutions of the Communist International and the Balkan Communist Federation'. They were further asked 'to expose the true objectives of all those who appear under the mask of Socialism', and to call the oft-postponed Third Regular Congress of the party within four months. To carry out these tasks, the Central Committee were given the power 'to suspend any rules of the party Charter, which they consider obstructive to the fulfilment of these tasks'.[5]

Exercising their 'dictatorial powers', the Central Committee went forward with the purge of the party. To quote an official party announcement:

[3] Yiannis Kordatos, Serafim Maximos, Thomas Apostolides.
[4] *To KKE, 1918–1931*, p. 268.   [5] *Rizospastis*, 9 February 1924.

. . . the knife of the Central Committee began to cut off the rotten parts of the body. This action has been approved by the Balkan Communist Federation. . . . Yesterday, the Central Committee expelled eight members; there are many more to be thrown out because they are a disgrace to the party. For this reason, the Central Committee has dissolved the Piraeus party organization, and has appointed a committee to reinstate only those members who deserve the honour of being Communists.[6]

These efforts of the Central Committee received the official blessings of the BCF in a resolution which was triumphantly published by *Rizospastis* on 30 September 1924. The Greek translation even included in parenthesis the transliteration of some key Russian words, as though to emphasize the genuine character of the document. For the second time within a year the leaders of the KKE had sought support from a foreign organization to strengthen their position against dissident party members. Comintern support went even further. Manuilsky and Smeral, two leading members of the Executive Committee of the Communist International (ECCI), came to Greece to lend a hand and facilitate both the purge and the preparation of the Third Regular Congress. The first objective was accomplished without much difficulty. As to the second, 'insufficient representation, and the long absence of several members of the Central Committee, did not allow the proper organizational and political preparation of the Congress. Therefore, the Congress[7] was unanimously proclaimed not as the Third Regular but as the Third Extraordinary Congress.'[8] This was a subtle way of saying that the continuing intra-party squabbles did not allow the meeting of a fully-fledged Congress. In any event, 'with the invaluable contribution of the representatives of the Communist International and the Balkan Communist Federation', the Congress which convened in Athens between 26 November and 3 December 1924

accepted unanimously all the resolutions of the World Congresses of the Comintern and the BCF and especially the Twenty-One Conditions for the admission of new parties to the Communist International. In accordance with these Conditions, the Congress changed the name of the party from *Socialist Labour Party (Com-*

---

[6] *Rizospastis*, 5 April 1924.

[7] The Congress elected a fifteen-member Central Committee with P. Pouliopoulos as its Secretary, the highest post in the party hierarchy.

[8] *Rizospastis*, 14 December 1924.

munist) to *Communist Party of Greece (Greek Section of the Communist International*).[9]

The cell system

The Third Extraordinary Congress marked a turning-point in the party's history. By adopting the Twenty-One Conditions the party became *formally* what it had already been in practice, a *section* of the Communist International. Furthermore, it entered the period of *bolshevization*. Communist writers of that period use the general title *Na putyakh bolshevizatsii Partii* (Towards the Bolshevization of the Party) to describe the party policies following the Third Extraordinary Congress.[10]

Bolshevization was the magic word coined by the Fifth World Congress of the Comintern. The slogan 'to the masses', put out by the Third World Congress of the Comintern, had failed to produce any spectacular gains for the various Communist parties. The failure was blamed on the lack of proper party organization. Bolshevization was expected to eliminate in the future the 'right deviations' and the 'ultra-left trends' which presumably had prevented the Communist parties from scoring any substantial political successes during the previous two years.

The KKE had had more than its share of right and left 'deviations'. Bolshevization was expected to transform the weak and crisis-ridden party, as if by magic, into a powerful and cohesive political organization. With pathetic eagerness the Third Extraordinary Congress embraced the Comintern thesis on bolshevization. As this organizational structure still forms the framework of the KKE, it may be useful to look into this structural metamorphosis at its early stages.

Up to the Third Extraordinary Congress, the party maintained the traditional organization of other Greek political parties, composed of sections and groups following the administrative subdivisions of the Greek state. The Extraordinary Congress, copying in this the directives of the 7th Balkan Communist Conference, established the system of cells. This was far more than a mere redistribution of the party membership. The members were now expected to perform 'daily'

---

[9] Ibid. The second part of the title was deleted in 1943.
[10] Cf. Ch. Kabaktsiev et al., *Kommunisticheskiye Partii Balkanskikh Stran* (Moscow, Gosizdat, 1930), p. 185; also G. Zinoviev, *Mezhdunarodniye Perspektivi i Bolshevizatsia* (Leningrad, 1925), p. 96.

specific tasks 'in the different branches of party activity'.[11] This requirement of 'constant daily work' was in effect the essential element of the cell structure. The members should no longer expect to act as part-time revolutionaries, leaving the daily work to a few *stelekhi* entrusted with the party's political activity. The party, members were told, was not an ordinary political organization designed to operate primarily in the electoral arena. Its members were not potential supporters at the polls, they were 'active soldiers of the world proletarian army'.

The cell, composed of three to five members, offered the organizational framework for the total utilization of the members. In such small groups no one could escape notice by losing himself in the crowd. The cells, integrated in a closely-knit structure, permitted the close supervision of party members. Such cells were to be formed at the factories and the shops where people spent most of their waking hours. In addition, party members belonging to labour unions should form 'fractions' within each union local.[12] The task of 'fractions' was to promote party policies within the labour organizations. In outlining the everyday activities of the cells, the Extraordinary Congress stated:

Par. 16. As soon as the cell is formed, members must familiarize themselves in detail with the duties they have to perform in the new organization. The secretary of the cell will be appointed by the local party committee. . . .

Par. 18. Every week, the cell shall convene. Regular topics on the agenda must be: (1) Analysis of the important party slogans; (2) checking the individual work of each member; (3) conducting educational work in the cell; (4) examining the admission of new members or candidates; (5) discussing problems concerning the factory, residential district, etc.

Par. 19. The secretary of the cell is responsible to the party for the regular functioning of the cell. He must know all about the living conditions of the members, keep their addresses, observe closely their individual Communist activity, call together the weekly meetings, direct the educational work of the cell, etc.[13]

The mere passing of detailed resolutions on the organization of the party could not accomplish its bolshevization overnight.

[11] *Theses and Resolutions; adopted by the Third Congress of the Communist International* (New York, Contemporary Publishing Association, 1921), p. 80; hereinafter cited as *Theses, Third World Congress.*

[12] *To KKE, 1918–1931*, pp. 358–9.   [13] Ibid., p. 359.

As some Communist writers observed a few years later, the resolutions on bolshevization were 'inefficiently applied in the practical work because of the inexperience of the party leadership, particularly in connexion with anti-war propaganda, and the national question'.[14] Furthermore, the party organization 'passed through many complications because the Party had very little contact with the factory workers'.[15] This assessment was accurate. The party remained a small organization with little political support even among the workers.[16]

The Third Extraordinary Congress did not produce the bolshevization of the party with the speed and efficiency hoped for by the Comintern leadership. However, it marked a milestone in party history. It introduced fundamental changes in the party organization; it formally integrated the party within the Comintern structure; and it unanimously adopted a policy of support for the establishment of a Macedonian and a Thracian state as a 'matter of principle'.

Legal and illegal activity

In January 1926 the party was formally outlawed for the first time. Till then, the leading political circles in Greece had largely ignored the social-revolutionary pronouncements of the Communists. Most Greek politicians at the time knew little if anything of Communist doctrine. The usual reaction of the authorities to Communist agitation was to arrest a party member for delivering 'revolutionary speeches' and exile him for a few months, with living expenses paid by the Government, to one of the sunny, though lonely, Aegean islands. In general, the attitude of official Greece towards the Communists was mild, police measures were spasmodic and amateurish. Class-struggle concepts were foreign to the Greek mentality at the time; but when *Rizospastis* launched, in broad daylight, a fierce campaign for Macedonian and Thracian independence, openly advocating the separation of national territories inhabited by Greeks, nationalist-minded Greek political leaders took a closer look at

[14] The term 'national question' refers to the Communist agitation for an independent Macedonian state.

[15] Kabaktsiev, op. cit., p. 186.

[16] According to an official report of the ECCI, the Greek Communist party had, at the end of 1924, 2,200 regular members and 450 candidates (Report, ECCI, 5 May 1925, quoted in Kabaktsiev et al., op. cit., p. 186; see also *Fifth Congress; Abridged Report*, p. 268).

Greek Communism. The evidence that this decision of the Communist Party had been reached by order of a foreign organization called the Comintern made it even more 'traitorous' and 'monstrous' in the eyes of the Greek leaders, and, it must be said, of the great majority of the people. In the circumstances, the Communist Party could no longer be shrugged off as a group of wild yet largely harmless politicians whose ideology was more or less a personal matter. In a wave of arrests, Pouliopoulos, Apostolides, and several other leading party members were sent to prison; Maximos was exiled to the island of Skyros. The remaining members of the Central Committee immediately met in secret and elected Eleutherios Stavrides as the acting Secretary in place of P. Pouliopoulos, who had been elected to the post by the Third Extraordinary Congress.

The arrest of so many of its leaders had an unexpected side-effect within the party. Since 1924 the first graduates of the KUTV, the Communist University of Eastern Peoples, had begun to filter into Greece from the Soviet Union.[17] The 'Koutvies'—one of them the future leader of the KKE, Nikolaos Zachariades—were trained, Russian-speaking Communists whose loyalty to Stalin was to play an important role in the following years. For more than a year their relations with the leaders of the KKE had been far from affectionate. Their intimate contacts with the Soviet Embassy in Athens, implying that they were trusted more than the regular party leaders, were a constant source of irritation. Apparently on instructions from their patrons, they had remained in the background, ready to offer their loyal services to the party as ordinary soldiers, without any apparent intention of pushing themselves forwards to the party leadership. All this changed with the arrest of party leaders in the early months of 1926. The 'Koutvies' took their first serious step towards the summit of the party hierarchy.

The detailed instructions of the Comintern to all its 'sections' constantly to combine 'legal with illegal work, and never commit the error of depending on a permanent legal basis for their

---

[17] The KUTV was a school for the training of students from Asia in Communist theory and tactics. Students from the Balkan countries were also sent to it on the assumption that the conditions in the Balkans resembled those of Asia, and did not warrant enrolment of such students in the school of Sverdlov for students from the West.

existence'[18] proved of little avail. In 1926 the outlawed KKE tried to implement Comintern instructions, but was plunged headlong into a situation far too difficult for its organization to handle.

Stavrides, the acting Secretary, sought desperately to strengthen the party by familiarizing members with the rules of the game under conditions of 'illegality'. His remarks in the first *Dheltion* (Bulletin) of the Central Committee are worth noting. Copying the Comintern directives on the subject, Stavrides instructed party members to form cells at their place of work, not at their domicile. Every three members working at the same enterprise ought to form a cell. Fewer than three should still form a cell and then try to attract more adherents. In areas where party members worked in small businesses and shops street cells should be formed by those Communists employed in neighbouring establishments.[19] The organization of the cells at the place of work offered certain advantages. As the members spent most of their active time where they worked, they could communicate easily, they could indoctrinate new adherents while they were working, and they could meet in an emergency without delay and exploit grievances on the spot.

Writing on the question of 'centralization', Stavrides stressed the importance of 'democratic centralism', which, he said, has to become even more rigid under conditions of illegality. 'Even the most minor signs of factionalism within the Party must be suppressed mercilessly, because factionalism is contrary to centralism and bolshevik discipline.' Even those orders and directives which appeared to members to be 'faulty' ought to be carried out without question because 'only the leading members who are educated and can form opinions are in a position to decide what is good for the Party'.[20]

The role of party 'fractions' within other, non-Communist organizations was described in the *Dheltion* with unusual clarity:

The fractions are party organizations within other organizations of workers, whether legal or illegal. The fraction—unlike the cell—is not based on the place of work but on the participation of a member in a given non-party organization. The fraction is composed of all party members belonging to the same non-party organization. Even

---

[18] *Theses, Third World Congress*, pp. 111-12.
[19] *Dheltion*, No. 1, February 1926, pp. 4-9.   [20] Ibid.

C

a single Communist in an organization is a party fraction. By non-party organizations, we mean trade unions, co-operatives, conventions, conferences, councils, administrations, committees, meetings, etc.

The fraction channels party views into the organization. The fraction has its own organization, discusses issues, reaches decisions in connexion with matters which interest the organization in which the fraction operates, but it always obeys the party directives.[21]

As a rule, he added, the fraction should meet before the meeting of the non-party organization and decide on a course of action. At the general meeting the members of the fraction should not act as an organized group but as individuals who happened to have similar views. By adroit manoeuvring, party members were expected to swing to the party point of view many non-Communist members not too sure about their convictions or about the significance of the issues involved.[22]

Stavrides also dealt with the establishment of 'legal' front organizations in a memorable paragraph: 'The KKE, though an illegal organization, must form, whenever possible, legal organizations in order to use them for propaganda and agitation among the masses. Co-operatives, art, sport, and other organizations may be among such "legal" organizations.'[23]

These detailed—and candid—instructions on party 'bolshevization' and illegal activity failed to avert the party's virtual disintegration in 1926. Communist leaders have discovered again and again that what appears on paper to be an almost perfect blueprint for action or organization is not easily translated into reality. In a letter written in 1926 by the Comintern representative to the KKE, a Rumanian known as Bantulesco, we find a candid description of the party's failure to implement the concepts of bolshevization:

. . . Unfortunately, the KKE did not have the experience of its sister parties and, therefore, the present conditions of terrorism have resulted in the complete disintegration of the party activities. . . . In the trade unions we have not begun to work. . . . We have difficulties even within the circle of the Central Committee of the party. . . . Many decisions remain only on paper because most members of the

[21] *Dheltion*, No. 1, February 1926, pp. 4–9.
[22] It is interesting to note that the use of 'fractions' is again provided by the new (1961) Statutes of the CPSU in Sec. IX, Article 67.
[23] Ibid.

Central Committee live underground and do not try to go to the factories and implement our decisions. . . . On the other hand, lack of a conspiratorial spirit has hindered the work of the Central Committee and has facilitated the job of stool pigeons. . . .[24]

This revealing document by a Comintern official accurately describes the actual state of party affairs in 1926 when the party had been forced for the first time 'underground'.

[24] *Dheltion*, No. 1, February 1926, pp. 11–12; also Kabaktsiev, op. cit., p. 187.

3. Stalinism and the Greek Communists

'Liquidarists' and Stalinists

The KKE had been forced underground in 1926 by the dictatorial régime of General Theodore Pangalos, who had overthrown the legitimate Government of Andreas Michalakopoulos by a *coup d'état* in June 1925. The Pangalos régime came to an end on 22 August 1926 when General George Kondylis, a Venizelist officer, led another successful *coup* while Pangalos was spending a holiday on the island of Spetsae.

Immediately after the overthrow of Pangalos, *Rizospastis* was allowed to resume publication, and most of the imprisoned and exiled party members were released. On 24 August the Central Committee warned the party members against any illusions of returning to the type of party organization which existed before the introduction of bolshevization and democratic centralism. 'The Party will of course exploit the liberties which have been restored.' The Central Committee decision went on: 'it will fight for their preservation and broadening; but this does not mean that it will go back to the old ideas of legality.'[1]

As soon as the party members returned from prison or exile, a new crisis broke out. This time, the offensive was spearheaded by the 'Koutvies', whose influence had substantially increased during the period of 'illegality'. They were mostly supported by those who had visited the Soviet Union as party emissaries or to receive medical treatment—those known in party parlance as 'Hadjis', that is, visitors to the 'Holy Places' of Communism. The attack was directed against the 'petty-bourgeois intellectuals' who, in the eyes of the Koutvies and the Hadjis, presented a permanent obstacle to the bolshevization of the party.

The stage was set for a clash with the Koutvies when, on 9 September 1926, Pouliopoulos was re-elected Secretary of the Central Committee. He refused to accept the post and at the same time rejected a proposal that he should become a party

[1] *Rizospastis*, 24 August 1926.

candidate for the parliamentary elections of 7 November. Stavrides later disclosed that Pouliopoulos thought he would be in a better position to fight against the Koutvies if he held no responsible post in the party hierarchy.[2] This marked the beginning of a two-year fight between the Koutvie–Hadji faction, led by Andronikos Khaitas, and the 'Liquidarists', headed by P. Pouliopoulos.

The fight against the Greek 'Liquidarists' was expected to be another major step towards the bolshevization of the party. It was waged with the blessing of the Comintern leaders, who were determined to free all Communist parties from those who, being of petty-bourgeois origin, had proved so susceptible to nationalist and other 'bourgeois prejudices'. In Greece the responsibility for the purge was entrusted to those who had been trained in the bolshevik way of thinking, had little regard for national sensitivities, and were specifically prepared for the task.

In the opinion of the Koutvies and Hadjis, the party had suffered constant crises since 1918 because of the influx of 'petty-bourgeois' intellectuals. Many among those intellectuals, it is true, were rather naïve ideologists who joined the party with boundless enthusiasm for the cause, only to be gravely disillusioned after two or three years of party membership by the cynicism and duplicity of Comintern methods and objectives. It must be noted that for most of those leaders the touchstone was the so-called national question, the establishment of a Macedonian state. To advocate what amounted to a transfer to Bulgaria of territories inhabited by Greeks proved too much for most of those 'petty-bourgeois intellectuals' who had never ceased to regard themselves primarily as Greeks.

As the struggle between the Liquidarists and their opponents went on it became clear that this was not an isolated phenomenon, peculiar to the Greek section of the Comintern. It was indeed an outgrowth of the momentous conflict raging at the summit of the Communist world. Those were the years of Stalin's relentless drive to absolute power by the gradual elimination of his former comrades. Men of Stalin's personal choice were soon to be installed as party leaders in the various 'sections' of the Comintern.

[2] Stavrides, op. cit., p. 201.

The Third Regular Congress convenes at last

It may be recalled that it was on 9 February 1921 that the intention to hold the Third Regular Congress was first announced by the party leaders. Time and again, the Third Regular Congress had to be postponed while one crisis after another shook the weak foundations of the small and ineffective party. By 1927, after successive purges, new leaders had emerged at the top of the party hierarchy. Most of them were men free of 'petty-bourgeois weaknesses and prejudices', deeply committed to the Comintern. They felt sufficiently strong to face the hazards of a Regular Congress, and 'with the help of the Executive Committee of the Communist International'[3] they decided to call the oft-postponed Third Regular Congress of the KKE to meet in Athens in March 1927.

At the Congress three factions emerged. A Communist book[4] published a few years later identified the three major factions at the Congress as 'the Pouliopoulos group, which demanded a "purge" of the "inefficient" elements and declared itself against the admission of ordinary workers', the Khaitas group, which 'upheld the principles of the Comintern on the organizational question', and the group of the 'Centre' headed by Maximos, 'which vacillated between the other two groups'. Since the Khaitas group was identified with the views of the Comintern, it is not surprising that in the end the Congress accepted almost every single point made by this faction.

One of the major topics before the Congress was the so-called organizational question. The bone of contention in this case was whether the party should develop first of all 'a leading nucleus of cadres' or open its ranks to 'a mass influx of workers'. Pouliopoulos, who participated actively in the deliberations of the Congress, came out against 'the mass admission of proletarians' because 'the workers within the Party now form the lowest stratum of the proletariat'. Instead, he advocated that 'the Party must first have a leading nucleus in order to be able to absorb workers'.[5] The Congress rejected Pouliopoulos' views as a 'total misconception of the role of a Communist party'. Led in this by the Khaitas group, the Congress gave full approval to

[3] *K. I. pered Shestim Vsemirnim Kongressom* (Moscow, 1928), p. 213.
[4] Kabaktsiev et al., op. cit., p. 188.
[5] *To KKE, 1918–1931*, II, p. 42.

the admission of more workers, while at the same time it voiced serious reservations as to the advisability of placing too much emphasis on Marxist education. These two points were closely related. The influx of ordinary workers was expected to offset the influence of the 'petty-bourgeois intellectuals' and boost the prestige of the Koutvies and the Hadjis. Many among them had always felt inferior to the well-educated intellectuals; to the uneducated workers they would appear as fountains of wisdom. Besides, these workers, hardly literate, would be *tabulae rasae* on which the Stalinist version of Marxism could be easily engraved. With the changing role of the Comintern under Stalin, Communists everywhere were expected to obey orders rather than be versed in Marxist theory. The Congress fully endorsed the views of the Stalinists on the grounds that 'a wide admission of workers from the factories, and the ensuing change in the composition of party membership, was an indispensable prerequisite for the bolshevization of the Party'.[6] The only problem was that the workers were not pressing at the gates to join the party.

In its report to the Sixth World Congress, the Executive Committee of the Communist International included the following assessment of the KKE's Third Regular Congress:

The Third Regular Congress was an important event in the life of the party. With the assistance of the Executive Committee of the Communist International, the possibility of greater development of active work was assured. The Congress paid much attention to the question of intra-party opposition which tried to apply open Liquidarism under the guise of theoretical-radical phraseology. This opposition was crystallized into a Menshevik-Trotskyist group which tried to break up the party. . . . This fractionist struggle retarded the party work, but at the same time it completely isolated the petty-bourgeois, intellectual-opportunist elements from the working masses and, equally important, it raised the ideological level of the party.[7]

The changing role of the party

At the Central Committee Plenum which convened in July 1927 a new development became dimly yet unmistakably evident: the KKE, from being a section of the Communist International, was gradually being transformed into an appendage of

---

[6] Kabaktsiev et al., op. cit., p. 131.
[7] *K. I. pered Shestim Vsemirnim Kongressom*, p. 213.

the Soviet Government. The Plenum accepted and reproduced in exact translation the entire resolution of the ECCI 'On the Danger of War', dated 29 May 1927, which called for the 'mobilization of the masses for the defence of the Soviet Union against imperialist aggression, under the slogan "the international proletariat defends its fatherland against the attacks of the imperialists" '.[8] It was a clear-cut call for a transfer of loyalty from one's own country to the Soviet Union as the 'fatherland' of the international proletariat. The defence of the Soviet Union was declared to be the foremost duty of the Greek Communist Party.

On a more practical level, the Plenum gave specific instructions 'for systematic anti-militarist work in the Army and Navy', noting significantly that 'the importance of our Party as the Bolshevik party of the Greek proletariat will be determined by our activity on the war issue, and by the results of our anti-militarist struggle'.[9]

In the meantime Pouliopoulos, apparently unaware of the fundamental changes taking place in the Kremlin and the international Communist movement, continued his attacks against the Stalinist group. Finally, in a statement published on 24 August 1927, he openly sided with 'comrades Trotsky, Zinoviev, and Kamenev', and declared Stalin's theory of 'Socialism in one country' as anti-Marxist and anti-Leninist.[10] One month later, on 25 September, Pouliopoulos was expelled from the party as 'an enemy of the proletariat'. His expulsion was immediately approved by the Comintern, a fact given wide publicity by the Central Committee of the KKE.

As soon as the top Liquidarists were eliminated, the Stalinist group turned against the 'Centrists' of the Maximos group, who were also accused of representing 'the united opposition of Trotsky–Zinoviev–Kamenev'. The KKE was faithfully imitating the internal convulsions of the Communist Party of the Soviet Union. At the Fourth Regular Congress, which convened in Athens on 10 December 1928, the Stalinist faction delivered the final blow against the Maximos group. Responding to the strong words of the Comintern emissary, who asked the Congress 'to finish the job by eliminating, once and for all, the trends which exist or existed within the Party',[11] it expelled

---

[8] *Rizospastis*, 22 August 1927.   [9] *To KKE, 1918–1931*, II, p. 243.
[10] Ibid., p. 192.   [11] Ibid., p. 309.

by unanimous decision 'the agents of the united opposition, Maximos, Sklavos, Khainoglou, Hadjistavrou, Papanikolaou, Nikolaides, and Polychronakos, former members of the Central Committee'.[12]

The representative of the Comintern, in his closing remarks, praised the party for the 'complete annihilation of Liquidarism', but he criticized 'the signs of inertia, hesitation, or vacillation displayed by certain comrades, which ought to be watched carefully by the Party, and suppressed in time'.[13] Thus the stage was already set for future purges, should the need arise.

In a significant paragraph of one of its resolutions the Fourth Regular Congress declared that the KKE fully accepted 'all party, organizational, and governmental measures taken by the Comintern, and by the Soviet Government against Trotsky and the other leaders of the Trotskyist opposition'.[14] For the first time in its troubled history the KKE had gone beyond the observance of Comintern directives to accept the decisions of the Soviet Government and the CPSU. By this alone, the Fourth Regular Congress of December 1928 marked another important milestone in the tortured growth of the party which had been founded in a shabby little hotel in Athens only ten years earlier, by people who in 1928 had long ago left its ranks.

Techniques of subversion

In line with Stalin's theory of the 'Third Period' (the alleged preparation for war against the Soviet Union), in the summer of 1929 the Comintern launched an international anti-war campaign scheduled to culminate in mass demonstrations on 1 August. The Central Committee of the KKE, dominated now by the Stalinists, took up the cue at the 2nd Plenum, which met on 10 June 1929, and resolved that 'the main task of the party consists in a struggle against the preparation of war by the Greek bourgeoisie and the imperialists, the defence of our Socialist fatherland, and *the transformation of the imperialist war into a civil war for the establishment of a workers' and peasants' government*'.[15] Most interesting is the reference to 'the transformation of the imperialist war into a civil war'. In 1929 no war

---

[12] *To KKE, 1918–1931*, II, p. 326.
[13] Ibid., p. 312.
[14] *Kommounistiki Epitheorisi*, January 1929, pp. 40–41; hereinafter cited as *Komep*.
[15] *To KKE, 1918–1931*, II, p. 354; author's italics.

was being contemplated against the Soviet Union—certainly not by Greece—nor was the KKE capable of fomenting civil war. Yet it would be an error to dismiss Communist policy statements only because they appear to have been unattainable at the time. The Greek Communists put this 'transformation' into effect later, during the country's occupation by the Axis. The civil war which ruined Greece in the forties and left a painful legacy was an integral part of the KKE's programme of action since 1929.

In line with the party's 'main task', the Plenum gave detailed instructions for the subversion of the armed forces. Its aim, they said, was 'not the democratization or the improvement of the bourgeois army but its *disintegration*. Our partial demands aim at bringing about this disintegration.' The fact that the length of military service for draftees was being reduced at that time was dismissed by the Plenum as irrelevant. With disarming simplicity, it declared that 'the reduction in the length of military service does not aim at relieving the young of a heavy burden, neither does it prove the peaceful intentions of the bourgeoisie'. Why? 'Because such a peaceful policy is today impossible for a capitalist state.' Slavish conformity to the Stalinist theories about the imminence of war often led the KKE to foolish conclusions.

Outlining practical measures for the subversion of the armed forces, the Plenum decided 'to pay particular attention to the broadening and strengthening of an illegal organization of Communists in the Army, beginning with the establishment of anti-militarist committees in all units'. Other proposed measures included the establishment of cells in 'war factories and the means of transportation and communication, in key areas near arsenals, and in villages located near military installations and camps'; the organization of 'fraternization parties for workers and soldiers, farewell parties for draftees'; and the organization of 'special lectures for party members and members of the Communist Youth (OKNE) who are about to be drafted, in connexion with their party duties in the armed forces'.[16] Outside the armed forces, the party was instructed to form 'united Committees' in the labour unions, to undercut the elected leadership of the unions, and 'mass strike detachments for mass revolutionary fighting against terrorism'.[17]

[16] *To KKE, 1918–1931*, II, pp. 369–73.　　　　　[17] Ibid., p. 367.

These detailed instructions, so impressive on paper, failed to produce any tangible results. The agitation against the Greek Government's alleged war preparations, totally unsupported by the facts, left the Greek public unimpressed. The call for the defence of 'our Soviet Fatherland' was too outrageous to be considered seriously by anyone but the party's seasoned Stalinists. N. Zachariades, referring to the failures of the party, later placed all responsibility on the KKE leaders of that period 'when the Party suffered only damage and losses due to the infamous sectarian and stupid "militant demonstrations" which were ordered without any real political meaning or purpose'.[18] In all fairness, the leaders of that period (1929–31) did their best to implement the directives emanating from Moscow. They failed because the directives had no relevance to existing conditions in Greece; yet Zachariades, in the usual pattern, attributed the failure to the inefficiency of the agents, not to the faults of the theory. Two decades later he himself was to receive the same treatment.

The KKE and the Greek trade unions

Throughout the 1920s the Greek trade unions, whether pro-Communist or 'reformist', failed to gain widespread support among the workers. By 1927 no more than 25 per cent. of the labour force had been 'organized' by the unions. Communist influence over the General Confederation of Greek Workers (GSEE) was at least partly responsible for the reluctance of many workers to join the unions. In March 1927 the non-Communist (reformist) labour leaders gained control of the GSEE executive committee at the Confederation's Third Regular Congress. Of the 410 unions represented at the Congress some existed only on paper, yet, on the whole, the turn of events at the Congress represented the prevailing trends among Greek workers at the time. Its resolutions called for affiliation with the Amsterdam International and denounced the revolutionary tactics and objectives of the Communist-controlled labour organizations. For the KKE this was another blow coming at a time when the party was facing the effects of government persecution and internal quarrels.

To counter the ascendancy of non-Communist elements in the GSEE, the KKE established 'action committees' and

[18] N. Zachariades, *Provlimata Kathothigisis* (mimeographed copy), p. 125.

'fractions' in the trade unions, charged with the responsibility of 'exposing' the reformist leaders. The impact of these committees and 'fractions' remained fairly limited, and their work was vigorously opposed and at times effectively frustrated by the reformist leaders. Nevertheless, the existence of these 'revolutionary' groups within the trade unions provided the KKE with a convenient 'base' for propaganda and agitation, and could in time be used to split off and form separate, Communist-controlled, unions, or at least disrupt the work of a national GSEE congress.

The Fourth Regular Congress of the KKE, which met in December 1928, took up the question of labour-union control and resolved that the organization of a 'class-conscious United General Confederation of Labour, supported by militant, 'class-conscious' trade unions, was 'a basic problem' for the party. The party 'fractions' in the reformist trade unions and in the organization of the GSEE were instructed by the Congress to intensify their attacks against the reformist leaders, 'unmask the subjugation of Greece by foreign capitalists', and strengthen the 'anti-imperialist trend' which, according to the party leaders, was rapidly developing among the workers. The party congress also asked the 'honest workers and labour leaders' to press for a 'united Pan-helladic Labour Congress, the only body where broad unity could be achieved'.[19]

Unable to force its will on the majority of Greek workers, the KKE finally decided to go ahead with its plan for a separate confederation. In February 1929 a 'Congress' of 289 pro-Communist labour leaders, claiming to represent some 650 unions and labour centres, agreed by a nearly unanimous vote to set up a 'United General Confederation of Greek Workers' (EGSEE). The ten dissenting votes came chiefly from some 'liquidarists', who argued that only through co-operation with other left-wing elements in the existing labour unions could the party exert effective influence.

The 'Congress', following in this the advice of the party, decided to establish formal ties with the Communist-controlled Revolutionary International of Labour Unions (RILU). The split lasted until 1936 when, in the context of the Popular Front policy, the Communist EGSEE dissolved itself, thus ending a seven-year split of Greek labour.

[19] 'To 40 Taktiko Synethrio', *Komep*, January 1929, pp. 308–43.

The party's influence wanes

The formal split in the Greek labour movement was another indication of the party's progressive drift to extreme 'left' positions under the impact of the Stalinists. This party line was an echo of the Sixth World Congress of the Comintern and its 'Third Period' theory. It left the Greek workers unimpressed.

To what extent Communist influence had ebbed in Greece was revealed on 1 August 1929, when the KKE, following Comintern orders, called for a massive anti-war demonstration. For a whole month the preparation of the 'First of August' militant demonstration became the KKE's chief preoccupation. On 1 August the Communist campaign fell flat on its face. Out of more than 150,000 workers, only 12,000 took part in the twenty-four-hour 'general' strike, 'and of them nine-tenths were tobacco workers', that is, old party faithfuls. 'The strike of 12,000 workers', the Central Committee wrote sadly, '*cannot be regarded as a success*.' Furthermore, 'the demonstrations of the First of August had failed completely'.[20] The Central Committee searched for a plausible explanation of the resounding failure. Their rationalization differed from that presented later by Zachariades. Yet they both shared a common feature: neither attributed the failure to the fallacy of the 'Third Period' theory or to the marked lack of interest shown by the majority of Greek workers in the Communist slogans. The Central Committee, absolving itself of any responsibility, attributed the failure to three factors: the inefficiency of the 'illegal organs' entrusted with the preparation of the demonstrations; the 'treachery' of the non-Communist workers 'who played an active role as agents of the bourgeoisie in the preparation of war'; and the 'rightist' deviations within the party.

The first vague reference to a 'rightist' deviation had already appeared in the deliberations of the Plenum in June. With the collapse of the 'First of August' campaign, the 'rightist danger' began to grow, at least in the minds of members of the Politbureau. In a statement published shortly after the fiasco, the Politbureau, the executive organ of the Central Committee, attacked the 'rightists' for alleging that 'the campaign had failed to such an extent precisely because the general interpretation of the period and of the condition of the masses is

[20] *To KKE, 1918–1931*, II, pp. 380–5.

erroneous'.[21] In fact, the interpretation given by the 'rightists' was much closer to reality. But to the Greek Stalinists, to question the validity of the directives emanating from Moscow was akin to treason.

In spite of the admitted failure to influence the broad strata of workers and peasants, the 3rd Plenum, which met secretly in Larissa on 27 January 1930, unanimously decided 'to mobilize the working class and the poor peasants for the general political strike and for *armed incursions* into the towns'. At the same time it outlined the formula for the preparation of a general strike: '. . . Fomenting of partial strikes, broadening these struggles, organizing militant demonstrations of the strikers, armed demonstrations of the poor peasants, mass activity of soldiers and sailors, and then passing into mass political strikes.'

In spite, or perhaps because, of its inflammatory proclamations, the KKE's influence among the workers and peasants was falling to a low ebb. The Comintern representative, addressing the 3rd Plenum, revealed that the membership of the KKE had gone down to only 1,500. The circulation of party publications which 'last year was at the 3,000 mark has now come down to 1,666'. In Athens, he added, 'the Party has only 170 members, and in Piraeus, the biggest industrial centre of the country, only seventy members'.[22] The 3rd Plenum attributed 'this isolation of the Party from the masses' to tactical errors in the application of the 'United Front from below' formula. Not a word was uttered about the three major causes of the party's decline: the improved conditions in Greece under the Venizelos administration, the unreality of a 'mass turn to the left' claimed by the Third Period theory, and the party's open agitation for a Macedonian and a Thracian state.

Ignoring the waning influence of the party, the 3rd Plenum, under the urging of the Comintern representative, resolved at its secret meeting to intensify the militant drive towards a general political strike. The first of May was set for the major step in the process. The party was instructed to organize 'joint demonstrations of workers and peasants who shall come from their villages in groups, and form self-defence detachments'.[23]

[21] *To KKE, 1918–1931*, II, pp. 385–90.
[22] *Communist International*, 31 March 1930.
[23] *Rizospastis*, 24 April 1930.

The all too obvious call for a revolutionary mobilization was pronounced to be 'a vital necessity for the worker-peasant masses'. The results of the 'mobilization' showed that such a vital necessity existed only in the imagination of the Communist leaders.

Only 3,300 workers, in all, took part in the strikes. For the first time, there was a red May Day strike without the participation of the tobacco workers. In the demonstrations only 1,300 people took part. . . . Although we had specifically incited the agrarian masses to demonstrate, march into the towns, and refuse to pay their debts, there was no response.[24]

However, the Politbureau refused to admit that the 'mass turn to the left' was only a figment of Stalin's imagination, at least as far as Greece was concerned. To say this boldly to the Comintern officials was beyond the power of the Greek Communists. Instead, they found a convenient scapegoat in the familiar 'rightists'.

The struggle 'without principles'

The lurking presence of a 'rightist danger' was first mentioned at the 2nd Plenum in June 1929, only six months after the purge of the Liquidarists and Centrists. In the following months unspecified rightist deviations were held responsible for the resounding failures of the party's revolutionary activity under the Third Period theory. At the 3rd Plenum of January 1930 the Comintern emissary alluded to the fact that 'the critical condition of our movement could not but cause intra-party friction. Within the Politbureau two factions are being formed, fighting each other, although their struggle is not always open.' He warned the plenum that there were no grounds for such intra-party fighting, and in his report to the Comintern suggested that the ECCI 'should prohibit the struggle of the two factions'.[25]

Nevertheless, the feud continued covertly throughout 1930. It differed from previous party conflicts in that both factions were faithful to Stalin and the Comintern. The cause of friction lay elsewhere. The Comintern representative had diagnosed it correctly. It was 'the critical state' of the Communist movement in Greece. If the theory was to be sacred and infallible, then the party leadership had to bear the blame for the failure. Two

[24] *To KKE, 1918–1931*, II, p. 448.   [25] Ibid., p. 561.

groups were formed, each trying to shift responsibility to the other faction. One group was headed by Khaitas, the other by George Siantos and Kostas Theos. Personal feuds were at the root of this strife, not ideological differences. To quote the term used by N. Zachariades and the Comintern documents, it was 'a struggle without principles'.

The fight came out into the open at the end of the year, when Khaitas published an article in *Neos Leninistis* in which he asserted that 'because of the inaccurate appraisal of the situation and its development in the immediate future, the call for a general strike was prematurely launched as an action slogan . . .'. After all the recent party failures one could hardly argue with this belated discovery. Khaitas did not challenge the correctness of the Third Period theory, nor did he question the desirability of a general political strike as a prelude to further revolutionary struggles. The clue to his thinking was the term 'action slogan'. In Communist practice an 'agitation slogan' is not elevated to the category of an 'action slogan' until the ground has been sufficiently prepared. In fact, Khaitas was right. Conditions in Greece were not ripe for a general political strike, nor had the party the necessary influence. But his rivals in the Politbureau, aspiring to secure for themselves the blessing of the Comintern, rallied to the extremist positions which they thought coincided with the Comintern directives. At the same time they turned to the Comintern as the supreme arbiter.

The answer of the Comintern, which arrived a few weeks later, caused a ludicrous incident. On 1 February 1931 the Politbureau triumphantly announced that 'the ECCI had allowed an open debate on the questions which concern the Party at the present time'.[26] This was interpreted as an indirect approval of the Siantos–Theos position. Three weeks later, *Rizospastis* published a complete translation of the Comintern letter. In it the ECCI ordered 'both groups to stop all discussion within the party organization and in the party press'.[27] This was the opposite of what the Politbureau had previously asserted. Inevitably, this contradiction 'gave rise to questions'. The Politbureau sheepishly explained that 'the contradiction was due to the wrong translation of the same communication. The word "to stop" was wrongly translated as "to take place" .'[28]

[26] *Rizospastis*, 1 February 1931.   [27] Ibid., 24 February 1931.
[28] Ibid., 4 March 1931.

After the correct translation of the Comintern directive had been received the Politbureau turned round and 'decided unanimously to discontinue the intra-party fight'. The party organizations which had previously called for a 'merciless fight' against the Khaitas group now 'saluted the intervention of the Communist International which put an end to the acute intra-party struggle'.

In the same communication the ECCI had called the KKE to devote all its forces to the 'immediate revolutionary fight'. In spite of previous disappointments, the Comintern leaders saw in the economic depression in the United States, with its world-wide repercussions, new possibilities for revolutionary agitation. In its directive to the KKE, the ECCI ordered 'a careful appraisal of the situation and of the correlation of forces, and the application of co-ordinated and concrete methods of struggle: economic strikes, short protest strikes, revolutionary demonstrations, mass political strikes, etc.'. These specific methods of subversion and revolutionary agitation were to be co-ordinated with 'a universal struggle against the Social-Democrat and Reformist leaders, while working for the conquest of the Social-Democrat workers and the Reformist trade unions, according to the general tactics of the United Front from below'. These instructions were coupled with an exhortation 'to bring the workers to the struggle against the danger of war, for the defence of the fatherland of the proletarians . . .'.[29] If instructions and exhortations alone could do the trick the world would long ago have turned Communist.

The Greek Communists, heartened by the prospects of an economic depression, resumed their revolutionary agitation only to end up with the worst fiasco in the party's history. Their anti-war demonstration on 1 August 1931 was attended by only 150 persons. The Politbureau, with obvious embarrassment, admitted that its appeal to the masses 'had found no response for this fight'.[30]

The Comintern installs the KKE's 'New Leadership'

With these new failures in the summer of 1931, both groups were utterly discredited. In August the Greek authorities

[29] *Tezisi, Rezolyutsii i Postanovleniya XI Plenuma IKKI* (Moscow, Ogiz Moskovskii Rabochii, 1931), pp. 17–30; hereinafter cited as *Tezisi, XI*.
[30] *Rizospastis*, 17 August 1931.

arrested Andronikos Khaitas, but he managed to escape in mysterious circumstances. He made his way to Moscow, where he stayed for a while until he was appointed to the University of Kuibyshev as a member of the faculty. In 1935 he was executed as a Trotskyist. On 16 September 1931 Theos too was arrested by the Greek authorities. Siantos had left for Moscow a few weeks earlier. With the protagonists out of the way, the Comintern decided to put an end to the endless squabbles by appointing a trusted agent with absolute power, responsible only to Moscow. The person chosen for this position was Nikolaos (Nikos) Zachariades.

Zachariades was a graduate of the KUTV, the Communist University for Eastern Peoples. On various occasions since his first return to Greece he had displayed personal courage and an unswerving devotion to the cause of Communism. Ambitious and intelligent, with a passion for organization and secrecy, a winning personality, and a hot temper, he was the man to take over the leadership of the disjointed party and lead it back towards the demanding task of revolution. Shrewd and calculating, he had carefully avoided entanglement with the losing side during the successive intra-party squabbles. In 1928, after his release from prison, under a twelve-month sentence for agitating in favour of Macedonian independence, he had again left for the Soviet Union, where he had remained during the 'struggle without principles'.

There is no evidence available to this writer proving that the visit of Anatoly Lunacharsky, the former Soviet Kommissar of Education, who was in Athens from 1 to 5 September 1931, had any immediate connexion with the appointment of Zachariades to the leadership of the party. It was, however, a rather peculiar coincidence. Two months later, the *Neos Rizospastis*—which had conveniently replaced *Rizospastis*, banned by a court order for slanderous attacks on the then Minister of Justice, Nikolaos Avraam—published an Appeal from the ECCI, addressed to the members of the KKE: 'The Party, in order to fulfil the tasks before it, must at last begin its bolshevization by immediately liquidating the criminal and unprincipled struggle, and by creating a homogeneous Party under a united leadership.'[31] The Comintern Appeal stressed anew the importance of organizing party cells in the factories, and added that 'the

[31] *Neos Rizospastis*, 3 November 1931.

Party shall wage a fight without delay for the right of self-determination including separation . . .', this being an oblique reference to the question of Macedonian independence.

A brief 'decision' of the Politbureau announced on 10 November the 'radical change' in the party leadership, and called all party organizations 'to begin immediately the work of carrying out all the suggestions contained in the Appeal of the Communist International'.[32] Within a month, 'unanimous' declarations began to arrive from all the district and local party organizations pledging the 'unswerving' and 'unqualified' allegiance of the members to the anonymous 'New Leadership'. With ludicrous uniformity, all these resolutions condemned 'the destructive, factionalist régime which had been created by the two groups (Khaitas–Eftihiades and Theos–Siantos) when the two groups tried to put the blame on each other for the failures of our Party, although they were both equally responsible. . .'.[33]

The letters which were exchanged between Kostas Theos and the New Leadership gave a first indication of what the 'radical change' really meant. For the first time the leader of a defeated faction was forced to use the most self-degrading expressions of repentance in confessing his 'errors'. In the past all dissenters had the courage to support their views without resorting to repulsive breast-beating. In a letter to the 'New Leadership' Theos sheepishly recognized as 'absolutely correct' the criticism levelled at his group and at himself personally by the ECCI, and concluded: 'I regard as absolutely necessary my removal from the party leadership. . . . I declare that I shall cut all ties with the old group and I place myself at the disposal of the New Leadership of our Party, and of the ECCI.' Never before had a leading member of the party knelt before the victorious faction to beg forgiveness. Theos' letter was only one illustration of the new *mores*. The answer of the New Leadership gave an even more striking taste of the new methods. This answer had the cold quality of steel:

The letter of comrade Theos, although a step in the right direction, cannot be accepted as satisfactory. . . . Theos, in his letter, continues to appear to minimize and conceal his errors instead of recognizing them courageously in a bolshevik manner and thus contributing resolutely to their elimination.

[32] *Neos Rizospastis*, 10 November 1931.   [33] Ibid., 12 December 1931.

Only 'the ruthless uprooting of his mistakes, and the most resolute, open struggle against the criminal factionalism' would be accepted as satisfactory repentance. Total capitulation was the price of reluctant forgiveness. The case of Theos was, of course, a primitive and imperfect application of the Stalinist techniques of human degradation; however, it should not pass unnoticed. Nikos Zachariades,[34] the trusted agent of Stalin, still hiding behind the label of the New Leadership, had already shown that he was a master of the new techniques. With the dawn of 1932 the KKE entered a new period in its twisted history.

Yiannis Zevgos, a leading party member in the following years, with pretensions to be a seasoned theoretician, wrote in the introduction to a collection of party documents published in 1936 by the KKE under the title *To Kommounistiko Komma, 1931–1936; Pente Khronia Agonon (The Communist Party, 1931–1936; Five Years of Struggle)*:

Then [December 1931] the Executive Committee of the Communist International intervened, dismissed the opportunist leadership, installed a new leadership of the Party, and addressed an Appeal to party members, in which it outlined the duties of the Party and called the members to fight for the eradication of factionalism and for the development of a Bolshevik party. This intervention of the Communist International marked the beginning of a new period in the development and the struggle of the Party.[35]

[34] See biographical note No. 1.
[35] *To Kommounistiko Komma, 1931–1936; Pente Khronia Agonon* (Athens, *Rizospastis* Edition, 1936), p. 111; hereinafter cited as *Pente Khronia*.

4. The KKE and Greek Politics

First experience at the polls

However self-centred it was, the Communist Party did not operate in a vacuum. Many of its policies were shaped by Comintern directives, but in most cases their implementation was materially affected by a multitude of internal factors. The story of the KKE cannot be told in artificial isolation from the political life of the country.

For the first fifteen years of its existence the party remained a marginal force, with no significant effect on the country's political developments. Greece was, and in large measure still is, an agrarian and petty-bourgeois country. In the twenties even those few thousands of industrial workers who could qualify as 'proletarians' were in effect former peasants. Many retained strong ties with the countryside, and this often shaped their political and social outlook. In spite of their low standard of living, few were emotionally prepared to heed the Communist call. Extensive land reforms, dating back to the early years of the twentieth century, had resulted in a multitude of propertied peasant households with a strong emotional attachment to their land-holdings, regardless of how large or how small they were. The 'petty-bourgeoisie', strongly nationalistic and property-minded, remained conspicuously unimpressed by Communist appeals 'to join the struggle against the capitalist yoke'.[1]

The perennial quarrels and the constant changes in its leadership and political orientation, though largely unknown to the general public, could not but lessen the party's effectiveness as a political force. Its increasing subordination to a foreign organization exposed it to the charge of being nothing but a foreign agent. This, together with its advocacy of 'Macedonian independence', which to most Greeks appeared to be a veiled attempt to transfer to Bulgaria, a traditional enemy, territories inhabited by Greeks, offset most of the advantages offered to a revolutionary party by the country's political and economic vicissitudes and tribulations in the twenties.

[1] *To KKE, 1918–1931*, p. 131.

Throughout this period the party's constantly changing membership remained extremely limited. As late as 1928 its leadership openly deplored the failure to attract 5,000 new members, as required by a decision of the Third Regular Congress of 1927. The recruitment of 'large numbers' of factory workers remained wishful thinking. According to the Comintern records, the party's membership during the twenties never exceeded 2,500 throughout Greece.

From the outset, the party leaders realized that only by exploiting political, economic, and social issues with little or no relation to Marxism–Leninism could they expect to broaden the influence of their party and make their mark on the political life of the country. Whatever successes they scored in the twenties were the product of skilful exploitation of practical problems besetting large segments of the Greek people. Their failure to become something more than an irritant was caused by their stand on the Macedonian question and their blind attachment to Communist slogans forced on them by the Comintern.

The first test of the party's political appeal came in November 1920, when the Greek electorate went to the polls for the first time since the end of the war. The party leaders, having no illusions as to their electoral prospects, declared at the preelectoral party conference that

the Party does not believe it can ever win power through elections but only through revolution. Yet it must always take part in elections because the electoral campaign offers excellent opportunities for propaganda and agitation; besides, the rostrum of Parliament is an excellent forum for the propagation of the Party's views to the people.[2]

In 1920 there was one major issue which appeared most suitable for political exploitation: the possibility of war with Turkey. The prospect of a military campaign in Asia Minor held little appeal for many Greeks who had spent more than eight years in uniform, growing old and tired through a succession of campaigns which carried them from the rolling hills of Macedonia and Thrace in the Balkan Wars of 1912–13 to the plains of South Russia during the Western campaign against the Bolshevik régime. To others, however, the territorial gains along the Aegean coast of Asia Minor, sanctioned by the Treaty

[2] Stavrides, op. cit., p. 37.

of Sèvres, represented a high point in the realization of the Grand Idea, the age-old aspiration to bring foreign-dominated Greek minorities under the protective mantle of the Greek state. The Liberal Party, under the leadership of Eleutherios Venizelos, the architect of Greek territorial expansion since 1912, advocated the preservation of territorial gains acquired under the Treaty of Sèvres in Asia Minor, at all costs, even if it meant another war with Turkey. The pro-royalist conservatives held the opposite view.

In a bizarre alignment with the Greek conservatives and royalists the Communists raised the anti-war cry. Their fierce proclamations, however, were lost in the thundering anti-war campaign of the conservative, anti-Venizelist camp. In the election of 1 November 1920 the conservatives won by a landslide. Venizelos left Greece, a voluntary exile. The candidates of the Greek Socialist Labour (Communist) Party mustered almost 100,000 votes. Under the majority system none of the party candidates tasted victory at the polls, as these votes were scattered. Nevertheless, the popular support received by SEK(k) candidates in the election of 1920 was to remain a high point in the party's political fortunes for more than three decades.

The general strike of 1923

The defeat of Venizelos did not avert a war with Turkey in Asia Minor. Forced by the course of events, the Royalist Government followed the policy they had so violently condemned before the election. To raise the considerable funds required for the campaign in Asia Minor, the Government resorted to inflationary practices. By the time the front collapsed in August 1922 the finances and the credit of the country had sunk to a low level, and by the end of the year the drachma had lost 94 per cent. of its gold value. Prices soared to unprecedented heights.

With the collapse of the front in August 1922, the royalist Government was overthrown in a revolution led by General Nikolaos Plastiras, one of the heroes of the Asia Minor campaign. Greece lost all the territories acquired under the Peace Treaties of 1919 except for an area of 3,315 sq. miles in Western Thrace. She had to accept one and a half million new inhabitants—refugees and exchanged populations. Four hundred and thirty thousand Turks and Bulgarians left Greece under exchange treaties.

The abrupt influx of one and a half million refugees and displaced persons into a country of no more than six million people was bound to cause serious economic and social dislocations. Most of the refugees from Asia Minor were city-dwellers, members of the professions, artisans, or merchants. Uprooted from their age-old homes in Asia Minor, they were faced with a painful readjustment in a poor and crowded land. Some were diverted to agriculture; others gathered around the main cities and towns, swelling the urban proletariat. The gigantic task of absorbing this mass of destitute humanity, amounting to almost 20 per cent. of the country's population at that time, can hardly be overestimated. It is not surprising that for many years the Communists found a relatively ready response to their agitation among the refugees.

Nevertheless, after the initial dire hardships, the refugees proved to be a valuable addition to the nation. This adjustment was not accomplished overnight. In 1923 the chaotic conditions caused by defeat and revolution offered the Communist leaders ample opportunity for agitation. In response to the Comintern's 'detailed instructions', the party leaders attempted to foment a strike wave in the major urban centres, particularly in Athens and Piraeus, as a prelude to a general political strike. To carry out their assigned task, they skilfully exploited the party's influence in the General Confederation of Greek Workers. In the Executive Committee of this nation-wide organization the Communists were strongly represented. By being active in the trade unions, party members, without using their party label, had managed to be elected to the executive posts of some of them. In turn, they had promoted to the Executive Committee of the General Confederation leaders with pro-Communist leanings. This, however, had caused several important unions to sever their ties with the General Confederation. The party leaders, fully aware of these facts, proceeded with subtlety and caution. In the end the Greek Communist Party, with no more than 1,000 members at the time, succeeded in mobilizing more than 150,000 workers—almost the entire Greek labour force.

It was no problem for the Communists to call a strike of the Communist-led unions; but such a 'success' would have been of questionable value. The strike wave should have originated in the non-Communist unions. Then the Communist-led unions would have joined in, thus assuring complete success. It is doubtful whether the party leaders expected to force a revolutionary change in Greece through the weapon of general political strike, although some incurable optimists among them probably hoped to exploit the unsettled conditions following the Plastiras revolt and repeat the feat of the Russian Bolsheviks. True, at the time of the revolt against the Royalist Government and King Constantine there were many opportunities for Communist agitation. But the Communist Party was beset by its own inner conflicts, too weak and disorganized to act in the tradition of the Russian Bolsheviks of 1917. No amount of detailed instructions from the Comintern could offset the party's ineptitude and lack of public support. By fomenting a widespread strike wave, the party leaders wanted to show the Comintern, as well as the Greek people and the traditional parties, that the Greek Communist Party, though small in membership, exercised strong influence over the workers and was a political force to be taken seriously.

The agitation started in the Federation of Railway Employees, which was not a member of the General Confederation. The Communists had a 'fraction' in the leadership of that union, but the majority in the Secretariat was made up of non-Communist elements under the leadership of its Secretary-General, G. Stratis, a station-master in the Peloponnesian Railways (SPAP), a man of moderate views, supported by the great majority of the union members. To force Stratis' hand, the Communists skilfully exploited two issues with no relation to Communist ideology: the demand for higher wages to cope with the continuing rise in the cost of living, and the demand for the reinstatement of those employees who had been dismissed by Plastiras for their affiliation with the royalist parties. Both claims had the overwhelming support of the union members.

Stratis, aware of the Communist objectives, faced a serious dilemma: whether to side with those favouring a strike, and thus play the Communist game, or to oppose the strike and risk losing his influence, to the benefit of the Communists. He chose the first alternative and gave the signal for the strike.

As soon as the railway employees went on strike, the

Communist 'fractions' in other non-Communist unions began to agitate for the broadening of the strike wave. It was easier to push those unions into the vortex of the strike wave than to keep them out, since members had ample grounds for purely economic grievances. By exploiting the discontent of union members, Communist agitators succeeded in convincing the 'masses' that their unions should enter the strike movement without delay. The reluctant labour leaders, who considered a strike at that moment to be a direct blow against government efforts to bring about some semblance of economic order, were forced to succumb to the general clamour.

With most of the non-Communist unions already on strike, it was fairly easy to make the strike general. In a show of 'solidarity', the Communist-led unions entered the arena. Then, following a decision of the Communist Party, the General Confederation of Workers proclaimed a general 'Pan-helladic'[3] strike.

Mobilization for the strike completed, the Communists felt that the time had come for a mass demonstration. Probably under the direction of the Comintern emissary who was then visiting Athens, the party leaders showed a remarkable appreciation of the basic principles of mass mobilization. As soon as the strike wave reached its peak, they called a mass demonstration in Passalimani Square, in Piraeus. The location of this square, far away from any important government buildings or installations, made control by the authorities fairly easy. To march from Passalimani Square to Athens for a showdown was a physical impossibility, because of the distance involved. The demonstration, if left to work itself out, would have been an exercise in futility. The Government, however, chose to break it up by force. Eleven workers were killed, many wounded. No Communists were among the casualties.

After the events at Passalimani several non-Communist labour leaders and liberal politicians made joint efforts to find a compromise solution, and the strikes were gradually called off. The Communists kept clamouring that the events at Passalimani were 'the beginning of much bigger, more difficult, more bloody, more acute struggles between the workers and the bourgeoisie'.[4] Yet for more than a decade this was to remain

---

[3] Pan-helladic in contrast to Pan-hellenic, which was considered to be a term nationalistic in character.　　　　[4] *Rizospastis*, 11 August 1924.

the highest point in the party's influence among the Greek workers. The wide participation in the general strike, achieved through clever exploitation of ordinary grievances, did not reflect the party's political strength. This was tacitly recognized by the second Extraordinary Congress which convened in Athens on 16 September 1923, to map out party strategy in the forthcoming parliamentary elections. In a memorable paragraph of its 'electoral platform' the Congress gave one of the most candid descriptions of the party's attitude towards parliamentary elections:

The Communist Party of Greece (KKE), the party of class struggle and social revolution, rejects categorically all democratic dogmas. On the basis of historical experience, the Party declares that it is impossible for the proletariat to come to power by common consent. On the contrary, the Party knows that the dictatorship of the bourgeoisie cannot be vanquished except by force; it must be replaced by the dictatorship of the workers and peasants until the final victory of Communism. For this reason, electoral activity has only secondary importance for our Party. It is useful only for the propagation of the Communist principles and of the party programme among the masses.[5]

The Congress reconciled itself to the fact that under the majority system no Communist candidate had a chance of being elected, except through electoral coalitions with other political parties. Such coalitions, however, had been ruled out by the Comintern; it was a period of 'United Front from below only'. Without the convenience of political 'allies', the Communist candidates were crushed at the polls. They received only 20,000 votes in a total of more than 800,000.

The first Communist deputies in Parliament

For another three years the Communist Party remained on the sidelines of Greek political life, a group of perennially quarrelling politicians with revolutionary pretensions. In the plebiscite of April 1924, which resulted in the establishment of a Republic, the Communists made an unsuccessful attempt to force a three-way choice, with 'a workers' and peasants' government' as the third possibility. When their demand was ignored by the Liberal Government the party leadership decided to vote in favour of the Republic. Characteristically

5 *To KKE, 1918–1931*, p. 252.

they argued that the struggle of the Communists and that of the partisans of the Republic against the Monarchy were only 'parallel'; but just as two parallel lines never meet, their co-operation with the Republicans did not go beyond their common desire to abolish the Constitutional Monarchy.

The plebiscite of April 1924 resulted in the defeat of the Constitutional Monarchy. Since their votes merged with those of the Republicans, there is no way of telling to what extent the Communists contributed to the establishment of the Republic. Judging from the results of the preceding parliamentary election of November 1923, their role could not have been decisive, nor even significant.

Their first opportunity to enter Parliament came with the election of 7 November 1926. The dictatorial régime of Theodore Pangalos had been overthrown by General G. Kondylis, who, in an effort to contribute to an honest and fair election, had agreed to stay, with his group, out of the contest. As a further guarantee of the fair representation of the country's political forces, the major parties had agreed for the first time to use the proportional electoral system.

There was one cause for apprehension. The so-called Republican Battalions, established by Pangalos to act as his henchmen, had turned against the dictator and helped General Kondylis to oust him from office. As long as the 'Republican Battalions' retained their strength and organization there was always a possibility that they might turn against the Government and attempt another *coup*. Kondylis carefully prepared their disbandment. In the early hours of 9 September regular troops converged on the barracks in Athens where the Battalions were stationed. Before dawn the barracks were surrounded, and after brief skirmishes Colonels Napoleon Zervas and Leonidas Dertilis, the leaders of the Battalions, agreed to surrender to avoid further bloodshed.

Although General Kondylis immediately issued a proclamation hailing his 'threefold victory against the Battalions, the Royalists, and the Communists whose co-operation is indubitable', the role of both the Royalists and the Communists had the overtones of comic opera. The Communists did call for a demonstration in support of Kondylis against the Battalions, and several hundred people did gather in the area around Omonia Square, in the centre of Athens. Another demonstration of Royalists, protesting against the instability and the constant disorders of the Republic, had gathered near by. By 10.30 in the morning an armoured car belonging to the Battalions drove down Stadiou Street towards the Central Post Office building. There it stopped in the middle of the square, while its occupants entered the building, leaving the car unattended. The Communist-led demonstrators promptly surrounded the armoured car. With the help of a taxi-driver, some of them set it in motion and triumphantly drove it at the Royalist demonstrators, who on seeing the oncoming monster prudently ran for cover. After this first victory the Communist *condottieri* drove through Stadiou Street to Constitution Square, then down Ermou Street; finally, in the vicinity of Monasteraki Square, the vehicle ran out of petrol and was ignominiously abandoned.

In the meantime the Communist-led demonstrators, emboldened by the retreat of the Royalists, marched towards Constitution Square. It was already almost noon, and by then the Battalions had agreed to surrender. Kondylis, quite unappreciative of the 'help' given him by the Communists against the Royalists, sent some troops to disperse the civilian demonstrators. A few die-hards tried to put up a semblance of resistance, but they, too, were soon put to flight. The next day *Rizospastis*, with unconcealed bitterness, wrote that 'Mr. Kondylis should know that if the Royalists failed to win power yesterday it was due to the democratic forces of workers and peasants and to the policies of their party'.[6]

Kondylis had asserted in his proclamation that the Communists had taken advantage of the disorders to try 'to win power'. To this, *Rizospastis* replied: 'We have never concealed the fact that our strategic objective is to win power by force. But this is our strategy; our tactics, based on present conditions, categorically rule out the seizure of power today.' This was a statement of fact. In 1926 the conditions in which the KKE could win power did not exist. The Government was well armed, the armed forces loyal, the middle class and the peasantry faithful to the traditional institutions in spite of many disappointments, while the Communist Party was not only unarmed but also weak and torn by internal strife. *Rizospastis* was telling the truth.

[6] *Rizospastis*, 10 September 1926.

With the elements of potential disorder out of the way, Kondylis proceeded with the parliamentary election as planned. In the election of 7 November 1926 the electoral system of proportional representation was the decisive element in the Communist candidates' success at the polls. Eleutherios Stavrides, who had taken over the direction of party affairs after the persecution of the other party leaders by the Pangalos régime, was still in charge when the party's electoral programme was drafted. He realized that, to avoid alienating potential supporters, one issue most distasteful to the Greek electorate, the call for an 'independent Macedonia', should be kept out of the party programme. Without this irritant, the 'United Front' candidates managed to collect a total of 41,982 votes. Ten of them were elected.[7]

In a total of 286 parliamentary seats, ten deputies may appear unimportant. Yet the potential significance of these ten Communist deputies was far greater than their numerical strength might indicate. As the two major political groups—the Liberals and the Royalists—had gained 143 and 127 seats respectively, the ten Communist deputies and the six independents were in an advantageous bargaining position.

A wasted opportunity

Parliament offered the Communist deputies a valuable rostrum for propaganda under the protection of parliamentary immunity. Yet these opportunities were lost mainly because of the intra-party squabbles between the Stalinists and the 'Liquidarists'. As the party deputies in Parliament belonged to the latter group—with Theos the only exception—the first parliamentary success of the Communist Party was largely wasted.

[7] The first Communist deputies who entered Parliament in 1926 were:

Name	District
Anastasios (Tassos) Khainoglou	Evros
Athanasios Sinokas	Rodopi
Const. Constantinides	Dramma
Eleutherios Stavrides	Kavalla
Jack Ventura (Jewish)	Salonika
David Behar Solan (Jewish)	Salonika
Gregorios Papanikolaou	Salonika
Nikolaos Kyriakopoulos	Florina
Serafim Maximos	Larissa
Kostas Theos	Larissa

For purely factional reasons, the Stalinist group under Khaitas caused the prosecution of the Communist deputies by raising the issue of Macedonian independence, knowing quite well that the deputies would be held responsible for the party's agitation. In this way the Stalinists hoped to get rid of those they considered their opponents, while crying out against 'the persecution of the Communist deputies by the class enemy'. The final objective, of course, was to have those deputies replaced by members of the Stalinist group.

Irritated by the Communist clamour for the separation of national territories and unaware of the Stalinists' hidden motives, the majority in Parliament voted for removal of the immunity of those deputies, with the exception of Maximos, thus allowing their prosecution by the courts.[8] With characteristic cynicism, the Stalinist-dominated Plenum of the Central Committee which met on 15 February 1928 charged the parliamentary group with having failed because of its 'reformist' distortions of the party line, its tendency to hush up the official party policy on essential matters, and its 'reformist emasculation of the party line on the question of a united and independent Macedonia'.[9]

In point of fact, the causes for the failure of the parliamentary group should have been sought far deeper. First of all, to the Communists the rostrum of Parliament was nothing more than a convenient platform for publicizing Communist slogans. Without genuine interest in the work of Parliament, the party deputies were unable or unwilling to offer even remotely constructive opposition. Yet, to their discomfiture, they soon discovered that it was practically impossible to take a negative stand on every single issue. Many legislative proposals enjoyed the support of the very people the Communists hoped to influence and win over. Afraid that constructive participation in the work of Parliament might expose them to the attacks of the Stalinists in the Politbureau, the Communist deputies either abstained from the debates or resorted to evasive generalizations and empty attacks ending with the familiar invocation of the 'workers' and peasants' government', which they offered as a panacea for all the country's social and economic ills. More often than not, the opposition of the Communist deputies appeared ill-informed, trivial, or even idiotic.

[8] See more details in Chapter 5.   [9] *To KKE, 1918–1931*, II, p. 240.

Another cause for the failure of the Communist deputies was
that they were forced for the first time to come face to face, in
the responsible environment of Parliament, with the magnitude
and the complexity of the nation's problems. The easy solutions
offered by the party ideology appeared, when contrasted with
Greek reality, naïve or irrelevant. The subsequent course taken
by most of those deputies indicates that during their participation in Parliament they began to question seriously the practical
validity of the sweeping promises of Communism. As long as
they remained within the ivory tower of the party, they had
felt intellectually secure. Thrown into the whirlpool of real
political life, they had come to realize that 'things were not so
simple'.

The law against Communist agitation

Eleutherios Venizelos, the Liberal statesman, a voluntary
exile since his dramatic defeat in the election of November
1920, decided in 1928 to return to Greece and take over once
again the reins of the Liberal Party he had founded in 1910. In
the elections of 19 August 1928 the Liberals won by a landslide.

In 1928 Venizelos was no longer the man who had left
Greece in 1920, much less the revolutionary leader of the
Cretans in Therissos. During the long years of his exile he had
time to study and understand the significance of a 'proletarian'
state on the soil of Russia. He had come to realize that the old
political feuds which divided the Greek people, and for which
he was partly responsible, had lost much of their relevance and
historical meaning. Considering the defence of free institutions
against the revolutionary ideology of Communism to be a
paramount obligation of the political leadership, Venizelos
made a serious effort to reconcile the two major camps—
Liberals and Royalists—on a permanent basis. He failed because his followers could not grasp the change in the political
outlook of their leader, while his opponents mistrusted him too
much to accept his conservative and conciliatory statements as
genuine. Much later, in 1936, Panagis Tsaldaris, the leader of
the conservative Populists and Venizelos' major opponent in
the thirties, wrote an article on the eve of his death. In that
article, which he never had time to finish, Tsaldaris gave his
followers this solemn warning:

... Whether we like it or not, whether we admit it or not, a change has taken place; sooner or later, the political leaders as well as the Greek people will be forced to realize that there are no longer Republicans and Royalists, Venizelists and anti-Venizelists. There is only the great majority of the Greek people on one side, faithful to their age-old national traditions, following at the same time the development of world conditions, never rejecting progress and the benefits one can derive from it. On the other side, there is a minority seeking to overthrow the social order . . . , confusing progress with disorder, corruption, and immorality.[10]

Venizelos had already reached the same conclusion in 1928. At that time his opponents were unwilling to accept his revised outlook as genuine. Yet the Bill Venizelos placed before Parliament on 22 December 1928 was a clear indication that his return to the political arena was motivated by the desire to avert 'the dangers threatening the existing order, and prevent the social disturbances which might result from the inability of the political parties to provide the country with a stable government'.[11] By this Bill, agitation against the social order became for the first time a punishable criminal offence, a *sui generis* (Idionym) crime.

The proposed law was not severe: the maximum penalty did not exceed six months in prison. On the other hand, there was a danger that the ambiguity of the text in defining the basic elements of the 'crime' would leave the way open for arbitrary actions by local authorities; being ignorant of even the most basic features of Communist theory and practice, they were liable to interpret the most innocuous political movements as 'aiming at the overthrow of the existing social order'. The Bill's rough passage through the parliamentary seas was an indication of the mixed reaction to its merits, most of the opposition coming from Venizelos' own followers in Parliament. Finally, after a long and involved scrutiny by parliamentary committees, the individual articles and the proposed amendments were debated by the full chamber on 18 June 1929. The following day the Bill was enacted as Law 4229 and became popularly known as the 'Idionym Law'.

This 'Idionym Law' was not, of course, an original invention of the Greek Government. Once the revolutionary tide of the

---

[10] G. Vouros, *Panagis Tsaldaris* (Athens, Elliniki Ekthotiki Etairia, 1955), p. 567.
[11] Gr. Dafnis, *I Ellas metaxy thyo Polemon* (Athens, Ikaros, 1955), p. 375.

E

early post-war years had subsided and the international situation had regained a measure of stability, many European governments thought that the adoption of such measures against Communist agitation could avert future revolutionary upheavals. Not always coupled with consistent social legislation, these police measures enjoyed, as a rule, only a very limited success.

The party at its lowest ebb

The marked decline of Communist influence in the years following Venizelos' return cannot be attributed to the 'Idionym' Law. This law, often ineptly applied, never really became an effective obstacle to the recruitment of new adherents or to the dissemination of Communist propaganda. The causes of the decline must be sought elsewhere.

The first indication of serious trouble came at the election of 19 August 1928. The party's candidates won a grand total of only 14,325 out of more than a million votes. It was the lowest figure ever polled by Communist candidates in Greece.

The return of Venizelos had inspired confidence among a large section of the population in the urban centres and in the countryside. His promise to make Greece 'better than ever' captured the imagination of people who had been groping for years for effective leadership. At the same time a series of economic measures, and a British loan of nine million pounds, somewhat eased the economic pressure. On the other hand, the disputes within the Communist Party came out into the open with unbridled vehemence and alienated many of the party's sympathizers. To many of them Venizelos' known abilities offered a more realistic hope of improvement than the wild promises of the quarrelling Communists. The difficulties of the party were compounded by the poor record of the Communist deputies in the previous Parliament and by the appointment of unknown individuals as candidates, in accordance with the party policy of promoting 'genuine proletarians' to positions of leadership. Moreover, the party's obstinate stand for an 'independent' Macedonia branded it in the eyes of most Greeks with the mark of treason, while the Communist slogans about the defence of 'our Soviet Fatherland' sounded too ludicrous to be taken seriously by the Greek voters.

It is true that in the years 1919–34 'growth in membership

and polling strength was not always a measure of success . . . as a party might grow and win parliamentary seats precisely because it was in decay and falling into "opportunism" '. During those years 'the test of real success could only consist in a tangible approach towards the revolutionary conquest of power by the party'.[12] Even in this approach the party could find no cause for jubilation. It was never farther away from a revolutionary seizure of power. On 1 August 1929 its call for a massive anti-war demonstration and a general political strike was ignored by 92 per cent. of the Greek labour force, while another 'mobilization' for a 'red May Day strike' on 1 May 1930, to be coupled with 'armed incursions' of peasants into towns, 'mobilized' only 3,000 workers and no peasants at all. The 'decision' to admit 5,000 workers remained an empty wish, while the membership of the party fell to 1,666, with only 170 members in Athens and 70 in Piraeus. The KKE entered the decade of the 1930s in bankruptcy and political isolation.

[12] Franz Borkenau, *World Communism; a History of the Communist International* (New York, W. W. Norton, 1939), p. 177.

5. The Macedonian Question

A touchstone of loyalty

From the early days of the party no other issue has caused more trouble in its relations with the Greek people and within its ranks than the so-called 'national question', i.e. the party's continued agitation for a separate Macedonian state. For many years all efforts to broaden its political influence were undermined by its open advocacy of an autonomous or even an independent Macedonian state, to include the Greek portion of Macedonia, inhabited by almost a million and a half Greeks.

This thorny issue came up for the first time in the spring of 1921 when a party delegation, under George Georgiades, an able lawyer and then the foremost advocate of affiliation with the Comintern, went to Moscow to participate in the Third World Congress. During their stay in Moscow Vassili Kolarov, then Secretary of the Bulgarian Communist Party, spoke to Georgiades of the need to support the drive for Macedonian autonomy 'so that the [Bulgarian] Party will be able to win support from the Bulgaro-Macedonian refugees, and take them away from the reactionary camp'.[1] Georgiades was taken by surprise, but he managed to avoid any definite commitment. By the time he returned home, he was no longer an ardent advocate of Communism. Disillusioned by his experiences at the Congress, Georgiades reversed his former position and led the party's last major move to regain independence, crystallized in the decision of the February Conference (1922).[2]

In May 1922 the Bulgarian Communists made another attempt to promote their pet project. At the Plenum of the BCF Bureau, Kolarov presented the Bulgarian demand for an autonomous Macedonia in no uncertain terms and asked the other parties to come out in support of the Bulgarian position. Most of the area, which Kolarov insisted was inhabited by 'Bulgaro-Macedonians', lay outside Bulgaria within the borders of Yugoslavia and Greece. Yiannis Petsopoulos, the owner of

[1] Yiannis Petsopoulos, *Ta Ethnika Zitimata kai i Ellines Kommounistes* (Athens, 1946), p. 31.   [2] See above, pp. 8–10.

Rizospastis, who represented the Greek party at the meeting, opposed Kolarov's proposals and argued that

the Communist parties of the other Balkan countries cannot adopt the slogans which the Bulgarian bourgeois governments have been propagating since their defeat in 1913, especially at a time when hundreds of Komitadji bands, equipped and supported by these same governments, are active in the Greek and Serbian parts of Macedonia.[3]

Petsopoulos had reacted to Kolarov's proposals almost instinctively as any patriotically-minded Greek would have. He interpreted the demand for an 'autonomous Macedonia' as a veiled attempt to extend Bulgarian rule over territories inhabited by Greeks. At the first provocation his petty-bourgeois background showed through the newly-acquired Communist veneer. Petsopoulos failed to appreciate the reasons behind Comintern support for an 'autonomous Macedonia'. The agitation for 'autonomy' led by Communist agents was expected to win over thousands of people with uncertain loyalties in the very heartland of the Balkans. If the agitation succeeded in producing an autonomous Macedonian state the Comintern hoped to exercise considerable influence over it and use the new state as a convenient springboard for further expansion in the Balkans. At the very least, agitation in Macedonia would have caused trouble in three Balkan countries simultaneously.

When Petsopoulos came back, his conduct in Sofia was denounced by the pro-Comintern faction of the Greek party as an 'irrational' mixture of super-Communism, chauvinism, and reformism. Under pressure, he gave up the ownership of *Rizospastis*, which by now was, in effect, the party newspaper, supported almost exclusively by party members and sympathizers. Then he was expelled from the party.

The party supports the Macedonian demand

The Communist veterans who returned to Greece after the collapse of the Asia Minor front were the first to endorse the Bulgarian demand for a Macedonian state. At the National Council of the party in May 1923 their spokesman, Eleutherios Stavrides, successfully moved a resolution which included a demand for the recognition of 'the right of minorities to self-

---

[3] Petsopoulos, op. cit., p. 30.

determination'. This demand was not as innocent as it might
have appeared to the uninitiated. For the first time the Communist Party had formally accepted the Bulgarian thesis that there
existed in the heart of the Balkans a Macedonian nationality
aspiring to establish its own national state. To be sure, there
was no direct reference to the Macedonian question, yet everyone knew what the ostensibly innocuous proposal really meant.
The slogan of 'Macedonian autonomy' was formally accepted
a few months later by the party's representative to the ECCI in
Moscow. N. Sargologos was sent to Moscow in the autumn of
1923 to take part in the plenary sessions of the ECCI and of the
Executive Committee of the Balkan Communist Federation.
During the meetings of these two bodies Vassili Kolarov and
Georgi Dimitrov, the Bulgarian representatives, once again
pressed for the formal adoption of the 'Macedonian autonomy'
slogan, which they elevated to a 'matter of principle'.

The attitude of the Bulgarian representatives was all the
more surprising in view of the crushing blow the Bulgarian
party had suffered in October when, at the insistence of the
Comintern, it had instigated a revolt in Nova Zagora. With
only limited and rather reluctant support from the peasantry,
the Communist rebels had been crushed by the troops of the
Tsankov Government. Kolarov and Dimitrov, with a group of
2,000 faithfuls, escaped to Yugoslavia. Within a few weeks the
two Bulgarian Communist leaders, with some of their most
important lieutenants, were able to reach Soviet Russia, where
they took up residence near Moscow.[4]

Apparently these serious setbacks failed to discourage the
two Bulgarian leaders. Following the axiom that attack is the
best defence, they pressed with even greater vigour for the
acceptance of the 'Macedonian autonomy' slogan as a matter
of principle. To the previous argument that they needed this
slogan to attract the 'Macedonian refugees', they added the
theory that they also expected to attract the *komitadjis* of the
IMRO (Internal Macedonian Revolutionary Organization),
the nationalist organization agitating for a Macedonian state.
They attributed their defeat in the October uprising to the
co-operation of the *komitadjis* with Tsankov, the obvious implication being that had the Balkan Communist parties adopted the

[4] Dragomir Nenoff, *The Communist Party of Bulgaria* (MSS, Library of Congress),
p. 4.

slogan in time, the *komitadjis* would have sided with the Communists.[5]

With the support of Dmitry Manuilsky, a Comintern leader associated with the Balkan region, the slogan of 'Macedonian autonomy' was adopted by the ECCI and the Executive Committee of the Balkan Communist Federation as a matter of principle, obligatory, that is, for all member parties. The Yugoslav representatives Mirkovich and Miliokovich, in a rare display of defiance, refused to accept the slogan.[6] The Greek representative N. Sargologos, without any definite instructions from his party, accepted the slogan on its behalf, together with 1,500 gold sovereigns, part of the £3,000 yearly contribution of the Comintern to its Greek 'section'. Sargologos did not deliver the money. When he reached Greece he claimed that he had been robbed in Italy. Shortly afterwards he left for the United States.[7]

The party chose temporarily to sidestep the commitment assumed by Sargologos on the 'national question'. Pressed by several leading members who wanted to postpone a definite decision on the subject, the Central Committee submitted a memorandum to the ECCI in Moscow requesting further information and clarification of certain points. Even the members of the three-man Central Committee, elected by the National Council of February 1924, held differing views on the subject. Kordatos, who had served as an army officer in Macedonia, argued that adoption of this cause would estrange the party from the masses in the northern Greek provinces and discredit it as an appendage of the Bulgarians. Serafim Maximos, disagreeing with Kordatos, insisted that 'the KKE should, first of all, obey the instructions of the Comintern'.[8] Thomas Apostolides, the third member of the Central Committee, refused to take sides, on the ground that he was not familiar with the situation in Greek Macedonia.

The matter was brought to a head by an invitation from Moscow. The Greek Communist Party was invited to send its representatives to the Fifth World Congress of the Comintern,

---

[5] Cf. Ch. Anastasoff, *The Tragic Peninsula* (St. Louis, Blackwell Wieland, 1938), p. 33.

[6] *Fifth Congress of the Communist International; Abridged Report* (published by the C.P. of Great Britain, 1925), p. 191; hereinafter cited as *Fifth World Congress, Abridged Report.*

[7] Stavrides, op. cit., pp. 177–9.　　　　　　　　　　　　[8] Ibid., p. 181.

scheduled to meet in Moscow on 17 June 1924. The invitation
included a strange addendum: the KKE representatives should
be prepared to discuss the 'national question'. To party
members the cryptic phrase meant only one thing: the question
of Macedonian autonomy.

Yiannis Kordatos, the senior member of the Central Commit-
tee, declined a suggestion that he should represent the party at
the Fifth World Congress, presumably to avoid acceptance of
'Macedonian autonomy' against his better judgement. Instead,
Serafim Maximos, accompanied by P. Pouliopoulos, left for
Moscow via Germany.

In Moscow the two Greek Communists were confronted not
only with the question of Macedonian autonomy but also with
that of Thrace—as though a Thracian nation had sprung up
overnight. Manuilsky, the Comintern's Balkan expert, introduced the topic. Speaking on the complexities of the 'national
question', he said:

The many mistakes committed by the various sections of the
Comintern in connection with this question are due to the fact
that many of our comrades are not yet rid of social-democratic
ideology. . . . Very characteristic is Com. Mirkovich's [Yugoslav]
attitude towards the Macedonian question. . . . In his articles, he
expresses the opinion that the Macedonian question is not by any
means a Balkan but a European problem which cannot be solved
before a victory of the European proletariat over the bourgeoisie
has been achieved. If the question is put in this way, what will be
the result? Only a passive attitude of the Communist Party to one
of the most burning questions which are agitating the various
Balkan nationalities at present.

Similar mistakes are made by our Greek comrades in connection
with the Macedonian question. A few months ago, when an armed
conflict seemed imminent in the Balkans . . ., the Executive Committee of the Balkan Federation issued a manifesto which called upon
the proletariat of the Balkan countries to stand up for Macedonian
independence. The Greek Communist Party not only did not
publish this manifesto, but even sent a reasoned protest against the
issue of such a document.[9]

Throughout the period of revolutionary agitation in Bulgaria,
mentioned by Manuilsky, the Greek Communist Party did
nothing to assist the Bulgarian Communists and the autono-

[9] *Fifth World Congress; Abridged Report*, p. 191.

mists of the Internal Macedonian Revolutionary Organization (IMRO) in carrying out their plans for Macedonia.[10] To Serafim Maximos, who had been one of the three members of the Central Committee, the meaning of Manuilsky's criticism was quite clear. The party was charged with deliberate failure to perform its duty as a loyal section of the Comintern. He therefore tried to present an explanation for the negative attitude of the Comintern's Greek 'section'. He told the Congress:

The position of the Greek party on the Macedonian question is not what Manuilsky says it is. Every national minority finds a defender in us, since the struggle of the national minorities is at the same time a struggle against the dominant class. . . . It is true that we sent a letter to the Balkan Federation protesting that in issuing the slogan of autonomy of Macedonia, it failed to take into consideration the conditions of its application to Greece.

After the Treaty of Lausanne, all the Turkish inhabitants of Macedonia were obliged to leave, and the Greek bourgeoisie installed 700,000 refugees in their place. The Greek Communist party opposed, and will continue to oppose, this violence, and the Treaty of Lausanne. We would be glad if the Turkish comrades did the same. But the fact remains that there are 700,000 Greek refugees in Macedonia. The workers and peasants of Greece were not, therefore, prepared to accept the slogan of the autonomy of Macedonia. . . .[11]

Maximos, still a Communist at heart, died in Vienna, a voluntary exile, in 1961. His opposition to Manuilsky at the Fifth World Congress of the Comintern was to remain his finest hour. It was a brief hour. Under pressure from the Comintern and from Pouliopoulos, he agreed to accept on behalf of the KKE Central Committee the resolutions of the Congress on the 'national question'. He asked only for moral support from the Comintern and the Balkan Communist Federation in overcoming the opposition he expected to encounter within his own party in Greece.

[10] On 6 May 1924 representatives of the Bulgarian Communist Party and the IMRO had signed an agreement to work together for Macedonian autonomy. The agreement was soon denounced by the IMRO, and after the assassination of the IMRO's leader, Todor Aleksandrov, it was completely discarded by his successor, Ivan Mikhailov. See also Ruth Fischer, *Stalin and German Communism* (Cambridge, U.S.A., Harvard University Press, 1948), pp. 465–70; also J. Swire, *Bulgarian Conspiracy* (London, Robert Hale, 1939), pp. 180–90; also Anastasoff, op. cit., passim.

[11] *Fifth World Congress; Abridged Report*, pp. 205–6.

The Fifth World Congress decided 'to propagate the slogan for a Balkan Federation of equal and independent worker-peasant republics', and assigned to the Balkan Communist Federation the task 'of uniting and leading the work of the Balkan Communist parties in connexion with the national and, in particular, with the Macedonian and Thracian question'.[12] This inclusion of a 'Thracian question' was accepted by Maximos without protest; in any event it seemed futile to object.

In November 1924, with the 'invaluable contribution' of the Comintern representatives and with Pouliopoulos leading the chorus, the Third Extraordinary Congress of the KKE overruled Kordatos' objections and accepted unanimously the slogan for an *independent* Macedonia and Thrace as a matter of principle, on which open disagreement was inadmissible. Following a pattern which has since become a hallmark of Communist tactics, the Greek Communists justified their support for the independence of Macedonia and Thrace as a means to preserve peace. 'The new imperialist war is approaching the Balkan peninsula with gigantic steps,' they said in the manifesto on the 'national question' which was issued by the Congress. 'As long as the present dismemberment and oppression of Macedonia and Thrace continues, we cannot avoid imperialist wars. . . . That is why we fight for *the unification of the three sections of Macedonia and Thrace* and for their becoming independent.'[13]

One sentence, practically hidden in the blazing rhetoric of their manifesto on the 'national question', read: 'If we do not smash the bourgeois national yoke which plagues Macedonia and Thrace, we cannot smash the bourgeois social yoke which is plaguing us.'[14] Clearly, the establishment of an independent Macedonia and an independent Thrace was considered to be a prerequisite for the sovietization of Greece. In the trials of KKE officials which took place later on, this central proposition was overlooked. Many of their defenders argued that the 'autonomy slogan' did not constitute treason, since the party did not advocate the alienation of national territories. It was, they said, a 'promise' of what the party planned to do if and when it came to power. Yet the manifesto clearly showed that the party had *unanimously* assumed the obligation to fight for the

---

[12] Ch. Kabaktsiev, *Balkanskaya Kommunisticheskaya Federatsia* (Moscow, Gosizdat RSFSR, 1930), p. 222.

[13] *Rizospastis*, 14 December 1924; author's italics.   [14] Ibid.

separation of national territories not after but before its coming to power. This decision was to plague the development of the party for many years.[15]

The support given by the Communist International to the establishment of a Macedonian and a Thracian state cannot be fully understood unless viewed in the context of the social composition prevailing at the time in the Balkans. All the Balkan countries were primarily agrarian and all included several ethnic minorities, in spite of extensive population exchanges before and after the First World War. Communist agitation could not be expected to go very far if addressed exclusively to the limited industrial proletariats of the Balkan states. The peasantry and the ethnic minorities were better potential targets for penetration. The discontent and the aspirations of the ethnic minorities, in particular, offered considerable opportunities for political agitation. Furthermore, most ethnic minorities were at the same time primarily agrarian. The Third Extraordinary Congress of the KKE combined the slogans of 'an independent Macedonia and Thrace' with the slogan of 'the workers' and peasants' government' under the all-inclusive slogan of the 'United Front of workers, peasants, and oppressed minorities'. The seventh section of the resolutions adopted by the Congress noted:

In the Balkans, the support of the minorities by the KKE in their struggle for liberation has today a decisive importance for the social revolution. . . . The United Front of workers, peasants, and oppressed minorities against the bourgeoisie for the union of all the Balkan peoples in a Balkan federation is the fundamental slogan of the Greek Communist Party. The KKE fully applies this thesis to the question of Macedonia and Thrace.[16]

By identifying the 'national question' as an integral and essential part of the revolutionary process, the Greek Communists had accepted the dialectical basis for elevating the establishment of a Macedonian and a Thracian state to the lofty level of a 'question of principle'. The independence of these new states, however, was viewed as only a temporary, transitional stage. The final objective was the establishment of a much larger entity comprising all Balkan peoples in a Communist federation. The section of the Congress resolutions referring to

---

[15] Petsopoulos, op. cit., p. 32.
[16] *To KKE, 1918–1931*, pp. 354–5; also Zinoviev, op. cit., p. 96.

the workers' and peasants' government and the Balkan federation was quite explicit:

Our struggle for power is directed against the bourgeois-fascist republic, for the *armed* imposition of the workers' and peasants' and refugees' government. By winning political power, and maintaining it by our armed forces, we shall produce the solution we want through our own workers' and peasants' constitution. Nationalization of heavy industry, workers' control over light industry, nationalization of the banks and of the export trade; expropriation of big estates, of church property, nationalization of all land and its distribution to landless and poor peasants for cultivation; abolition of taxes, of mortgage and usury debts; support for peasants who have small holdings and do not exploit the workers; gradual transition to collectivism.

True peace for the Balkan peoples can be achieved only through the establishment of the Balkan federation of the workers' and peasants' republics. Our struggle against the capitalists and the landlords places before us the problem of power. To win power is the axis of our struggle.[17]

Greek reaction to the Communist stand

The KKE's formal declaration that it would 'fight for the self-determination of the peoples of Macedonia and Thrace, including their separation from Greece'[18] was bound to provoke a strong reaction on the part of the Greek authorities. The first trial of party members accused of treason opened in Salonika on 1 August 1925. Twelve of the most prominent members of the Salonika organization were in the dock. One of them was Nikos Zachariades, the future leader of the KKE. During the trial the Communists made the most of their opportunity of airing the Macedonian slogan. Zachariades, in particular, was extremely vocal in declaring his party's determination to uphold the decisions of the Comintern on Macedonian and Thracian independence. The defendants received prison sentences ranging from twelve to eighteen months. Few remained in prison more than a year.

From a national standpoint, the trial was a tactical error. By conducting it in Salonika, the Government gave world Communism and the autonomists of the IMRO an opportunity of claiming that the Greek Government was persecuting 'Macedonian' patriots—though only two of the twelve defen-

[17] *Rizospastis*, 14 December 1924.   [18] *Rizospastis*, 7 February 1925.

dants were even born in Greek Macedonia, a Jew named Saporta and Gregorios Papanikolaou, who, incidentally, had fought for union with Greece before 1912.

The second trial took place in Athens. P. Pouliopoulos and Serafim Maximos were the two major defendants. Presumably during the interrogation of party members the authorities had learned that Maximos and Pouliopoulos had been in Moscow and had accepted the 'autonomy' slogan.

On 4 January 1926, shortly before the two Communist leaders and their co-defendants were brought to trial, Pangalos proclaimed the establishment of a dictatorial régime. Under martial law the case of Pouliopoulos and Maximos came under the jurisdiction of the court martial, where the death penalty could be imposed.

During the trial the main argument of the defence was that the Greek Communists were merely advocating what they planned to do *after* they came to power; this, the defence contended, was their political platform, and the platform of any party should be judged by the people, not by the courts. The Greek authorities ought to have known that this argument was without foundation: the party itself had formally declared, on several occasions, that the separation of Greek Macedonia and Thrace was a prerequisite to its coming to power.[19]

International Communism succeeded in inducing Professor Aulard, a well-known French historian and chairman at that time of the humanitarian 'Ligue pour la Protection des Droits d'Homme et du Citoyen', to send a long telegram to Pangalos imploring him to prevent the imposition of a death sentence, which, in Aulard's words, would be 'a stigma on Greek justice and civilization'. At the same time the international Communist organization MOPR (International Organization of Workers' Assistance) contacted prominent French attorneys and asked them to go to Greece and defend the two Greek Communists. For procedural reasons these French lawyers were not allowed by the court to take part in the trial, but, in the meantime, the Communists had succeeded in presenting Maximos and Pouliopoulos to the world as victims of political persecution. In the end the trial was discontinued and postponed indefinitely.

[19] See above, p. 60.

Parliament and the Macedonian issue

After the overthrow of the Pangalos régime Kondylis decided to hold a parliamentary election in November 1926 under the proportional representation system. As has already been noted, this system offered the KKE its first real chance of entering Parliament. Eleutherios Stavrides, who continued to be in charge of party affairs, since most of the other leaders were still in prison or exile, realized that to include the 'Macedonian and Thracian independence' slogan in the electoral platform of the party would jeopardize all hope of success in the election. Stavrides was sensitive on this particular question for personal reasons. He intended to stand for election in the district of Kavalla in Thrace. He knew that his chances would be very slim indeed should he advocate the separation of Thrace from Greece.

Stavrides further realized that party candidates could not possibly depend for their election to Parliament on the support of party members alone. According to the official Comintern records,[20] the KKE had in 1926 approximately 2,500 members. Candidates therefore needed the support of many sympathizers outside the party. The recent military *coups*, the inability of the economy to recover under the added burden of almost one and a half million refugees from Asia Minor, and the continuing feud between the two major political camps—the Royalists and the Liberals—over the constitutional question, offered the Communists some ground for political exploitation provided that the question of Macedonian and Thracian independence was shelved for the time being. On 9 September Stavrides, in his capacity as acting Secretary of the Central Committee, called a meeting which adopted an electoral programme containing no reference to the 'national question'.

Stavrides, realistically assessing the chances of party candidates entering Parliament, pressed for a programme which, by its relative moderation, could attract a sufficient number of voters. Although this programme contained several social and economic demands of a purely Communist character, some of the imprisoned or exiled leaders released by Kondylis, on returning to Athens, expressed strong opposition to its 'modera-

---

[20] *Fifth World Congress; Abridged Report*, p. 268; also *K. I. pered Shestim Vsemirnim Kongressom*, p. 216.

tion'. Under pressure from extremist elements, a joint conference of the full Central Committee and the Communist
Youth (OKNE) was held in Athens in October. The conference
denounced the decisions of 9 September as 'erroneous, rightist,
reformist'.[21] Stavrides could no longer impose his views on the
party. Yet his manoeuvre to keep the 'national question' out of
the electoral programme proved successful. Even the most
extremist Communists realized that to incorporate it at so late
a date would attract too much attention and could possibly
deprive party candidates of the support they could otherwise
expect on the basis of their political and social programme.

As noted previously on page 48, in the election held on 7
November 1926 the Communist candidates received 41,982
votes, 4·38 per cent. of the total. Of the ten Communist deputies elected under the proportional system eight represented
districts in Macedonia and Thrace. It was unquestionably a
major political success for the fledgling party. Yet the opportunities presented by the parliamentary forum were thrown overboard. When the fight between the so-called 'Liquidarists' and
the pro-Stalinist faction within the KKE ended with the defeat
of the former, the Communist deputies in the Greek Parliament
came under attack by the Stalinists.

It may appear strange to the uninitiated that the leadership
of the party should want to cause trouble to its own deputies in
Parliament. Yet the KKE parliamentary group presented a
peculiar problem to the Stalinist leaders. Of the ten deputies
only Theos belonged to the Stalinist group. At the time when
the candidates for the 1926 election were nominated, the
Koutvies and Hadjis were still struggling for supremacy in the
party. Consequently, those nominated belonged to what may
be called the old guard. Now that the Stalinists were firmly in
control of the Politbureau they decided to force the removal of
these deputies from Parliament. To this end they exploited a
convenient set of circumstances and procedures. According to
the parliamentary by-laws, elected deputies were the lawful
occupants of their seats regardless of political disagreements
with the party leaders. The only procedural way to remove
these deputies from Parliament was to have them convicted of
some criminal offence. The most likely issue to get them into
trouble was the old, familiar 'national question'. Therefore the

[21] *Rizospastis*, 27 October 1926.

Politbureau once again raised the banner of 'Macedonian and Thracian independence'. The Greek authorities, unimpressed by fine dialectical distinctions and unaware of intra-party disagreements, could only see the agitation for the separation of national territories inhabited by Greeks. It is customary in Greek politics to consider the leading deputies in Parliament as the leaders of their respective parties. Consequently, the Communist deputies were held responsible for the offences committed by the Politbureau.

The reaction of the Greek political leaders was exactly what the Politbureau had anticipated. On 7 December 1927 Theodore Turkovassilis, then Minister of Justice, put before Parliament an indictment against the 'United Front deputies', S. Maximos, K. Theos, El. Stavrides, J. Ventura, N. Kyriakopoulos, A. Sinokas, and Behar Solan.

Only a few days earlier the Public Prosecutor of the Athenian Court of Appeal had asked Parliament to allow the prosecution of the other three Communist deputies, G. Papanikolaou, C. Constantinides, and Anastasios (Tassos) Khainoglou, 'charged with undermining the constitution'.[22] This was the opening scene of a rather injudicious effort to unseat the Communist deputies.

A demand that the parliamentary immunity of the Communist deputies should be lifted to allow their criminal prosecution was supported by all members of the coalition Government. Yet when the matter came up for discussion in Parliament on 12 December 1927, those who participated in the debate did not follow strictly-defined party lines. This was the first time the Greek Parliament discussed the Communist problem in Greece, openly and comprehensively. The statements of those who spoke showed a mixture of ignorance and awareness, excessive fear and unwarranted complacency.

George Ladas, an eminent Liberal deputy, criticized the Government for focusing public attention on the question of Macedonian independence as though the Communist Party had sufficient power to threaten the territorial integrity of the country. He reminded his colleagues that the Communist deputies would in all probability be replaced by other Communists in by-elections. The only result would be, he added, 'to

---

[22] *Efimeris ton Sizitiseon tis Voulis*, First Period, Second Session, 1927–8, pp. 253–452.

create new heroes and see them occupying ministerial posts in a few years'.[23]

Of the twelve Members of Parliament who took the floor, nine voiced their opposition to the prosecution of the Communist deputies, mostly on the grounds that they had committed no crime by merely advocating an unpopular policy. Only one deputy, Evangelos Makhairas, spoke with full comprehension of the underlying issues. He was a worker, a former Secretary of the General Confederation of Greek Workers. To the utter astonishment of those who took note of his speech, Makhairas suggested that the Central Committee of the KKE, for reasons of its own, wanted to provoke the prosecution of the Communist deputies. He called the attention of Parliament to the fact that the Central Committee had issued inflammatory proclamations in favour of an independent Macedonia and had organized provocative demonstrations outside Parliament, knowing full well that its actions could only infuriate the deputies. 'Even the simplest of men knows', Makhairas went on, 'that if the Communist Party really wanted to avert the prosecution of its deputies it would have kept quiet, as it does whenever it considers it to be in its own interest.'[24] Makhairas cited *Rizospastis* in support of his argument—but how many Greek politicians at that time had opened *Rizospastis* even once? He referred to the disputes between the leadership of the party and the Communist deputies, and he specifically mentioned that Maximos had been called to appear before the Comintern and had refused. 'I am convinced', he concluded, 'that the Communist Party no longer wishes the presence of these deputies in the Parliament. . . . I believe we should not help the Communist Party to accomplish its own designs.' Makhairas was the only one of those who took part in the debate who was really informed. Yet his speech failed to influence in any appreciable degree the thinking of the ponderous orators who followed him to the rostrum. Apparently those Greek politicians considered the speech of a mere worker unworthy of their attention.

In replying to the charges, Serafim Maximos, the recognized leader of the parliamentary group, carefully avoided taking a clear-cut stand on the 'national question'. Shortly before the opening of the debate, Khaitas had informed the Communist

[23] *Efimeris ton Sizitiseon tis Voulis*, loc. cit., p. 362.
[24] Ibid., p. 452.

F

deputies that, by decision of the Central Committee, they were expected vigorously to uphold the slogan of Macedonian and Thracian independence, 'regardless of the consequences'. Maximos, fully aware of the motives behind this decision, ignored Khaitas' admonition. When he was asked by George Papandreou, the prominent Liberal leader, to state his position on the Macedonian question, Maximos replied that the KKE was only in favour of self-determination, and that the term 'independence' had never been used by the party. Piles of party documents testified to the contrary.

Ioannis Metaxas, the Royalist leader, pressed the point further with his familiar bluntness and insistence:

Metaxas: What do you mean by self-determination? Do you suggest asking the Greek inhabitants of Macedonia whether they want to leave Greece?

Maximos: We cannot ask the Greeks only; we have to ask all Macedonians.

Metaxas: In other words, you mean we should ask all the inhabitants of Macedonia, Greeks, Serbs, and Bulgarians, if the majority wants to have self-determination; and if the majority wants self-determination, then you will force the inhabitants of Greek Macedonia to attach themselves to the new state, although they may have voted against it. Is that correct?

Maximos dodged the question. He muttered that he was not qualified to talk about the limits of Greek territories to the north because he lacked the necessary information. He admitted, however, that Greek Macedonia was 'inhabited mostly by Greeks . . .'. 'In fact,' he added, 'with the exception of a very small minority, almost the whole population is Greek.'[25] Maximos was faltering. Alexandros Papanastassiou, another prominent Liberal leader, remarked that 'there seems to be disagreement within the KKE on this subject', and drew the attention of Parliament to the fact that 'prominent party members like Kordatos and others have been either expelled from the party, or have withdrawn on their own accord precisely because they disagree on this question'. Maximos made a last feeble effort to conceal the party's internal dissensions. 'We are at this moment', he said, 'defending the party line, and we are not inclined to bring our intra-party differences into this discussion. . . .' He ended his speech without answering the question of whether the

[25] *Efimeris ton Sizitiseon tis Voulis*, loc. cit., p. 368.

Communist Party favoured the separation of Greek Macedonia and Thrace.

The other members of the group followed the same general line in their speeches. They agreed that Greek Macedonia was inhabited by Greeks, but they objected to the exchange of populations which 'had changed the ethnic complexion of Macedonia'. Stavrides, invited by the Chairman of the Parliament to take the floor, declined; he was already thinking of leaving the party. Of all the Communist deputies, only Theos spoke like a 'true Communist'. He brought the most vulgar Communist slogans from the gutter to the parliamentary rostrum, and began to hurl scurrilous insults at all the other parties. Parliament had to adjourn for five minutes so that order could be restored. Theos' conduct leaves the distinct impression that he was deliberately trying to infuriate Parliament and alienate even those deputies who were inclined to vote against granting permission for the prosecution of the Communist deputies. To the uninitiated, his outrageous performance appeared puzzling. Viewed in the light of his connexion with the Stalinist group, which wanted to replace the United Front deputies with other, more reliable Communists, it becomes crystal clear.

Parliament unwittingly played into the hands of the Stalinist group. One hundred and twenty-six deputies voted and by substantial majorities removed the parliamentary immunity from the Communist deputies. A separate poll was taken for each deputy. The two Jewish deputies from Salonika received the largest number of unfavourable votes (95 to 31). Only Maximos escaped, because less than two-thirds of those present and voting had approved the removal of his immunity.[26] These Communist deputies were not prosecuted; eventually they were reinstated. The net result of the unfortunate incident was to provide the Communists with sensational propaganda material.

The New Leadership and the 'national question'

In 1945 Zachariades, as a concession to Greek nationalist feelings, asserted: 'Since 1931, when I became its leader, the Greek Communist Party *has rejected* the slogan [of Macedonian and Thracian independence] and now once again declares that

[26] *Praktika ton Sizitiseon*, First Period, Second Session, 1927–8 (Athens, National Printing Office, 1928), Vol. II, p. 299.

Macedonia is and shall remain Greek.'[27] He evidently counted on the fact that the great majority of the Greek people knew little of the party's past history, including the unequivocal resolution of the 4th Plenum, passed under the 'New Leadership' of Nikos Zachariades.

The 4th Plenum, which met in December 1931 in Khalkis, was in effect the first formal meeting of the so-called New Leadership of the KKE which had been installed by the Comintern in the autumn of that same year. At that meeting the Comintern representative, a German Communist known as Gruwe, referring to the perennial 'national question', lashed out at the previous party leaders without exception, accusing the KKE of 'not participating actively in the revolutionary struggle for national liberation of the peoples who are oppressed by the Greeks'.[28] In response to Gruwe's strong words, the Plenum passed one of the most unequivocal resolutions on the 'national question' ever approved by the KKE:

Greece is an imperialist state which has conquered by force whole areas inhabited by other nationalities (Macedonia and Thrace); in the name of the basic principles of Bolshevism, the Communist Party of Greece proclaims for Macedonia and Thrace the slogan of self-determination, including separation from the Greek state, and actively supports the revolutionary struggle of the population of these areas for their national liberation.[29]

This resolution formed the basis of party policy for another three and a half years. Then, in the spring of 1935, there was a drastic change.

For more than a decade the KKE's agitation for a Macedonian and a Thracian state had tinted the party image with a heavy shade of treason. To many Greeks with leftist political and social ideas, co-operation with the Communists appeared odious because of the party's commitment to the separation of territories inhabited by Greeks. Any serious effort to establish a United Front from below and from above was doomed to fail as long as the party remained 'the party of treason'.

In April 1935 the 3rd Plenum of the Central Committee formally dropped the slogan for an independent Macedonia and

---

[27] *Laiki Phoni*, 25 October 1945; author's italics. Cf. infra, p. 222.
[28] *Pente Khronia*, p. 42.
[29] *Neos Rizospastis*, 5 March 1932.

in its place adopted the slogan of 'complete equality for the minorities'. The party had suddenly discovered that 'in the portion of Macedonia under Greek control, Greek refugees have been settled, and the majority of the population today is Greek. The change in the ethnic composition of Greek Macedonia, *in close connexion with the anti-Fascist and anti-war struggle*, requires the replacement of the old slogan.'[30] The real explanation for the party's change of heart on its most controversial policy is provided by the italicized portion of the preceding quotation. The assertion that the party had abandoned its long-held position on the Macedonian issue because the ethnic composition of the area had changed was naïve to say the least. The exchange of populations and the settlement of refugees in Macedonia had changed the ethnic composition of the area at least ten years earlier, when the Turkish population left for Turkey and was replaced by Greeks from Asia Minor. Even Serafim Maximos, in his confrontation with Manuilsky at the Fifth World Congress of the Comintern in 1924, had recognized that Greek Macedonia was populated by Greeks. The real reason for dropping the 'Macedonian' slogan was the Comintern policy of an all-out effort to form a United Front from below and from above. In Greece the slogan for an independent Macedonia and Thrace was the most serious obstacle to this. Besides, a United Front was of far greater political significance than any advantages offered by the Communist agitation among the 'Macedonians'. The *komitadjis* of the IMRO had long ceased to co-operate with the Comintern. In fact, the IMRO–Comintern co-operation had lasted only for a few months in the summer of 1924. With the assassination of Todor Aleksandrov and the rise of Ivan Mikhailov to the leadership of the IMRO the abortive alliance had come to an end. Mikhailov became the instrument of Italian foreign policy in the Balkans. The Communists, for several years after the collapse of their brief 'alliance' with the IMRO, had continued to hope that their support for 'Macedonian independence' might strengthen the Bulgarian Communists and expand their influence among the 'Macedonians'. Gradually they came to realize that in supporting the slogan for independence they

[30] *Dheka Khronia Agones, 1935–1945* (a collection of documents published by the CC of the KKE, 1946), p. 66; hereinafter cited as *Dheka Khronia Agones;* see also *Komep*, No. 17, 1 December 1935.

were merely serving the objectives of the Italian Fascists.[31] The slogan was finally dropped. The KKE endorsed the change with a sigh of relief. As we shall see, it returned to the discredited slogans in desperation many years later, in 1949, at the moment of its gravest crisis.

[31] Swire, op. cit., pp. 34, 182–5, 215–42.

Part II

THE 'MONOLITHIC' PARTY

6. Mending the Broken Fences

The first steps of the New Leadership

Events moved with unprecedented speed in the autumn of 1931. Lunacharsky came to Athens in September. The ECCI 'Appeal' and the first mention of the 'New Leadership' appeared in early November. Before the end of December the 4th Plenum of the Central Committee met in Khalkis on the island of Euboea. 'Plenum' was a misnomer. Most of the leading members of the Central Committee which had been elected by the Fourth Regular Congress were no longer present or active. The 4th Plenum was in effect the first meeting of what was left of the Central Committee, under the control of the New Leadership.

Not surprisingly, the Comintern representative, Gruwe, played an extremely active role at the meeting. He fiercely attacked the previous leaders for their factionalist struggles 'in violation of international discipline', and enumerated their errors which had caused 'the failure of the Party's mass political struggle'.[1] Gruwe went on to say that seven whole years after the word 'bolshevization' had appeared on its records the party had not yet completed the process. He listed the establishment of a 'united, monolithic leadership', the organization of cells in factories, and the organization of an 'illegal party apparatus' as the three indispensable prerequisites for successful bolshevization. He explained that the organization of an illegal apparatus did not mean the liquidation of the party's legitimate machinery; the party, he stressed, should always be able 'to combine legitimate and illegal methods of action'.[2]

---

[1] *Pente Khronia*, pp. 31–40. [2] Ibid., p. 41.

The fact that the 'New Leadership' had been *installed* by the Comintern, as Yiannis Zevgos wrote so candidly in 1936, did not prevent the local party organizations from declaring unanimously, in resolution after resolution, their 'absolute confidence' in it. Though it took Zachariades approximately two years to emerge openly as the 'Leader', the party was already well on its way to becoming monolithic. But this was not accomplished overnight. Before completing the process of bolshevization, the New Leadership resisted suggestions that a party congress should be held. 'The Party,' they said in an editorial published in *Neos Rizospastis*, 'estranged from the masses, beaten and broken by the criminal factionalist struggle, cannot hold a Congress now.'[3] According to the 4th Plenum, 'the next Congress should not become an arena of factionalist struggle, but should be based on the centralized efforts of a united and monolithic party'.[4] The New Leadership needed time 'to apply the principles of truly bolshevik democratic centralism in party life, to an extent hitherto unknown to the Greek Communist Party'.

Democratic centralism had occasionally been cited in the past as the guiding organizational principle of the KKE. The bitter quarrels of the previous years had shown that the party had neither democracy nor centralism. The New Leadership hoped to correct this by introducing 'the truly bolshevik democratic centralism' in which *centralism* was the most essential ingredient.[5] One of its first moves was to return to the systematic exploitation of 'everyday problems'. For the first two years of the 'Third Period', the Comintern slogans for the defence of the Soviet Union had left the 'masses' all over the world largely unimpressed. The Stalinist-dominated 11th Plenum of the ECCI, under the pressure of overwhelming evidence, acknowledged that Communist parties ought to combine 'their struggle for the dictatorship of the proletariat with the struggle for the *everyday needs* of the workers'.[6] With remarkable speed the KKE's New Leadership responded and gave the signal for a change in direction, decreeing that 'neglect of the immediate

[3] *Neos Rizospastis*, 17 December 1931.
[4] *Pente Khronia*, 2nd Edition, 1946, p. 37; hereinafter all references are to the 2nd Edition unless otherwise indicated.
[5] Cf. *Bolshaya Sovietskaya Entsiklopedia*, Vol. XIII, 1954, pp. 655–6; see also the 1961 Charter of the CPSU.
[6] *Tezisi, XI*, p. 18; author's italics.

demands of the workers and peasants, refusal to lead, organize, and broaden these demands, must be considered as the most flagrant opportunism'.[7] The KKE's support for the 'everyday demands' had an openly-acknowledged objective: 'To conquer the workers who are still under the influence of the agents of the class enemy, to attract them to the path of revolutionary struggle, to liquidate the organized basis of the capitalists within the masses'.[8] To use a favourite Communist expression, the 'decisive link' at that time was to gain power by exploiting the mounting economic and social problems besetting most of the world in the wake of the American economic depression.

As the waves of economic depression reached Greece in the early thirties the economic gains which had marked the first two years of the Venizelos administration were virtually wiped out. Unemployment and inflation hit the weakest segments of the population. It required little imagination to realize that the everyday economic problems of the workers offered the Communist Party many opportunities for political penetration. By espousing the practical demands of the workers and peasants, the Communists stood a good chance of broadening their contacts with the 'masses', and bringing the party out of the wilderness of political isolation. In true Leninist–Stalinist fashion this was a shrewd, expedient move to exchange realism for the blind observance of abstract theories. But this was not a real change in the revolutionary methods or in the objectives of the Communist Party. On the central subject of the United Front, the party line, like that of the Comintern, remained unaltered: 'United Front from below'.[9] The New Leadership,

[7] *Pente Khronia*, p. 19. [8] Ibid., p. 39.

[9] For a seasoned Communist, 'United Front' has a special and definite meaning. It may take two forms: 'United Front from below' and 'United Front from below and from above'. The first term refers to a Communist Party's efforts to attract the support of ordinary people and infiltrate into existing non-Communist organizations and social groups. Such efforts presumably never cease, not being subject to tactical changes. The term 'United Front' becomes politically significant primarily in the form of 'United Front from below and from above'. Whenever this last formula is applied, it involves the co-operation of a Communist Party with the leaders of other political parties or labour organizations under a minimum programme of common acceptance, which as a rule leaves out familiar Communist dogmas, while the party 'agitators' make every effort to infiltrate the 'allied' organizations, expanding the party's 'mass basis' at the expense of its 'allies'. In the words of an old Bolshevik, Zinoviev, who gave us the above outline of the United Front tactics, this Communist formula 'is not a method of genuine political coalition' but 'a strategic manoeuvre' (*Fifth World Congress, Abridged Report*, p. 29).

by its decision of 28 December 1931 on the 'question of unity', called on the Communist-controlled labour unions to bring 'under the banner of the struggle for their demands, not only the workers who already belong to these unions, but also those who belong to the reactionary trade unions, and also the masses of the unorganized workers'. The instrument to be used was the familiar 'United Front committees', controlled by Communist 'fractions', and cutting through trade-union and political lines.

The New Leadership was apparently annoyed by the fact that during the preceding years a great number of economic strikes had been led by what the Communists called 'counter-revolutionary Socialist–Fascist and Trotskyist–Fascist organizations'. In simpler language, the new Politbureau recognized obliquely that the calls for a general political strike, the defence of the Soviet Union, and the like had made little impression on the Greek workers. Instead, they had turned to the Reformist leaders who were concentrating their efforts towards the improvement of the living conditions of the workers. Even modest improvements resulting from the efforts of the Reformist unions were viewed by the Communists as a blow to the prestige and the future prospects of their party. It was no surprise, then, that the Politbureau, at its meeting of 28 December 1931, launched a vicious attack against the non-Communist labour leaders. 'The Communist fractions in the Reformist unions', the Politbureau directed, 'must place themselves at the head of the workers in the struggle for their demands, strengthen their ranks, unmask the treacherous role of the reactionary leaders, and bring the majority of the Greek workers under the banner of the class struggle and of the revolutionary tactics.' The Politbureau, in accordance with the rules of the 'United Front from below', proclaimed that labour unity should be achieved 'on the basis of revolutionary class struggle, against the employers and their state, and against their wilful agents, the Socialist–Fascists, the Liquidarists, the Trotskyist–Fascists, and the "uncommitted" leaders'.[10] The Politbureau concluded by declaring grandly that these 'reactionary labour bosses have no place in the ranks of the revolutionary camp'. Less than two years later, the same Politbureau, following new Comintern directives, was to address hypocritical appeals for co-operation[11]

[10] *Pente Khronia*, pp. 44–46.   [11] *Rizospastis*, 9 September 1934.

to all those who in December 1931 'had no place in the ranks of the revolutionary camp'.

Although the exploitation of the everyday demands of the workers was expected to achieve 'trade-union unity', the Communists were against what they called 'an artificial dedication to the concept of unity'. The only kind of 'unity' they wanted was 'revolutionary unity', the gathering 'of the great masses of workers under the banner of the class struggle for the overthrow of capitalism'. To those who might have been misled by the Communist appeal for 'unity', the Politbureau gave an unusually candid and explicit warning. Unity becomes 'revolutionary', they said, only when the Communists enjoy absolute control over the 'unified masses'.

It is in the interests of the working class to have revolutionaries, Communist workers, as leaders. We are not petty-bourgeois democrats; we are revolutionaries! Whenever there is a question as to how the trade union elections should be conducted, we favour the way which assures the election of a homogeneous committee of revolutionary workers.

If anyone, even after this statement, naïvely thought that unity still meant equality for the participating groups, the KKE attacked such an 'absurd notion' by saying: 'We must smash the idea that there can be equality among the various groups. *We* always claim the leadership of the working class.'[12] This was not mere rhetoric. The claim to absolute monopoly of leadership is one of the constant concepts of Communist ideology, confirmed once again in no uncertain terms by the 1961 Programme of the CPSU. In 1931 Nikos Zachariades, schooled in the Leninist–Stalinist way of thinking, was setting an ambitious course for his party. To translate these far-reaching objectives into reality, the party needed the proper organization, he said. And to this end he devoted his efforts in the following years.

The ABC of Communist organization

When Japan invaded Manchuria in February 1932, the Communist parties all over the world were mobilized to create a war atmosphere. Japan's aggressive action was interpreted by the Comintern leadership as the first act in the imperialist

[12] *Pente Khronia*, pp. 52–54.

war against the Soviet Union. The various 'sections' of the
Comintern were instructed to intensify their 'anti-militarist and
anti-war struggle'. The KKE's leadership, faithfully obeying
these instructions, decided to make the 'struggle against war,
the defence of the USSR, etc., the central slogans for the May
Day demonstrations for the whole period of the campaign'. In a
more ominous statement the Politbureau called on the Communist organizations of Athens, Piraeus, and Salonika to concentrate on 'the branches of transport, of war and chemical
industries, and on the discovery and sabotage of war supply
convoys'.[13] Making the defence of the Soviet Union the central
point of its campaign had proved unwise for the party in the
past. Zachariades may have realized that the call would not
move many Greek workers this time either; but he had to
conform to the Comintern directives. The outcome was predic-
table. The party failed to organize any mass demonstrations on
May Day (1932), even in the 'basic proletarian centres' of
Athens, Piraeus, and Salonika.[14]

The May Day fiasco, reminiscent of other similar débâcles
which had heralded the downfall of previous 'leaderships',
caused Zachariades and his colleagues to take a long, hard look
at the party and its organization. They bitterly and openly
deplored the 'terrifying inefficiency' of the cadres, the continued
instability of the party membership, 'the legalistic under-
estimation of the conspiratorial measures'.[15] The instability of
the membership, in particular, had occupied the thoughts of the
New Leadership ever since they took over the reins of the party.
Many members joined the party only to desert its ranks in
disillusionment or disgust shortly afterwards. It was not enough
to recruit new members, cautioned the New Leadership. 'We
must learn how to hold these new members, how to make them
militant Communists.'[16] The failure of the May Day 'mobilization' had brought home the fact that a mere change at the
summit of the party hierarchy was not enough. The entire
organization needed a careful and thorough overhauling. To
set the stage for this task, the first Pan-helladic organizational
conference of the KKE met in June 1932. With provocative
clarity this conference outlined the *modus operandi* and the
organizational set-up of the KKE. Its decisions, based on the

[13] *Pente Khronia*, p. 81.   [14] *Neos Rizospastis*, 12 May 1932.
[15] Ibid.   [16] *Komep*, No. 5, March 1932.

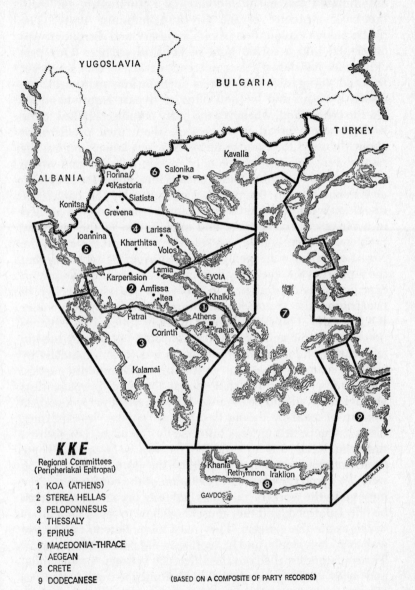

YUGOSLAVIA

BULGARIA

TURKEY

ALBANIA

Kavalla

Florina ⑥ Salonika
Kastoria
Konitsa Siatista
Grevena

Ioannina ④ Larissa
⑤ Kharthitsa
Volos

Karpenision Lamia
② Amfissa EVOIA
Itea Khalkis

Patrai ① Athens
Corinth Piraeus ⑦
③

Kalamai

⑨

KKE
Regional Committees
(Peripheriakai Epitropai)

1 KOA (ATHENS)
2 STEREA HELLAS
3 PELOPONNESUS
4 THESSALY
5 EPIRUS
6 MACEDONIA-THRACE
7 AEGEAN
8 CRETE
9 DODECANESE

Khania
Rethymnon Iraklion
⑧
GAVDOS

(BASED ON A COMPOSITE OF PARTY RECORDS)

accumulated wisdom of international Communism, still form
the basic structure of the Greek Communist Party. The
unscrupulous exploitation of public misery and discontent was
developed into a sordid kind of political science. 'Our past
experience has shown', the conference declared, 'that whenever
we tried to organize the workers outright into party cells, the
results were nil and we had often to depart empty-handed.'
On the other hand, whenever the party organizers talked to the
workers 'about bread, about wages, about their problems or
about the need to organize themselves into labour unions, the
results were favourable not only in our political and union
work but also in turning these contacts into a basis for recruiting
new members into the party'. Consequently, the conference
resolution went on, 'the starting-point in contacting the workers
in a factory is the support and exploitation of the everyday
problems concerning the workers . . .'.[17] In other words, the
New Leadership was openly and unequivocally declaring that
the support of the 'everyday demands' of the workers was only an
expedient device designed to serve the party's objective of
penetrating the factories and bringing more workers under
KKE control. This cynical but at the same time subtle exploitation of economic and social problems could not be entrusted to
amateurish zealots, whose enthusiasm was seldom matched by
political acumen or a firm grounding in Communist tactics.
The conference decided that special teams of 'propagandists
and agitators' should be organized. These select party members
were to be paid by the party for their services. In exchange,
they were expected to work full-time for the party. For the first
time the KKE was to establish its own *apparatchiki*. These
professional agitators and propagandists had to know their job
well. To quote the pertinent resolution of the conference, 'they
must go to the workers' meetings carefully prepared; they must
be fully informed, and they must know how to speak on matters
which excite the workers. They must know how to talk in one
way to young people, and in another to old people or women.'[18]
The conference spelled out the difference between 'propaganda'
and *'agitatsia'*. Propaganda should be limited to small gatherings
of party members and the closest party sympathizers. Agitation,
on the other hand, aimed at the broad masses, could take a
variety of forms: 'organization of meetings outside the factory

[17] *Pente Khronia*, pp. 91–95.   [18] Ibid., p. 112.

gates, or at the place where the workers have lunch; regular publication and distribution of cell newspapers, and of the party press; posting or distributing posters, proclamations, articles; organization of factory picnics, lectures, discussions and the like'.

A spirit of expediency, practicality, and common sense was evident in every decision of the organizational conference. The senseless rigidity of the past was replaced by a programme of controlled flexibility. At the same time the fight against the 'reactionary provocateurs'—the police agents who had allegedly penetrated the party ranks—was elevated to a major task. Vigilance became 'a basic duty'. To combat the 'menace' of police agents, the New Leadership ordered a 'systematic check' on all members and a fight against idle talk. The party cells were formally described as 'conspiratorial units'. The organizational conference was unusually explicit on this point:

The cell is *above all illegal*, that is, it exists and operates *underground*. . . . Its members do not appear as party members. The members of a factory cell must never show that they have any special association while they are at the factory; they must avoid keeping company. . . . At a workers' meeting only one comrade from the cell may appear and speak, usually the member who is least likely to be betrayed and persecuted. In many instances, this comrade must not even identify himself as a representative of the cell, but must appear to be an ordinary factory worker, or a representative of the trade union, and the like.[19]

One may wonder how these agitators could proselytize new members without revealing their identity and their connexion with the party. There lies an essential element of the Communist *modus operandi*. The special party *apparatchiki* were instructed to talk about 'wages and bread', with no reference to Marxist ideology or even to the Communist Party. Those workers who showed themselves to be most receptive and trustworthy were then to be singled out by the trained instructors and subjected to a more intensive and detailed indoctrination. Participation in strikes and demonstrations would help to identify such potential recruits.

The spirit of 'vigilance' was not limited to the relations of the party with the 'outside world'; it spilled over into intra-party relationships as well. The organizational conference decreed

[19] *Pente Khronia*, p. 94.

that whenever a party cell had more than ten members it must
be subdivided into sections; 'it is advisable that the members of
one section do not know the members of the other sections of a
factory cell'.[20] The implications of this statement are all too
obvious.

During the period 1932–6 the KKE, led by Nikos Zachariades, concentrated heavily on the organization of the party
along these lines. The Communists scored a few initial successes;
but, as we shall see later, when the real test came during the
Metaxas dictatorship the party organization collapsed.

The KKE gains some ground

Less than a year after its appointment by the Comintern the
New Leadership could point with some satisfaction to the
improvement in the party's fortunes. The first test came during
the parliamentary elections of 25 September 1932. For the
KKE, which had drifted from the triumphant mobilization of
100,000 people in 1920 to the ludicrous demonstrations by 150
faithfuls in August 1931, even a return to the numbers of 1926,
when the United Front candidates mustered 42,000 votes,
must have seemed an over-ambitious objective in September
1932. Yet the Communist candidates, under the cloak of the
United Front, received 58,223 votes in the parliamentary elections.

This expansion of Communist influence was a product of the
economic depression rather than the skilful management of
party affairs by the New Leadership. The international economic crisis had swept away Greek stability. The British Government's decision on 21 September 1931 to abandon the gold
standard precipitated a serious economic crisis in Greece. The
Venizelos administration tried in vain to soften the blow to the
Greek economic structure. Prices began to rise rapidly, driving
the poorer strata of the population to despair. In the first
months of 1932 a wave of economic strikes inflicted further
damage on the tottering economy. The Opposition pressed for
parliamentary elections as the only remedy. Venizelos finally
agreed. But realizing that public sentiment was running against
his Liberal Party, he proposed the reintroduction of the proportional electoral system in the hope that this would avert an
electoral alliance of all his opponents. It is not difficult to see

[20] *Pente Khronia*, p. 95.

that the majority system would have forced on the opposition parties just such an alliance as their best hope of succeeding at the polls. On 20 May 1932 the Bill establishing the proportional system was approved by a majority in Parliament. Once again, as in 1926, this system made the election of Communist candidates possible. Ten of them were returned in the elections in September. Compared to the party's rapidly falling influence only the year before, this was no mean achievement. Yet the New Leadership voiced dissatisfaction because 'the greatest part of the masses which deserted the Venizelist camp were led astray by the demagogy of the Populist Party, while the great majority of the people remained faithful to parliamentarism'.[21]

To be sure, more than 1,110,000 voters out of a total of 1,170,000 had ignored the appeals of the United Front (Communist) candidates. In the Parliament which resulted from the September 1932 election none of the major parties had a working majority to form a homogeneous government. After much wrangling Venizelos agreed to give limited support to a Cabinet headed by his opponent Panagis Tsaldaris, the leader of the Populist Party. Thus, for the first time since the anti-royalist revolution of 1922, a purely anti-Venizelist Government came to power. Ten days later, after authorizing the Government to issue urgent legislative decrees, Parliament adjourned. By the time it reconvened on 12 January 1933, Venizelos had decided to withdraw his limited support from the Tsaldaris Government. On 14 January Parliament voted the Populist ministry out of office, and two days later approved a coalition Cabinet headed by Venizelos. But the old Cretan statesman had no intention of leaving the fate of his Government to the mercy of the day-to-day whims of a whole host of small political parties. Within ten days after the coalition Cabinet was sworn in, Venizelos made two drastic moves. He brought back the majority electoral system of the 1928 elections and issued a decree for the dissolution of Parliament. At the same time a new election was announced for 5 March 1933.

The Communist Party took a very active part in the campaign for this election, under the familiar cloak of the United Front; its slogans 'for bread, work, and freedom', 'for an end to the persecution of taxpayers in the villages', 'for the application of the Social Security law', and 'for the increase of today's

[21] *Neos Rizospastis*, 1 October 1932.

starvation wages' were all geared to exploit the everyday economic problems of the lower-income groups. Only as an afterthought was the slogan 'for a Soviet, Socialist Greece' occasionally used. In the election of 5 March 1933 the Communist-led United Front received 52,958 votes out of a total of 1,141,331. None of the Communist candidates was elected; yet the fact that the KKE had mustered almost as many votes under the majority system as it had under the proportional system the previous September was very significant. The voters knew that under the majority system only the candidates of the major parties had any chance of winning. If they voted for the candidates of small parties they felt that their votes would be virtually wasted. In 1928 this reasoning was at least partially responsible for the abrupt decline in Communist votes. In 1933 the followers of the 'United Front' were faithful enough to stick to their party in spite of the electoral system. Though hardly a triumph, this was a considerable improvement.

The Communist leaders were, of course, not primarily interested in counting votes. What mattered most was 'the penetration of the factories to recruit new militants for the Party'. In discussing the electoral results the Politbureau deplored the fact that such penetration had not taken place because the party organizations had failed 'to take full advantage of the electoral campaign'. From the point of view of long-range strategy, supporters at the polls were welcomed by the KKE for psychological reasons. But such followers were unreliable, to say the least. The party wanted militant members, persons steeped in Communist ideology, willing to follow the gyrations of Communist policy without demur.

In its public pronouncements the party hailed the 'success' of the 'United Front' in spite of the electoral system, but at the same time suggested that the 'objective conditions' warranted even greater successes, which eluded the party only because of the errors committed by the lower cadres and the weaknesses of the local party organizations. To be sure the 'objective conditions' for greater gains did not exist, and the party leadership must have been aware of this. But the continuous reference to weaknesses and errors and the unending demands for greater successes had by now become the familiar features of the Stalinist parties.

In extolling the 'successes' of the party at the polls, the

Politbureau went so far as to say that the *coup d'état* which General Plastiras, a Venizelist stalwart, attempted on the night of 5 March, when the reports from various electoral districts showed a decisive majority in favour of the Populist Party, was partly due to 'the great electoral victory of the United Front of workers and peasants'. This assertion was ludicrous. Plastiras was not concerned with the non-existent victory of the United Front. He wanted to wipe out the victory of the Populists. His effort was abortive mainly because Venizelos himself told Plastiras that he considered the establishment of a dictatorship unwise. 'If you become dictator', he told Plastiras in a dramatic conversation on the night of the election, 'you will fail dismally within three months, because you will be unable to solve any of the economic problems which are uppermost in our minds.'[22] The KKE tried to take credit for the mobilization of the people of Athens, who demonstrated the following morning, demanding the preservation of the *status quo*. In a bombastic declaration the Politbureau asserted that 'the working people of Athens poured into the streets, thus forming the United Front, and with gigantic demonstrations and clashes wiped out the Plastiras dictatorship in a few hours'.[23] No such credit was due to the Communist Party. With total disregard for the intelligence of their readers, the members of the Politbureau admitted in the same document that the party agitators had been unable to induce 'the masses to continue the struggle in order to overthrow the new Fascist Government', that is, the caretaker Government which had been formed to restore public order. In fact, the Politbureau admitted that 'the Party had been altogether unable to intervene effectively in the events which broke out'. The 'thundering reaction' of the people of Athens, as the Politbureau termed the demonstration of 6 March, had proved that there was no popular support for a military dictatorship. The people of Athens had poured into the streets to demonstrate their support for democratic institutions, not to follow the Communist agitators to 'the revolutionary overthrow of the capitalists, to a Soviet, Socialist Greece'.[24] Though its fortunes were improving, the party was still a secondary force in Greek political life.

[22] Eleutherios Venizelos' statement before the Greek Parliament on 15 May 1933.

[23] *Pente Khronia*, p. 154.   [24] Ibid., p. 155.

More centralization

The KKE's inability to influence the events of 6 March 1933 to any appreciable degree was blamed by the party leadership on the unpreparedness of the party organizations. In all fairness, however, one must say that in 1933 the Communist Party had not yet gained the mass influence necessary for it to play a central role in Greek politics. It was not a question of organization. The majority of the Greek workers and peasants remained indifferent, if not hostile, to the party. Three tenets of Communist propaganda and agitation—the anti-religious propaganda, the 'Macedonian' slogans, and the theories of collectivization and control under the dictatorship of the proletariat—were repellent to people as religious, nationalistic, and individualist as the Greeks.

In any event, on 21 April 1933 the Politbureau once again called for more centralized organization and formally introduced the system of 'instructors'. The previous system of sending party officials 'as messengers' to the local branches for a day or two was replaced by the permanent presence of trusted representatives of the Politbureau, and the establishment of a 'network of organizers for the actual direction of the district and local party organizations'.[25] The Politbureau re-emphasized that the cell was 'a strictly illegal body', meaning in this context conspiratorial or clandestine. Party organizations, at all levels, were once again urged 'to combine legal with semi-legal and illegal methods of work'. It must be noted that while the Politbureau was organizing the 'illegal' apparatus, the Communist Party was legally recognized and operated freely in the political arena.

The theory of 'bourgeois-democratic revolution'

The building up of a closely-knit organization relying on a network of paid 'instructors' was only one part of Zachariades' plan for strengthening the KKE. Organization alone, he argued, though essential, would not suffice. Party work should be adjusted to the conditions prevailing in Greece. The party needed its own strategy and tactics, worked out to suit 'the Greek reality'. At the 6th Plenum of the Central Committee, which met in January 1934, Zachariades presented his resolu-

[25] *Pente Khronia*, pp. 156–7.

tion on 'conditions in Greece and the duties of the Party'. For many years afterwards the 6th Plenum of 1934 and this particular resolution were regarded by Greek Communists as the most significant milestones in the KKE's ideological evolution. Although party propaganda implied that the new concepts were the product of Zachariades' political genius, the celebrated resolution was merely a restatement of Stalin's theories on Communist strategy and tactics in the underdeveloped parts of the world.

The resolution of the 6th Plenum asserted that

Greece is one of those countries which, in the Programme of the Communist International, are considered to be 'countries with a medium level of capitalist development . . . with a considerable residue of semi-feudal relationships in agriculture, and a certain minimum of material resources for a socialist reconstruction, but without a completed bourgeois-democratic transformation.[26]

What was the practical significance in 1934 of placing Greece in this category? First of all, the KKE was expected to concentrate its fire on the alleged exploitation of the people by foreign capitalists and, secondly, to direct its attacks against the small group of 'local reactionaries' at the summit of the economic pyramid. 'Liberation of the oppressed people from the yoke of imperialism and local reaction' was the task 'assigned by Comrade Stalin to the Communists of these countries'.[27] This was a first step. 'In my opinion', Stalin had said in 1926, 'the first stage is the revolution on the general national front directed mainly against foreign imperialism and supported by the national bourgeoisie; the second stage is the bourgeois-democratic revolution . . . the third stage is the establishment of Socialism.'[28] More precisely, 'the transition to proletarian dictatorship is possible, as a rule, only after a series of preparatory stages, and only as a result of an entire period of inverting the bourgeois-democratic revolution into a socialist one'.[29] In other words, the initial stages of the revolution should have a 'bourgeois-democratic' character. This was the essence of the resolution passed by the 6th Plenum in 1934:

The promotion of slogans which can unite the wide masses of the people around the proletariat—slogans such as 'land for the

[26] *Pente Khronia*, p. 206.   [27] *Voprosy Ekonomiki*, No. 1, 1953.
[28] *Pente Khronia*, p. 206.   [29] *Imprecor*, No. 133, p. 2642.

peasants', 'liberation of the oppressed nationalities'—is a necessary prerequisite for the transformation of the popular, worker-peasant, bourgeois-democratic revolution into a socialist revolution which, in this way, will complete the victory.[30]

During the 'bourgeois-democratic' stages of the revolution only slogans with the widest possible appeal were to be used. The 6th Plenum assigned to the party cadres 'duties' which seemed to have little direct relationship to Marxist theory or the ultimate Communist objectives. These tactics were successfully checked in the thirties. But in 1941, when the Greek state collapsed under the blows of the Wehrmacht, the KKE took advantage of the favourable circumstances created by the disintegration of the Greek political world and established the National Liberation Front (EAM). The party agitators of the war period carefully avoided any mention of Marxism–Leninism; they relied heavily on demands for and promises of social justice while playing freely on the nationalist feelings of the people. Many, including some democratic leaders, were deceived by these tactics; yet the leadership of the KKE had openly declared as early as 1934 that this 'bourgeois-democratic' movement was only 'a prerequisite for turning the indignation and dissatisfaction of the masses towards the path of the socialist revolution, leading them to the final victory, to the dictatorship of the proletariat'.[31]

To carry out this preparatory task, the Communist Party needed allies. In such alliances the Communists were instructed to conceal their identity and their ultimate objectives while trying to establish their 'hegemony' over their 'allies'. Establishing such a hegemony behind a screen of deception is a very subtle operation. Its success depends on the dexterity of local Communist leaders in discrediting those opponents who expose the Communist game; and in helping to plant reliable party agents in key positions while promoting individuals with wide popular appeal to positions of prestige but little power. In later pages we shall discuss in detail how these tactics were applied by the KKE during the Second World War.

The 6th Plenum made it abundantly clear that the stage of 'bourgeois-democratic' revolution should be swiftly turned into a Communist revolution. It resolved that:

---

[30] *Pente Khronia*, p. 209.　　　　　　　　　[31] Ibid., p. 208.

The hegemony of the proletariat in the bourgeois-democratic revolution will assure, with the practical support of the international proletariat, the swift transformation of the bourgeois-democratic revolution into a socialist one. The workers' and peasants' soviet government will become a government of the proletarian dictatorship.[32]

Experience has frequently shown that this 'swift transformation' is more often than not a long-drawn-out painful process without any guarantee of ultimate success.

[32] *Pente Khronia*, p. 207.

7. Subversion through Co-operation

Back to the 'United Front from above' formula

Students familiar with Communist policies since the October Revolution have pointed out that the formula of the United Front 'from below and from above' has been applied whenever the Communist leaders have felt that they lacked the strength to go it alone or that they could advance faster and farther by riding on the shoulders of other political forces. In 1933 Communist expectation of an early collapse of capitalism as a result of the economic depression began to fade once again. At the same time the emergence of Hitler in Germany at last gave some substance to the oft-repeated fears that a 'capitalist' onslaught was being prepared against the 'only Socialist state'. The first sign that Moscow was reverting to the formula of 'United Front from below and from above' was given by the 'Appeal' sent by the ECCI to all Communist parties on 5 March 1933. With this Appeal, the Comintern invited its sections 'to make one more effort to form a United Front together with the social-democratic masses through the mediation of the social-democratic parties'.[1] Those who had been denounced by the Communists as 'traitors, with no place in the movement', the day before, were magically transformed by a single Comintern directive into leaders whose co-operation was not only necessary but even desirable.

In Greece the movement for a United Front scored some initial success. The resolution of the 6th Plenum in January 1934 on the need for a 'bourgeois-democratic' stage in the revolutionary process, together with the decisions of the KKE's Fifth Regular Congress three months later, paved the way for a renewed effort to establish a common front with the leaders of non-Communist trade unions and political groups. In March 1934 the Fifth Congress unanimously accepted the

[1] *Kommunisticheskii Internatsional pered VII Vsemirnim Kongressom; Materiali* (Moscow, Partizdat, 1935), p. 41.

resolutions for the formation of a popular anti-Fascist front and, with equal unanimity and 'complete bolshevik unity', approved the political work of the Central Committee 'since the Appeal of the Communist International of November 1931'. Also unanimously, the Congress re-elected the 'New Leadership' headed by Nikos Zachariades.[2] For the first time in the history of the KKE a Congress had convened to sanction a major change of policy without a change in leadership, and without any internal fighting. This remarkable unity was the end product of two years of careful preparation. By crowding out the old, unreliable cadres and, under various pretexts, promoting new and loyal members to positions of leadership, Zachariades had brought the entire party organization under his control. The hallmark of a cohesive Communist Party was then, and still is, its readiness to make 'the most rapid and unexpected change'[3] from one policy to another without breaking up. After two years as the leader of the party Zachariades could point with pride to the unanimity of the Fifth Congress as proof of his successful handling of party affairs.

Throughout the summer of 1934 the KKE carried on a well-planned campaign to induce various labour and peasant leaders to join in a popular anti-Fascist front. Finally, on 5 October 1934, an agreement was signed by the Communist Party of Greece (M. Tatasopoulos), the United General Confederation of Greek Workers (G. Siantos), the General Confederation of Greek Workers (I. Kalomiris), the Independent Trade Unions (Laskaris), the Agrarian Party (A. Tanoulas, A. Vogiatzis, E. Pagouras), the Socialist Party (Stratis Someritis), and the Labour Social-Democratic Party (G. Pyrpasopoulos). Of these seven organizations, the first two were Communist; the last three, in spite of their imposing titles, were groups with insignificant political influence. Only the remaining two labour organizations were of any practical importance.

Under the terms of the agreement the parties pledged themselves 'to fight together against any dictatorial-Fascist *coup* which might result from the present situation in our country, and to mobilize [their] organizations and public opinion against such an eventuality'. The parties further undertook to

---

[2] *Komep*, Special Supplement, 'Apophasis tou Pemptou Synethriou' (Decision of the Fifth Congress).

[3] The 1961 Programme of the CPSU, Section V.

avoid any criticism of and any attack on the participating organizations, and, on the insistence of the Communists, they agreed that the parties to the agreement should maintain 'full independence in carrying on their propaganda and disseminating their ideas'.[4]

Past experience had shown that the exchange of insults and recriminations with the non-Communist labour organizations had damaged rather than benefited the Communists. A truce to mud-slinging would do no harm, while the agreement to disseminate their ideas freely would, under the pretext of co-operation, give the Communist 'instructors' access to the non-Communist organizations and expose a greater number of people to Communist agitation. As soon as the non-Communist leaders realized why the Communists had pressed so vigorously for this particular clause they let the agreement lapse. In vain the KKE and the United General Confederation of Labour admonished the other leaders to show 'more anti-Fascist vigour and energy'. Finally, to clear the air, the KKE invited the other organizations to meet and discuss 'a final anti-Fascist agreement' on 7 December 1934. Only the Communist representatives showed up at the meeting.

The difficult art of deception

The Communists were stunned by the dismal failure of the 7 December meeting, where they had expected to make a decisive step forward in the building of the United Front. In November the 2nd Plenum of the Central Committee elected by the Fifth Congress had decided to tone down considerably all Communist propaganda and agitation and concentrate almost exclusively on such matters as 'the fight for wages, bread, land, and against taxes and debts'. In analysing the character of a Communist revolution in Greece and the dynamic forces needed for it they had concluded that an alliance with the peasantry and the petty-bourgeoisie was indispensable. To acquire such 'allies' the Communists needed to relegate their political concepts to the background and conceal their strategic objectives. Stalin had already intimated the imperative need to concentrate on whatever political or economic issues were currently causing widespread social concern. The November Plenum, in accordance with Stalin's instructions,

---

[4] *Pente Khronia*, pp. 180–5.

had passed resolutions granting unequivocal support to any
and all demands of interest to the target groups. In the agrarian
'platform', approved by the Plenum, out of eighty-three
'demands' only four, hidden in a torrent of words, were
Communist-oriented slogans: 'liquidation of Fascist organizations; abolition of the "Idionym" Law; struggle against Fascism
and war; defence of the Soviet Union'. The remaining seventy-
nine covered an unlikely assortment of 'everyday problems',
such as 'tax-free popular cigarettes of good quality', 'the
cancellation of interest-bearing debts owed to the banks by
working peasants', and 'American vine-plants supplied free by
the Government to villagers whose vineyards were destroyed
by phylloxera'.[5] The Communist leaders had hoped that the
decisions of the November Plenum had sufficiently calmed the
misgivings of their allies. The fiasco of 7 December abruptly
dashed all such hopes. In fact, the Communists had no one to
blame but themselves. They had not gone far enough in their
efforts to conceal their objectives. The detailed instructions of
the Plenum to the district party organizations had been particularly revealing. These local organizations were asked to send
to the villages groups of five, eight, or ten knowledgeable
'agrarian instructors' who, using the 'platform', would try to
establish 'in every village a strong bolshevik base, able to carry
out broad mass revolutionary work'.[6] At the same time the
Plenum had candidly acknowledged that the 'platform' was to
be used by the party as an instrument to foster co-operative
agreements with the peasant organizations.[7] The object of such
co-operation had already been revealed to the Greek public in
a translation of the Comintern *Programme*. It was 'to pave the
way for the socialist dictatorship of the proletariat through a
democratic dictatorship of the proletariat and the peasantry'.[8]
The November Plenum had been equally outspoken about the
ulterior motives for toning down Communist propaganda and
concentrating on the everyday demands of the workers and
peasants.

The only way to attract a wide public to the United Anti-Fascist
Front to fight the anti-Communist forces and avert an attack against

[5] *Komep*, No. 5, March 1935.   [6] *Dheltion*, No. 3, January 1935.
[7] *Komep*, No. 5, March 1935.
[8] *To Programma tis Kommounistikis Thiethnous* (Athens, Laiko Vivliopolio, 1932),
p. 83.

the Soviet Union [it said] is by organizing and fostering the masses'
most trifling complaints and, through the everyday struggle for
bread, lead them to do their duty in the fight against Fascism; only
by so doing can the Communists strengthen the vanguard detachments of anti-Fascists workers with new reserves.[9]

Once again the Communists were telling everyone willing to
listen that their party, while supporting the economic demands
of the workers, pretending to be their champion, was in effect
using their problems as a means to draw 'new reserves' to the
Communist ranks, and line up the masses against 'Fascism', a
label which, as the KKE's 'allies' well knew, had been indis-
criminately applied by the Communist Party to all those who
effectively opposed Communist subversion. It was not surprising that the leaders of the non-Communist groups who were
invited to the ill-fated meeting of 7 December 1934 chose to
ignore the invitation.

The Venizelist coup of March 1935

Late in the afternoon of 1 March 1935 a group of retired
officers of the Greek Navy went to the naval base on the island
of Salamis and, with the help of other conspirators, seized the
cruiser *Averoff*, the cruiser-destroyer *Helle*, three light destroyers,
and two submarines. This was the beginning of the Venizelist
coup d'état of March 1935.

Both the Government of Panagis Tsaldaris and the Communist Party had expected a drastic move on the part of the
Venizelists and were making preparations to meet the emergency—each with completely different methods and objectives.
For the Communist Party, a *coup* by the Venizelists presented
an excellent opportunity for agitation and revolutionary work.
The party leadership hoped that while the two 'old-party,
bourgeois camps' were engaged in fighting each other, the
KKE, as a third force, would launch a general political strike,
paralyse the economic life of the country, and, by gaining the
support of the 'masses' and, more important, of the soldiers in
both the Government and the rebellious army units, smash the
Venizelist revolutionaries while at the same time prostrating
the Government. Should the situation develop on these lines,
the Communists would then decide what 'higher forms of
struggle' should be applied. One month before the *coup* the

[9] *Pente Khronia*, p. 198.

Politbureau invited the secretaries of the most important party organizations to a special conference and discussed with them the possibility of a 'military Fascist *coup*'. The Politbureau gave the secretaries 'all the necessary practical instructions'.[10] In April, after the collapse of the Venizelist *coup*, the 3rd Plenum of the Central Committee ruefully admitted that 'the outbreak of the revolt did not find our Party in a satisfactory degree of ideological and organizational readiness, a fact which prevented us from playing a decisive role during the *coup*'.[11]

There were, of course, several objective reasons which prevented the KKE from turning the March *coup* into the beginning of the 'bourgeois-democratic revolution, as the first stage towards the dictatorship of the proletariat'. The KKE continued to be a numerically weak political group, distrusted by the great majority of the Greek people, who were strongly involved in the historically outmoded but politically very lively feud between Venizelists and anti-Venizelists. Its efforts to organize a United Anti-Fascist Front had foundered as soon as its 'allies' spotted the Communist game. One of the 'basic errors', in the opinion of the Central Committee Plenum, was 'the inability of the KKE to develop a broad United Front movement before the *coup d'état* and to organize it with the assistance of United Front committees *at the grass-roots*, in the factories, business establishments, ships, suburbs, villages'. In fact, the ultimate object of the KKE's co-operation with other non-Communist groups was to open the way for the establishment of such committees at the grass-roots 'which were expected to play a decisive role by becoming the nucleus, gathering around them broad masses, organizing them, leading their struggle, and thus implementing the anti-Fascist protocol of 5 October 1934, in spite of the treachery of the reformist and agrarian leaders'.[12] In 1935 the Communist leaders' plan to establish their control over large groups through the device of 'United Front committees at the grass-roots' failed to materialize because the non-Communist leaders withdrew from the alliance too soon for the KKE. A few years later, in 1942–4, the KKE again used the formula of the 'United Front from below and from above' and succeeded in consolidating its control over large groups behind the convenient structure of the National Liberation Front (EAM). In December 1944, when the KKE

[10] *Pente Khronia*, p. 280.   [11] Ibid., p. 289.   [12] Ibid., p. 281.

attempted to seize power by force, its non-Communist 'allies' saw with dismay that it had organized 'the grass-roots'; the withdrawal of the 'allied' groups from EAM had no effect on the KKE's influence over the rank and file.

Another serious 'error' listed by the 3rd Plenum of the Central Committee in April 1935 was the inability of the KKE to stir up a broad wave of strikes based on immediate, everyday economic and political issues before the *coup*, 'thus preparing and mobilizing the masses for the general strike. As a result, the call for the general strike, which was presented immediately after the outbreak of the revolt, remained suspended in the air, although it was correct.' In fact, it was not 'correct'; the Communist tactical rules warn against the calling of a general political strike without sufficient preparation.

A third serious error identified by the Plenum was the failure of the party organizations to use the Communist-led unions, 'as well as whatever reformist trade unions we could influence', as connecting links 'for the transmission of the Party's slogans and for action among the masses . . .'. Whatever the 'errors' committed by the party organizations, the fact remained that in the spring of 1935 the KKE was still a small though boisterous force, operating on the periphery of Greek political life, and handicapped by its position on the 'national question'. This serious burden was thrown off by the 3rd Plenum in April 1935. With the approval of the Comintern the Central Committee then replaced the controversial demand for an independent Macedonia by the demand for 'complete equality of minorities' within the framework of the Greek state. With this, the party was freed from its most damaging handicap.

The elections reveal some progress

The parliamentary election of 9 June 1935 gave the KKE the opportunity to test the effect of its new policy on the Macedonian question. The change in the party's position on this question was advertised from the rooftops, while the KKE, under the cloak of the 'Popular Front for People's Liberties', called for 'complete democratic freedom, humane wages, an eight-hour working day and social security, bread and work for the unemployed, and absolutely peace-loving policies'.[13] A rather peculiar demand was added which, if adopted, could

[13] *Pente Khronia*, p. 276.

only have weakened Greece's defensive preparations while Europe was inexorably drifting towards war: 'Neither the Government nor the Parliament have any right to proclaim mobilization or war. These two vital questions shall be decided by the entire nation, men and women, in two separate plebiscites.' Greece, deeply committed to and vitally interested in the *status quo*, had neither the will nor the strength to wage an aggressive war. War could come only as a result of outside attack. The delay that would have been caused by those two plebiscites could only have benefited the aggressor.

The Liberal Party (Venizelists), together with other smaller parties of Venizelist leanings, decided to abstain from the 9 June election on the grounds that their proposal that proportional representation should be reintroduced had not been accepted by the Government. The Venizelists realized that, after the failure of their March *coup* and the escape of Eleutherios Venizelos to the Dodecanese, public sentiment had largely turned against them. The proportional system would cushion the effect of a radical decrease in Venizelist influence and ensure the election of a larger number of Venizelist deputies than could be expected under the majority system.

The Venizelist call for abstention from the election passed largely unheeded, as 1,030,362 voters cast their ballots. The KKE's 'Popular Front' received 98,699 votes; under the majority system no Popular Front candidate received enough votes to be elected. Yet the increase of the party's electoral following from 14,000 in 1928 to almost 100,000 in 1935 under the majority system was a noteworthy achievement. This increase of pro-Communist votes should not be attributed to the abstention of the Venizelists; the elections of January 1936 proved that the KKE's political influence—free from the burden of the 'national question'—was steadily growing.

8. Preparing for the 'Approaching Decisive Struggles'

The targets for subversion

With renewed confidence after the results of the 9 June election, the Politbureau called the 3rd Pan-helladic Organizational Conference in order 'to prepare and organize the Party and all the workers for the approaching decisive class clashes'. The decisions of the conference gave the impression that the party leadership seriously contemplated a showdown by force. Its detailed instructions were not those of a political party. They read:

(*a*) Our Party must place primary importance on the concentration of forces in Athens, Piraeus, Larissa, Volos, Salonika, and Kavalla.

(*b*) The party organizations must concentrate their efforts on the *transport services*, and in the factories.

(*c*) All organizations, on the basis of the experience gained during the March *coup* and according to the instructions of the Central Committee, must take the necessary steps to prepare their members *for any eventuality*.

(*d*) [The party] must organize non-party mass organizations of anti-Fascist action, *militant* organs with many thousands of members . . . with intensive work in the army and among the anti-Fascist officers.

(*e*) [The party] must gain allies and above all win over the peasantry.[1]

The targets for party activity were the major urban centres, the means of transport, the armed forces, and the peasantry. Subversion of the armed forces and control of the transport system, chiefly the railways and the merchant marine, through party cells, fractions, and United Front committees, would place in the hands of the party the power to paralyse the country at a crucial moment. With armed units going over to the side of the revolution, a general political strike crippling the vital

[1] *Komep*, No. 8, July 1935; author's italics.

services, the transport facilities controlled by party functionaries, and the peasants coming to the urban centres to add the force of their numbers to the equation, 'Greece would be on its way to the bourgeois-democratic revolution with a swift passing into the next stage, the dictatorship of the proletariat'.[2] This was the 'concrete task' set before the party cadres, to be accomplished through the scrupulous application of the party's organizational directives.

To carry out this task, the KKE was directed by the Organizational Conference to promote a coalition of all 'democratic anti-Fascist' forces and then 'work untiringly to gain hegemony over the coalition'. Those who later, during the Occupation by the Axis, participated in the coalition of EAM painfully learned exactly what the KKE meant by the word 'hegemony'. It is worth noting that the tactics applied by the Greek Communists during the Occupation were largely formulated in 1935. In fact, their application *had started* in 1935. It was interrupted by the Metaxas dictatorship, only to be resumed with much greater effectiveness in 1941, when the German invasion destroyed most political and institutional structures in the country, leaving the field open for the tactics of the United Front.

The KKE intensifies its revolutionary agitation

While speaking to the 12th Plenum of the ECCI (1932), Otto Kuusinen, the well-known Communist leader of Finnish descent, said:

Comrade Stalin called our attention to the fact that the October Revolution, during the period of organizing for the storm, was concerned to take every step, or almost every step in its attack, *under the guise of defence.* . . . 'The revolution has to a certain extent veiled its offensive operations under the *guise of defence*, in order that the undecided and vacillating elements may more easily be swept into its whirlpool.' Our present slogans are well suited for the revolutionary attack if only we understand how to mobilize the masses for the attack.[3]

Kuusinen's open and cynical statement in 1932 that the Communists had used and should always use the guise of

---

[2] *Pente Khronia*, p. 207.
[3] Otto Kuusinen, *Prepare for Power* (New York, Workers' Library Publishers, 1932), p. 116; author's italics.

H

defence to veil their offensive operations has never really lost
its validity. In 1935, while protesting against 'the intensified
aggressiveness of the Capitalists', calling the people to join the
fight 'for the defence against the plutocrats and their government of hunger: and for defence against Fascism and war', the
KKE was simply disguising its offensive operations under the
cloak of defence.

To mobilize the 'masses' and sweep them into the whirlpool
of revolution, the Communists were again advised to exploit
the everyday problems of the working people. A paragraph of
the KKE Central Committee's directive 'on the Victory of the
United Front and the formation of the anti-Fascist coalition',
adopted soon after the Organizational Conference, succinctly
outlined the steps to be taken to prepare for 'higher forms of
struggle':

The Central Committee emphasizes the importance of the decisive
exploitation of the everyday limited struggles. As the experience of
the last year has shown to us, and as current conditions require, the
Communists and the vanguard workers must work untiringly for
the *unification* of the limited separate struggles, to turn them into
mass political strikes, and then proceed with the systematic ideological and organizational preparation of the general strike as a
decisive anti-Fascist weapon.[4]

Besides its significance as a concise outline of Communist tactics, this paragraph explains why a Communist party relies so
heavily on public discontent to initiate the revolutionary process. Removal of the causes of discontent through social and
economic reforms 'blunts the revolutionary fervour', as Stalin
once openly acknowledged, or, more precisely, deprives a
Communist party of the indispensable tactical conditions for
starting the process towards revolution.

In 1935 there were many causes for public discontent in
Greece. Unemployment, inflation, political instability, a debt-
ridden agriculture, taxation falling heavily on the lower-income
strata, an old-fashioned, small-market capitalism, could all
furnish the Communists with fuel for their revolutionary drive.
Disregarding their own advice on the gradual broadening
of the process, the KKE leaders decided to raise the struggle
abruptly to the level of a twenty-four-hour Pan-helladic
strike. The strike, scheduled for 25 July 1935, failed for want

[4] *Komep*, No. 8, July 1935.

of adequate preparation. This failure revealed that the KKE
had not succeeded in establishing strong ties with the organized workers. The Politbureau hastily asked the Communist-
controlled Executive Committee of the United General Confederation of Workers to call the Second Pan-helladic Trade
Union Conference. When the conference convened, it turned
out to be nothing more than a meeting of Communist cadres
entrusted with 'fraction-type' work in the trade unions. The
upshot of their deliberations was summed up in one sentence:
'We must prepare the working class with the weapon of the
mass political strike and then with the weapon of the general
strike.'[5] On 14 August *Rizospastis* published 'a resolution of
the United General Confederation of Greek Workers in
favour of immediately establishing trade union unity'.[6] In
another directive the Politbureau revealed its motives for
seeking 'trade union unity'. The struggle for such unity, it
said, 'is the basis for a strong Communist upsurge all over the
country . . . , for the active preparation of the working class for
the big new battles which are now approaching, and for the
winning of hegemony over the developing democratic anti-
Fascist movement'.[7] Note that this ominously-phrased directive was not '*agitatsia*' aimed at the general public. It was a
policy statement addressed to the party cadres, advising them
on the real objectives of the drive for 'trade union unity'.

Zachariades had already proved himself a reliable and
resourceful agent. At the 4th Plenum of the KKE Central
Committee, which convened on 28 September 1935 with the
participation of party secretaries from the local organizations,
Zachariades outlined 'the duties of the party with regard to the
decisions of the Seventh Congress of the Comintern'. All his
suggestions were 'unanimously' approved by the Plenum.

Zachariades explained that the three basic tasks set before the
Communist parties by the Seventh Congress could be summa-
rized in effect as (*a*) subversion of all non-Communist régimes—
Fascist, social-democratic, democratic; (*b*) strengthening of the
Communist Party through 'alliances' with other political and
labour forces in the capitalist countries; and (*c*) in the event of
a general conflagration, 'transformation of the imperialist war
into a civil war'.[8]

---

[5] *Rizospastis*, 13 August 1935.   [6] Ibid., 14 August 1935.
[7] *Pente Khronia*, p. 301.   [8] Ibid., p. 375.

The 'decisive link'[9] in the carrying out of these three tasks was the establishment of a United Front, which would permit the infiltration of broader groups.[10] The Seventh Congress had made this quite clear. Furthermore, the Communist parties were directed to form an underground revolutionary army known as the 'anti-Fascist mass defence corps', prepared to intervene at the decisive moment and turn 'an imperialist war into a civil war'.[11] The United Front was to serve as the convenient framework for 'the preparation of the workers for the second round of proletarian revolutions, for the welding of the proletariat into a single mass political army for the dictatorship of the proletariat and the power of the soviets'.[12]

The 4th Plenum dutifully translated and incorporated in its own decisions all these resolutions of the Seventh World Congress. A few years later, during the German Occupation (1951–4), the KKE made a serious effort to implement the directives enunciated by the 4th Plenum and the Seventh and last World Congress of the Communist International. The effort ultimately failed, but only after a bloody and protracted fight.

Target: 'Monarcho-Fascism'

In 1935 'monarchy' became the whipping-boy of the Greek Communists. Absolute monarchy as a form of government was abolished in Greece in 1864, and replaced by a constitutional monarchy resembling the British system. In Greek, constitutional monarchy is known as *Vassilevomeni Dimokratia*, which can loosely be translated as a democracy or republic under a king. In the Greek language there is only one word for both 'democracy' and 'republic'. The *Vassilevomeni Dimokratia*, too, had been abolished in 1924 and Greece had become a republic in the ordinary sense of the word. Consequently, in 1935 there was no ground, strictly speaking, for the use of the term 'monarchy'; but the compound of the words 'monarchy' and 'Fascism'—Monarcho-Fascism—made an effective weapon for political agitation. The Communists have usually shown remarkable sensitivity to the power of words as weapons.

---

[9] *Seventh Congress; Resolutions and Decisions* (Moscow, Co-operative Publishing Society of Foreign Workers in the USSR, 1935), pp. 33–44; hereinafter cited as *Seventh Congress*.

[10] *Pente Khronia*, p. 360.   [11] *Seventh Congress*, pp. 29, 44.   [12] Ibid., p. 34.

Of course, there was another more practical reason for the resurrection of the 'bogy' of monarchy. After the collapse of the Venizelist *coup* in March 1935 the movement for the restoration of the *Vassilevomeni Dimokratia* had gained momentum. Many had been disillusioned with the Republic, and their ranks were steadily growing. The Republic, in its decade of existence, had scored a very poor record. Half a dozen military *coups* and one dictatorship in the short span of ten years could hardly pass as a successful performance. When General George Kondylis, who had played a key role ten years earlier in the establishment of the Republic, openly joined those who advocated the restoration of the *Vassilevomeni Dimokratia*, the issue could no longer be shrugged off as the private wish of incorrigible Royalists.

Few among those who supported the restoration of the *Vassilevomeni* did so with a clear realization that the political instability under the Republic was playing right into the hands of international Communism. Those who understood the basic implications looked upon the return of the exiled King George II to the throne as a means of strengthening the defensive capabilities of the nation at a time when the storm of war was looming ominously on the horizon. Interestingly enough, the Communists, too, interpreted the proposed restoration as a defensive measure against 'the approaching second round of proletarian revolutions'.[13] They realized that a strong government, ensuring governmental stability, would take measures to improve economic conditions and remove some of the issues on which the Communists counted heavily for initiating and then speeding up the revolutionary process. Besides, a strong government could hardly be expected to sit back and watch the Communists prepare their revolution without taking steps to frustrate such preparations. Being fully aware of these possibilities, the 4th Plenum of September 1935 declared that 'the principal duty of the party is to establish the Popular Front of all the democratic and anti-Fascist forces of the people and of the armed forces . . . which will use *every means* of making the restoration of the Monarchy and the victory of Fascism impossible in Greece'.[14] While inviting the 'democratic' or 'republican' forces—again the same word in Greek—to join in the Popular Front, the KKE was admittedly not interested in the preservation of the Republic. 'The KKE declares that while

---

[13] *Pente Khronia*, p. 364.   [14] Ibid., p. 309; author's italics.

devoting all its forces today against Monarchy and Fascism, it will continue untiringly its work for the victory of the *only* genuine republic, the soviet republic.'[15]

A 'soviet republic' remained the ultimate objective. For the time being, however, the Plenum decided to support the establishment of a 'democratic government'. This appeared to be a major concession on the part of the KKE, considering its previous extremism. But was it? A few weeks earlier *Pravda* had published an article signed by Georgi Dimitrov in his capacity as the Secretary of the ECCI. In it hc said that 'in many countries, a government of the United Front will be, perhaps, one of the most important *transitional* forms. Such a government, however, cannot bring about a final solution. . . . It is therefore necessary that we should arm for the socialist revolution. . . .'[16] In other words, the United Front 'democratic government' was looked upon by the Communists as a transitional stage, useful in facilitating the arming of the Communists for their revolution. In line with these Comintern pronouncements, the KKE Plenum declared itself in favour of a democratic government and at the same time decided 'to form a mass militant defence corps, a strong weapon in the hands of the popular masses'.[17] The word 'defence' ought to mislead no one; Kuusinen's candid statement has provided a durable clarification.

The 4th Plenum is memorable for another reason: it elected Nikos Zachariades to the newly-created post of Secretary-General of the party. Till then there was only the post of the Secretary of the Central Committee. Zachariades had occupied this post since November 1931. It was not a permanent position, a secretary being elected by each new Central Committee. By the decision of the 4th Plenum, Zachariades was elevated to permanent, life-long office. It lasted till March 1956, when a Central Committee headed by Apostolos Grozos denounced Zachariades as a Stalinist and he was removed.

The formal elevation of Zachariades to the position of permanent leader of the Communist Party was a reflection of Stalin's policy of developing 'cadres and genuinely Bolshevik leaders in the Communist parties so that the parties may be able, in times of crisis, to find independently and quickly . . .

[15] *Pente Khronia*, p. 310.   [16] *Pravda*, 6 August 1935; author's italics.
[17] *Pente Khronia*, p. 310.

correct solutions for the political and tactical problems of the Communist movement'.[18] It was not a question of vanity. The great *vozhd* in the Kremlin wanted trusted agents at the helm of the various Communist parties, free of any pressures from the rank and file, and subject only to his control. In Greece members of the Communist Party were taught to address Zachariades by the title of *Archigos* (leader).

Vassilis Nefeloudis, a Communist of the younger generation, who owed his promotion to Zachariades, was elected by the 4th Plenum to the vacated post of Secretary of the Central Committee. The KKE was tightening its organization in anticipation of the 'approaching second round of proletarian revolutions'.

[18] Cf. the 1961 Programme of the CPSU.

9. Dictatorship or Revolution?

The return of King George II

The political manoeuvres which led to the plebiscite of 3 November 1935 on the restoration of the *Vassilevomeni Dimokratia* make a fascinating story by themselves, but we cannot discuss them here in detail. It is, however, worth mentioning that Panagis Tsaldaris, the Premier and leader of the Populists, the traditionally royalist party, gave rather half-hearted support to the champions of restoration. Not that he was against the idea, but he realized that the King could serve as a rallying-point for all patriotic Greeks only if he returned to the throne by an honest and incontestable plebiscite. Some of the champions of restoration were rather impatient; others not too confident. On 10 October 1935 Tsaldaris was forced out of office by three high-ranking royalist officers, 'representing' the Army, the Navy, and the Air Force, who intercepted Tsaldaris' car on the highway from Kifissia to Athens and demanded his resignation. Alexander Papagos, of later fame, was one of the three officers.

A new Cabinet, headed by General George Kondylis, took office and a plebiscite was proclaimed for 3 November. The results of the plebiscite showed an overwhelming majority in favour of restoration. Many felt, however, that there were some grounds for questioning, if not the majority itself, at least its size. In any event, the excessive zeal of extreme royalist groups tarnished the outcome of the plebiscite and allowed partisans of the Republic to dispute the claim that the plebiscite had settled the 'constitutional question' once and for all. This was a disservice to the King; to some extent it precipitated the events which nine months later led to the dictatorial régime of the Fourth of August.

King George returned to Greece on 25 November 1935 after twelve years in exile. His first move was to work out a plan for the reconciliation of the two major political camps, the Venizelists and the anti-Venizelists (Royalists), whose feuds had plagued the country for more than twenty years.

Two weeks after the King's return, the KKE held its Sixth Regular Congress. One may recall that the previous Congress was the one in which 'for the first time complete bolshevik unity prevailed', the Congress which had 'unanimously elected the new leadership of the Party'. In other words, the Fifth Congress of March 1934 had retrospectively sanctioned the Comintern's intervention in November 1931 and presumably awarded rank-and-file recognition to the New Leadership under Zachariades. In March 1934 the participants did their best to convey the impression that the Congress genuinely represented the will of the party. Yet a report to the Sixth Congress revealed that 'for reasons of vigilance, the New Leadership had prepared and convened the [Fifth] Congress without announcing its convocation to the cells and the district organizations'.[1] In March 1934 the New Leadership, still uncertain, had resorted to a rather exclusive meeting of selected and trusted cadres. By December 1935, however, Zachariades had carved out an unassailable position for himself in the party organization. He had already been elected, by the 4th Plenum, to the newly-created post of Secretary-General of the Party, while members who were personally loyal to the *Archigos* had been appointed to key posts in the party hierarchy. The Sixth Congress, besides confirming the elevation of Zachariades to the sacrosanct position of the 'Archigos', unanimously ratified all the decisions of the 4th Plenum. If anything new was added it was the assertion that the return of the King was the prelude to the establishment of a dictatorship. There seems to have been no real basis for this allegation. At that time the régime established in 1936 by I. Metaxas was still in the future. In December 1935 Metaxas was not even a member of the Government. There is no reason to believe that the King, in the early months after his return, had any intention of establishing a dictatorship. In fact, King George had dismissed General Kondylis precisely because he had taken up an extreme position and refused to put into effect the conciliatory measures favoured by the King, particularly the granting of an amnesty to all those connected with the March 1935 Venizelist *coup*. With the signs of approaching international upheavals all too evident, the King sincerely wished to pave the way for the reconciliation of the two major political camps. On the other hand, even Metaxas agreed with

[1] *Pente Khronia*, p. 386.

the King that conciliation was the only realistic course, and advised him through George Streit to pursue a policy of 'conciliation with Venizelos'.[2]

King George rightly felt that his conciliatory efforts could not succeed as long as he maintained the one-sided Parliament elected the previous June, when the Venizelist parties had abstained. A new parliamentary election was imperative. The King, as well as the leaders of the national political parties, with the exception of Andreas Michalakopoulos, agreed that the election should be held under the proportional representation system, to allow all political groupings to compete at the polls without the psychological limitations and pressures associated with the majority system. There is evidence that King George intended to proclaim a second election under the majority system, later, to provide the country with the strong government it needed for the turbulent times ahead.

In the election which took place on 26 January 1936, under the proportional system, 1,278,085 people voted. The traditional pro-royalist parties received 582,940 (45·6 per cent.) of the votes and the Venizelist camp 562,796 (44·0 per cent.). Between these two major political alignments, the Communist-led 'Popular Front' mustered 73,441; the Peasant Party (I. Sofianopoulos) 13,006; and the newly-formed National Unity (Enotikon) Party, under Panayiotis Kanellopoulos, 9,870.

The distribution of votes was reflected in the composition of Parliament. Out of a total of 300 seats, the Royalists held 143, the Venizelists 141, the Popular Front 15, the Peasant Party 1. With this almost equal representation of the two major camps, the power of decision passed into the hands of the fifteen Popular Front deputies. Without their co-operation neither major party could form a stable government or enact legislation.

It is not clear whether the supporters of the proportional system had anticipated this outcome. If they did, they were wilfully paving the way towards dictatorship or political stalemate; since both major political camps urged the use of the proportional system, they must be held equally responsible for what followed.

Eighteen days after the election the country was still without a government. All the King's efforts to form one had failed.

---

[2] Miltiades Malainos, *I Tetarti Avgoustou; pos kai thiati Epevlithi* (Athens, 1946), p. 26.

Finally, King George summoned the political leaders to a conference and asked them to set aside their differences and form a viable coalition. The two major parties, the Liberals (Venizelists) and the Populists (pro-royalists), agreed to start negotiations towards a coalition government which could muster overwhelming support in Parliament. Had the two major parties understood the historical significance of their actions they would have discarded their outdated feuds and formed a strong, stable administration. This was not to be the case. A narrow partisan attitude prevailed. If the decision to use the proportional system was the first step towards a dictatorship, the unwillingness of the two major parties to provide the country with a stable government was the second.

The Sofoulis–Sklavainas Agreement

While the two major parties continued, off and on, their desultory talks, they both made contact, separately and in secret, with the Popular Front deputies. The bourgeois politicians were seeking Communist support in their petty partisan feuds. The Populists did not get very far in their talks with the Communists. The Liberals were more successful. On 19 February a secret agreement was signed by Themistokles Sofoulis, representing the Liberal Party, and S. Sklavainas, representing the parliamentary group of the Popular Front. Under its terms, the Popular Front group in Parliament agreed 'to vote for the Liberal candidate for the office of the Speaker of the House, and support a government formed by the Liberal Party'.[3] The plan was quite simple. With the Popular Front votes added to those of the Venizelist deputies supporting the candidacy of Sofoulis, the Liberal leader would be elected to the office of the Speaker. Then, following an established parliamentary custom, the King would call Sofoulis and give him the mandate to form a Cabinet. The Popular Front agreed to give him a vote of confidence, thus providing the necessary majority. The Communists did not pledge their support without some significant strings attached. They included 'the repeal of Law 4229 (Idionym)', a general amnesty for all political prisoners and exiles, the 'abolition of the state security agencies', the suppression of all organizations having 'Fascist' objectives, the permanent establishment of the proportional electoral system, a

[3] See full text in *Rizospastis*, 3 April 1936.

reduction in the price of bread by at least two drachmas, a moratorium on debts to the state for sums exceeding 3,000 drachmas, a five-year unconditional moratorium on peasants' debts to private individuals and banks, and immediate application of the social security law. The transparent object of these demands was to perpetuate the conditions of political instability which had brought the KKE to the enviable position of king-maker, and to create for the party the image of a political force concerned with the economic problems of wide segments of the Greek population.

On 3 March 1936 General Alexander Papagos, then Minister of War in the Demertzis caretaker Cabinet, reported to the Premier that the corps commanders of the Army had visited him and declared that the Army could not remain passive in the event of collaboration between any of the bourgeois parties and the Communists. Apparently they were unaware of the Sofoulis–Sklavainas agreement, which still remained secret.

Some observers insisted at the time that Ioannis Metaxas was behind the Army leaders' *démarche*. Though the anxiety of the military might have been artificially intensified at the top, there is no doubt that a great number of officers at all levels were seriously concerned about the rumoured collaboration of the Liberals with the Communists. In any event, Metaxas felt that his aim of becoming Minister of War was approaching fulfilment. He had already secured the support of several members of the King's entourage. On 5 March General Papagos was forced to resign, and Ioannis Metaxas was appointed Minister of War in the Demertzis Cabinet. This was another significant step towards the dictatorship.

As soon as Metaxas took over the Ministry of War, the unrest among the military subsided. Those who had been deliberately fomenting the anxiety of the officer corps to assist Metaxas had no reason to continue their agitation. The many who were sincerely worried saw with satisfaction the appointment of a man of known abilities to the key post of Minister of War. The immediate end of the military unrest helped Metaxas speedily to win the King's confidence.

The next day, 6 March, Parliament voted to elect a Speaker. In the first ballot Sofoulis received 142 votes, Ch. Vozikes, the Royalist candidate, 137, and George Siantos, the candidate of the Popular Front, 13. The election required an absolute majority. On the second ballot the thirteen Popular Front votes switched over to Sofoulis, who received 158 votes and was elected Speaker of the House. The Communists had lived up to the first part of the Sofoulis–Sklavainas agreement. But the election of the Speaker through the support of the Popular Front deputies revealed with stark clarity how much power the Communists had over Greek politics. Immediately after the announcement of the results, the Royalist deputies left the Chamber. All the other parliamentary officers were elected unopposed by 152 Venizelist and Communist deputies. The public still knew nothing of the Sofoulis–Sklavainas agreement. Even Communist Party followers expressed astonishment at the collaboration between the Popular Front deputies and the 'bourgeois politicians'. The next day, *Rizospastis* published what appeared to be an explanation for the vote, but with no mention of the Sofoulis–Sklavainas agreement. The *Rizospastis* statement, signed by Sklavainas, simply stated that the action of the Popular Front deputies was prompted by their desire 'to avert the danger of Fascism'; Sklavainas added that the Popular Front deputies felt satisfied with the assurances given by Sofoulis in Parliament that a Liberal Government would 'take the necessary measures to protect the oppressed public liberties'. To calm any misgivings among the ideologists of his party, Sklavainas asserted that 'fundamental differences separate the Popular Front deputies from all bourgeois parties, including the Liberal Party'.[4]

Why did Sklavainas conceal the agreement he had signed with the leader of the Liberal Party? Evidently he realized that by disclosing it he would make it all but impossible for Sofoulis to form a government. It required little imagination to foresee that even Liberal deputies would refuse to support a government operating under the thumb of the Communist Party.

Metaxas becomes Prime Minister

As was expected, on 7 March Sofoulis was called to the Palace, where he received the mandate. At this crucial moment he made an unexpected move. In a frank talk with Panagis Tsaldaris he stated that 'under the circumstances, the two major parties should support a non-political government [i.e., one not composed of parliamentary deputies], after agreeing

[4] *Rizospastis*, 7 March 1936.

on its platform and composition'. It seems that Sofoulis, under pressure from powerful Liberal personalities, had decided against forming a Liberal government, with the Communists pulling strings behind the scenes.

Sofoulis declined the mandate, and the King accepted the recommendation of both major parties to form a non-political Cabinet. He re-appointed K. Demertzis as Premier, with Metaxas as Vice-Premier. Anyone familiar with the personalities involved could easily see that Metaxas was to be the real power in the new 'non-political' government.

The Communists took revenge against Sofoulis in an original fashion. On 3 April *Rizospastis* published the Sofoulis–Sklavainas agreement in its entirety. The disclosure fell like a bomb on the already tense political stage. If the Communists were set on strengthening the advocates of a dictatorial régime, they could not have used a more potent weapon. The publication of the notorious agreement was another big step towards a dictatorship.

The Communists did not stop there. When, a few days later, Parliament discussed a censure motion against Sofoulis on account of his agreement with the Communists, they revealed that the other major party, the Populists, had also asked for their co-operation. They even named Constantine Angelopoulos, a deputy, as the representative of the Populists in the negotiations. The prestige of the bourgeois parties sank lower when 188 deputies voted against the censure motion, thus indirectly condoning the agreement with the Communists.

On 19 March 1936 Eleutherios Venizelos, the man who had dominated the political scene for a quarter of a century, died an exile in Paris. His death markedly weakened the position of Sofoulis, who had been designated by Venizelos as his substitute. Many among the Liberal politicians turned to George Kafandaris, who had held the reins of the Liberal Party in the twenties, when Venizelos lived abroad in voluntary exile. Sofoulis, in a desperate manoeuvre to retain his control over the party, introduced a Bill practically stripping the King of his constitutional prerogatives. His manoeuvre failed, but it added fuel to the political bickering between the two major political camps.

On 13 April Premier K. Demertzis died quite unexpectedly of a heart attack. The next day, the King appointed I. Metaxas to the premiership. Metaxas was not an ordinary 'non-political' premier. His appointment caused grave concern in the ranks of both major parties. Metaxas had made no secret of his contempt for the traditional parties and the parliamentary system which had proved unable to provide the country with a stable government for months after the election. The two major parties decided to make one more effort. A new series of negotiations began, but on 22 April it was formally announced that the discussions had ended in deadlock. For the third time since January the major political parties had failed to find a solution. This time the talks had failed because Kafandaris had posed conditions unacceptable to the Populists for the settlement of a thorny issue, that of the officers who had been put on half-pay because of their involvement in the March 1935 *coup*.

The collapse of the bi-partisan negotiations strengthened the position of Metaxas. If the parties were unable to provide the country with a parliamentary government they could at least vest his Government with the cloak of legitimacy. On 25 April he appeared before Parliament and asked for a vote of confidence. Sofoulis immediately declared that the Liberal Party had decided to support the Metaxas Government. Kafandaris also stated that, in view of the danger of having no government at all, he, too, intended to vote for Metaxas. Tsaldaris, the leader of the Populists, who had never trusted Metaxas in spite of their common political orientation, declared that his party would give the Metaxas Government only a vote of 'tolerance'. The Liberal George Papandreou, and the Agrarian leader, Alexandros Mylonas, decided not to support the motion, while the left-wing Liberal Alexandros Papanastassiou stated that he would abstain in protest against the major parties, which had failed 'in their primary responsibility of giving the country a government'. The spokesman of the Popular Front said that his group would vote against the Metaxas Government. When the votes were counted 241 had given their formal support to Metaxas; sixteen voted against him and four abstained. Seldom before had a Greek Government received such an overwhelming parliamentary endorsement. The Government was further authorized to issue legislative decrees while Parliament was not in session. Then Parliament decided to adjourn till 30 September 1936. It did not meet again until after the Second World War.

Shortly before the adjournment Sofoulis introduced a Bill establishing proportional representation—which had produced the impasse in the first place—as the *permanent* electoral system of the country. This had been one of the provisions contained in his agreement with Sklavainas. Did Sofoulis expect to pacify the Communists and set the stage for future co-operation? It is not clear. In any event, the Bill was passed with the help of the Popular Front deputies. With this, all hope for new elections under the majority system, which alone could give the country a stable, democratic government, vanished. It was another major step on the road to dictatorship.

The KKE could boast that its efforts to weaken the democratic institutions had made considerable headway. Within a few months the parliamentary system had been disgraced. The political parties, which until recently could rightly claim that they commanded the support and the loyalty of the overwhelming majority of the Greek electorate, had been exposed as petty-minded, bickering groups of feuding politicians. While the democratic institutions were losing the respect of the people, both the advocates of dictatorship as the only defence against the 'bourgeois-democratic revolution' and those working for a revolution against the dictatorship were gaining unprecedented strength.

Metaxas had now openly joined the champions of dictatorship. In all fairness, one may say that once the proportional system had been established 'permanently' there was no democratic way to put an end to the political impasse. New elections would have merely produced similar results, while the Communists, taking advantage of the situation, would have continued building up their forces for a showdown.

The riots of May 1936

With the disintegration of the parliamentary system, the Communists felt that the time was ripe to put into effect the elaborate scheme of progressively expanding revolutionary activities which they had worked out in painstaking detail during the preceding years. The so-called 'popular revolutionary actions for the smashing of the Fascist offensive'—strikes, demonstrations, street fights, inflammatory proclamations—began to follow one another with increasing intensity until they came to an explosive climax on 9 May 1936, in Salonika.

Early in May tobacco-workers all over the country had gone on strike demanding higher wages. On the morning of 8 May five to six thousand tobacco-workers in Salonika formed a demonstration and marched towards the General Administration Building (Gheniki Dhiikisis) to present a petition to the Governor-General. The gendarmerie blocked the way to the G.A. Building. A violent riot broke out. Several people were wounded before the demonstration was broken up by force. Mounting tension gripped the entire city. In the afternoon groups of textile workers, who had joined the strike wave in the meantime, stoned a factory. Before midnight several other unions came out in a twenty-four-hour protest strike. The Government mobilized the railway employees, who were among the striking unions, and ordered the Third Army Corps to preserve public order by taking 'extraordinary measures'. A state of emergency was proclaimed.

The following morning several other unions joined in the strike. Almost 25,000 workers in Salonika alone stayed away from work that day. Shopkeepers, merchants, and artisans closed their shops. The tension was near to breaking-point. When the gendarmes attempted to arrest workers stationed at factory gates to prevent any strike-breakers from going to work, fresh bloody clashes took place. This gave the signal for a new demonstration. This time thousands of people from all walks of life poured into the centre of the city in a gigantic demonstration which reached the square in front of the G.A. Building shortly after 11.0 a.m. The gendarmerie tried to block the way, but was overpowered by the crowds. As the demonstrators tried to seize an armoured car, some gendarmes began to fire into the huge, pulsating mass. Twelve people were killed or critically wounded, while mounted gendarmes charged the people with drawn swords. The demonstrators fell back, leaving behind more than thirty-two people seriously wounded. Another 250 were badly knocked about.

As soon as the Government realized the seriousness of the situation, the gendarmes were ordered back to their barracks, and their units placed under the command of regular army officers. Army patrols were sent out to perform police duties. But the military units stationed in Salonika were composed mostly of local residents who had no intention of fighting against their own kin. One of the battalions which was sent to disperse

I

the demonstrators joined them. General Zeppos, the Commander of the Third Army Corps, was forced to give permission for a gigantic protest demonstration that same afternoon. The mob took possession of the streets, paraded, shouted, cursed, and cheered. Throughout the night government authority in the city of Salonika was non-existent. Of course only a small fraction of the thousands who flooded the streets of Salonika were Communists or even sympathizers. But this was immaterial. The numbers and the aggressiveness of the demonstrators showed that the people, angered by the brutal use of force and deprived of respected political leadership, had become 'masses' in the Communist sense of the word, a manageable multitude ready to follow self-appointed but determined leaders in any direction.

The next day more than 150,000 people attended the funeral of the victims. There were no incidents, because the authorities made no effort to interfere. Public authority was not restored until army units arrived from Larissa.

The Salonika eruption played straight into the hands of the champions of dictatorship. They now argued that the Communists were moving into a revolutionary stage. The Salonika riots were interpreted as a Communist dress rehearsal which had proved that, without proper counter-measures, the Communists would in the future be able to deliver even heavier blows against the Government. Some critics with vivid imaginations went so far as to say that Metaxas had deliberately allowed the situation to get out of hand in Salonika to awaken the public to the Communist danger. Whether this indeed was a trap set by Metaxas, it is hard to prove. In any event, the Communists supplied the material he needed to alert the country's patriotic forces. Impressed by their own success in Salonika, the Communists publicly claimed that the refusal of the army units in Salonika to fight against the civilian population was the product of their successful work through the Anti-Militarist Organization (AMI). They even predicted that in future clashes troops would cross the lines *en masse* and join the Communists 'for the final struggle against the Fascist menace'. In one of the many inflammatory proclamations of that period, 'the Central Committee of the KKE and the Parliamentary Group of the Popular Front' jointly declared:

Only a universal revolt, on the lines of Salonika, and with the co-operation of the Army, can impose the united and sovereign will of the People. . . . The people of Salonika gave the signal for the universal liberation struggle. With the forces of the people united in an invincible front, people and Army together, we must pour into the streets for the 24-hour strike. Let us everywhere form committees of public safety. The will of the people must triumph. The murderer Metaxas must be swept away. . . .[5]

An article in *Rizospastis* two days earlier had been even more outspoken. The Communist organ, commenting on the events in Salonika, said:

From now on, Greece will not find 'peace and tranquillity', no matter how much of the people's blood may be spilled, as long as plutocracy and Monarchy hold power. In the whole country, the people must stop all other work, pour out and take possession of the streets, and then, united with the army, impose their will: to oust the government of the murderers! A new government must be formed to apply the Agreement of the Popular Front with the Liberals, and satisfy all the demands of the strikers and of all the workers.[6]

In accordance with the party strategy of promoting, as a first step, a 'democratic-bourgeois revolution', the KKE carefully avoided any demands related to the party's ultimate objectives. However, its pronouncements were clearly a call to revolt. In the past similar inflammatory proclamations could be largely ignored by the authorities. After the events of Salonika the revolutionary pronouncements of the KKE seemed to possess ominous realism. They were not designed merely to stir up agitation, but reflected the official policy of the Communist Party. Zachariades himself, analysing the situation on 14 May at a secret meeting of the Central Committee, said:

We are moving towards new, serious, and more violent popular struggles. All our efforts must be concentrated on the overthrow of the Metaxas Government and the application of the Popular Front–Liberal Agreement. This Agreement remains even today the primary basis and the first step in the reorientation of domestic affairs towards a course which is in the interest of the People. Naturally, this application, which will bring about a complete change in our domestic conditions, depends primarily on mass activity and extra-parliamentary efforts. Therefore, today more than yesterday, our first duty is the comprehensive intensification of the limited, everyday, political and economic struggles of the masses.[7]

[5] *Rizospastis*, 15 May 1936.
[6] Ibid., 12 May 1936.   [7] Ibid., 20 May 1936.

The KKE's use of 'limited everyday political and economic struggles' had already scored substantial success. Within the first half of 1936 alone, the Communists instigated 344 strikes with a total worker-participation of 195,000 and a total duration of 1,990 days.

The Communists realized that the 'decisive link' in any revolutionary development was the attitude of the armed forces. As long as they remained loyal to the Government, a civilian uprising could be crushed by force of arms. For many months Communist agitators had intensified their 'political work' in the armed units, the military depots, the training centres. The Communist organization AMI, operating on a minimal political programme couched in terms of social justice and democratic freedom, had made considerable inroads in the armed forces, to the extent that responsible army authorities began to voice doubts as to the effectiveness of the country's defences in the event of foreign aggression. The First Army Corps, in a secret report submitted at that time to the Government, described in stark language the erosion of the ranks and proposed a number of 'measures of defence against the Communists'. It concluded: 'Without these measures no one can guarantee the cohesion of the army or its usefulness in the event of a threat against the honour and the integrity of our Motherland.'[8]

Equally ominous reports were pouring on to the Premier's desk from many other military units. However exaggerated, these reports left the strong impression that Communist references to a united action 'of the Army and the People' were not merely wishful thinking.

By the end of July the Communist leadership felt that the softening-up process had progressed sufficiently and the time had come to elevate the struggle to a 'higher level'. As a next step in the revolutionary process, the KKE proclaimed a general political strike for 5 August 1936.

The alternatives: dictatorship or revolution

Was the time ripe for a Communist-led revolution in Greece? Lenin once outlined the conditions which must prevail in a country before the struggle is pushed to the ultimate point:

The decisive battle may be deemed to have fully matured when all class forces hostile to us have become sufficiently entangled, are

---

[8] Original in Maniadakis' private archives.

sufficiently at loggerheads with each other, have sufficiently weakened themselves in a struggle which is beyond their strength; when all the vacillating, wavering, unstable, intermediate elements —the petty-bourgeoisie and the petty-bourgeois democrats as distinct from the bourgeoisie—have sufficiently exposed themselves in the eyes of the people, have sufficiently disgraced themselves through their practical bankruptcy; when, among the proletariat, a mass sentiment in favour of supporting the most determined, supremely bold revolutionary action against the bourgeoisie has arisen and begun vigorously to grow. Then revolution is indeed ripe; then, indeed, if we have correctly gauged all the conditions indicated above, and if we have chosen the moment rightly, our victory is assured.[9]

In this passage Lenin obviously refers to the final Communist revolution. In 1936, however, the KKE was preparing for the intermediate 'bourgeois democratic stage' which required the support of the 'vacillating, wavering, intermediate elements'. In this respect the second prerequisite for revolution in the Leninist formula was not directly relevant. Beyond that, the Greek Communists could point with satisfaction to the bankruptcy of the political parties, the infiltration of the armed forces, the petty feuds of the bourgeois political leaders, the weakening of the democratic institutions, and to the popular support indicated by the volume of strikes and, above all, by the events in Salonika. Everything seemed to indicate that the situation was fast approaching a climax. Several years later, in December 1942, George Siantos, one of the major Communist leaders of that period, recalled that 'the Sixth Congress of our Party *was absolutely certain that a rapid and decisive clash was forthcoming* between the people's anti-Fascist forces welded together around the KKE and the Fascist reactionary forces gathering around the King'.[10] But were the conditions present to ensure a Communist victory in such a clash? Siantos, in his appraisal of the 1936 party policies, suggested that the Communist aim of 'blocking a Fascist victory' was subject to the successful establishment of a United Front from above.

To achieve our immediate political objective [he said in December 1942] our Party worked to unify the working class into a single, class-oriented General Confederation of Labour. The Party also tried to unify the peasantry in a united, class-oriented agrarian

[9] Lenin, *Selected Works*, Vol. X, pp. 137–8.
[10] *Dheka Khronia Agones*, pp. 131–2.

party. Thirdly, it signed an agreement for the organization of a
Popular Front against Fascism, and also an agreement of the
Popular Front with the Liberals.

These efforts to institutionalize Communist control over the
non-Communist 'masses' had largely failed. The KKE had
been unable to achieve 'trade union unity' under the control
of its United General Confederation of Greek Workers. The
Agrarian Party of Greece (AKE), an organization created by
the KKE, remained a paper-organization, a title to be added
conveniently to any United Front coalition, but with no
influence among the peasantry. The Popular Front agreement
they had signed on 5 October 1934 had been thrown into the
waste-paper basket by the non-Communist leaders before the
ink was dry. The agreement with the Liberals in the spring of
1936 had been only a source of frustration. In 1942 Siantos
wanted to show that the defeat of the Communists in 1936
should be blamed on the unwillingness of the non-Communist
leaders to co-operate with the KKE in forming a truly united
front. He was speaking in 1942, at a time when the KKE had
again embarked on an ambitious effort to prepare for power by
establishing its controls through the device of a 'national
liberation front'. But in 1936, if the party really considered the
establishment of a United Front to be a prerequisite for successful revolutionary action, conditions were not 'ripe' for revolution.

It seems to me, however, that in spite of the Siantos statement, the Communist leaders in 1936 had realistically assessed
the correlation of forces—at least up to a point. True, the effort
to establish a United Front *from above* had failed in practice.
But, in the process, the Communists had made considerable
inroads into the ranks of the workers and the poorer intellectuals. The events in Salonika had apparently convinced the
Communist leaders that institutionalized control over the
'masses' through formal coalitions with non-Communist leaders
was not imperative, at least during the initial stages. Once the
United Front had become a reality 'in the street demonstrations', the formal agreements would follow regardless of the
personal views of the non-Communist leaders. The events in
Salonika had further shown that the numerical strength of the
party was irrelevant. The situation in the summer of 1936 was

indeed one of passive equilibrium, with the scales ready to be tipped by either side. Once the democratic leaders had abdicated their responsibilities, the initiative had automatically passed to the two extremes of right and left. Between them the majority of the people remained uncertain, frustrated, vacillating. True, in 1936 a Communist victory was by no means 'certain'. But when the Communist Party decided to call for a general political strike on 5 August 1936 they did so fully aware that a decisive act at a time of passive equilibrium could tip the scales in their favour.

A general political strike is admittedly a 'revolutionary weapon' in the Communist arsenal. Metaxas decided to move before the revolutionary process reached a higher and probably uncontrollable stage. Aware of the approaching showdown, he had used the preceding months to prepare the ground for the 'decisive clash'. But let us make no mistake. Just as a Communist revolution cannot succeed unless a number of objective conditions are present, in the same way no individual is strong enough to impose his own personal rule on a modern democratic state unless several powerful forces are willing to support his move or at least inclined to accept and tolerate his rule. In Greece the old political parties, unable to overcome their weaknesses and provide the country with an efficient democratic administration, were voluntarily withdrawing to the background of the political stage, leaving the field open to revolution or dictatorship.

The only effort of any promise made by the old parties to avert the establishment of a dictatorial régime by providing the country with a stable parliamentary government was the tentative agreement between Sofoulis and John Theotokis, a Populist of the extreme right. These two political leaders agreed early in July to co-operate in forming a coalition government. Theotokis accepted the proposal to reinstate the officers who had been put on half-pay after the March *coup*, and Sofoulis agreed that the Liberal Party should vote for a new electoral law establishing the majority system. The Liberal deputies, together with the thirty deputies who were associated with Theotokis, formed a comfortable majority, sufficient to support a coalition government and resolve the political stalemate. Sofoulis announced this agreement to the King on the morning of 22 July 1936. But when asked how soon it could be put into effect, he replied that the new government should be formed in October, soon after the opening of Parliament. In less than six months Sofoulis had moved from co-operation with the extreme left to co-operation with the extreme right. This hardly indicated a serious approach to the country's political problems. However, the agreement could have served a useful purpose if it were put into effect immediately. As its implementation was postponed for another three critical months, the champions of dictatorship had no difficulty in convincing the King that the agreement was too unreliable a political manoeuvre. That on 18 July, at the other end of the Mediterranean, in Spain, a civil war had broken out could not but furnish an impressive illustration of what 'could also happen in Greece'. At critical times impressive events assume disproportionate significance. In any case, Metaxas argued that the Communists should not be granted another three months in which to advance their revolutionary plans. A shrewd and able student of the intricacies of power, he was fully aware that in a situation of passive equilibrium success would crown the efforts of those who prepared more effectively for the showdown. The Communists had interpreted the disintegration of the parliamentary system as tantamount to the disintegration of the state itself. They failed to realize that Metaxas, from the first day of his elevation to the premiership, had begun to build up his own government machine. He had set aside all narrowly partisan considerations and appointed to key positions those who were determined to fight against the revolution, completely disregarding their political affiliations. The only relevant criterion was their ability and determination. While the old democratic shield was falling apart, Metaxas was welding underneath a new armour for the State. The Communists failed to perceive this quick but thorough transformation.

The Communists made another miscalculation. They knew that their following at the polls did not exceed, at best, 10 per cent. of the voting population. But when they saw the excited and defiant multitude pouring into the streets of Salonika, 'forcing' the Army and the police to retire behind barbed wire and thick walls, they resolved that with proper manipulation the whole country could be drawn into the whirlpool of revolution. In fact, the Salonika demonstrations had shown that the people, utterly disgusted with the petty feuds and the inefficiency of the old parties, were turning towards a radical solution of the political impasse. Such a radical solution was not necessarily the one offered by the revolution. Metaxas interpreted the lesson of Salonika more realistically.

If the conditions for a successful Communist-led revolution were absent in Greece in the summer of 1936, was the time ripe for the establishment of a dictatorship? It seems that it was. More and more people, however reluctantly, were reconciling themselves to the idea that only a strong, dictatorial régime could frustrate Communist plans. Influential papers, affiliated to both traditional political camps, published inspired articles calling for the establishment of a dictatorship. Even the old champion of the Republic, General Nikolaos Plastiras, wrote a letter to Metaxas from Beirut advising him to establish a dictatorial government. The leaders of the old parties, though on the surface they appeared to deplore such a possibility, were in effect pushing the situation step by step in that direction. The armed forces, which had been used repeatedly in the past as pawns in the feuds of the old parties, were no longer willing to play the political game. A new generation of military leaders felt only contempt for the politicians. The Communists believed that they had infiltrated into the Army sufficiently to turn the frustration of the military towards revolution. Yet the truth of the matter is that the majority of the officers and soldiers had no sympathy for the preachings of Moscow's agents; but neither did they have any respect for Parliament.

With large segments of the people and the armed forces moving towards the solution offered by a dictatorial régime, Metaxas possessed an additional advantage—the personal qualities of a dictator. He had a genius for organization and knew how to exploit the small weaknesses and the great passions of his opponents. An old soldier, he was more in his element when his decisions were not challenged or frustrated by bickering politicians. He was not popular as a political leader, but he had a well-deserved reputation, even among his enemies, as a strong and resourceful personality. To avert any British objections to his ascent to power—and British influence was then strong in Greek affairs—he had dispersed the old suspicions about his pro-German sympathies in the First World War by repeatedly giving convincing proof of his determination to lead Greece, in the event of another European war, 'into the camp to which

Britain belongs', as he had said at a meeting of top political leaders in 1934.

When the Communists called for a general political strike to commence on 5 August, Metaxas was ready for the showdown. Without waiting for the strike to begin he issued, on 4 August, with the King's approval, a proclamation suspending several articles of the constitution, thus establishing the dictatorship of the Fourth of August with a mere stroke of the pen. No one moved to challenge his authority.

The successful and painless establishment of the dictatorship was no accident. The political leaders who could challenge Metaxas and block his action had formally given up their right to lead the country by voting Metaxas to the Premiership and tying the hands of the King with their 'permanent' electoral law. They had lost the respect of their followers and secretly wished to see the dictatorship established so that they could leave the field as prisoners rather than deserters. Those who may find these remarks somewhat harsh need only read the publications of that period, full of petty exchanges and narrow-minded arguments among politicians who seemed to care only for their own small animosities and feuds. Realizing that they had lost the confidence of the people, they chose silence and succumbed without even a token resistance.

But what of the KKE? The Communists had prepared for the 'decisive clash' for months, if not for years. They had made 'the fight against the establishment of Fascism' their primary objective. After the events in Salonika they claimed to have the people and the Army behind them. Yet at the crucial moment the KKE remained motionless, as though the revolutionary wind was suddenly taken out of its sails. In 1942 George Siantos gave this explanation of the party's complete paralysis and disintegration:

Our Party fought as bravely as it could to avert the establishment of the dictatorship of the Fourth of August; but it could not block the way by itself, by its forces alone. The political line of our Party was correct but we had a number of organizational and technical short-comings, so that we were not able to push the people's anti-Fascist struggles even further at the appropriate moment. . . . Thus, Monarcho-Fascism *chose the right moment, before* the anti-Fascist forces *had time to prepare*, and suddenly, with one stroke, established the openly Fascist dictatorship of the Fourth of August 1936.[11]

---

[11] *Dheka Khronia Agones*, p. 132; author's italics.

The really relevant point in Siantos' analysis is that Metaxas chose 'the right moment' and established his dictatorship *before* the Communists had time to prepare for their revolution. There lies the crux of the matter. In August 1936 conditions were not yet ripe for the Communist revolution. What the Communists apparently expected was that *the actions of the Government would always be one step behind the evolution of the revolutionary process.* This was apparently their minimum expectation in calling for a general political strike, the maximum being a repetition of the Salonika experience on a nation-wide scale. By establishing his dictatorship on 4 August, Metaxas had outpaced the revolutionary process. The blow was too sudden. Those Communist leaders who were not arrested right away panicked and sought safety underground. The revolutionary agitation collapsed completely.

10. The Party under the Dictatorship

The 'illegal' party machine disintegrates

The sudden establishment of the Metaxas dictatorship cut short the KKE's first serious effort to win power. Metaxas, a seasoned tactician himself, fully exploited the initial element of surprise. Being aware of the complex nature of the KKE as a domestic political organization, an army of militants, a standard-bearer of a socio-economic ideology, a conspiratorial group, and an appendage of a foreign power, he took a series of diversified steps. He clamped down on the party cadres with unprecedented efficiency and resourcefulness, and at the same time initiated a number of social and economic reforms designed to undercut whatever social appeal Communism still had among the 'masses'. The settlement of peasant debts, a series of pro-labour decrees, the implementation of social security legislation, and the improvement of the economic situation all helped to blunt the sharpness of public discontent, while a climate of political and economic stability gave the ordinary citizen a feeling of security and confidence. In spite of strict controls over the press and the prohibition of all political activity, the dictatorship was one of the mildest régimes of its kind. Unlike other dictators of that period, Metaxas dissolved even his own small party. The régime, although largely accepted by the public, never became popular only because of the passionate devotion of the Greek people to liberty.

A thorough evaluation of the dictatorship falls outside the scope of this work. In this chapter we can only examine the disintegration of the Communist Party under the régime of the Fourth of August. The man who did most to bring about this disintegration was Constantine Maniadakis, Metaxas' Minister of Public Security.[1] He proved to be the right man in the right place. The stocky, blunt, and witty former officer of the Army Engineers concentrated his efforts on uncovering and neutralizing the Communist leadership instead of spasmodically per-

---

[1] In the 1950s he was repeatedly elected to the Greek Parliament.

secuting the rank and file. His major contribution to the techniques of sub-conventional counter-action was the effective
exploitation of the party's conspiratorial structure. This structure—with its cells and its rules of secrecy, vigilance, and
anonymity—was meant to provide the party with a protective
shield; instead, it became in Maniadakis' hands an excellent
tool for the disintegration of the party organization.

Zachariades had taken considerable pains to build the party
organization into watertight compartments connected with the
top leadership through a carefully-drawn network of 'contacts'.
Cell members—for reasons of security—were limited to knowing
only their own circle, communicating with the next higher level
through the cell secretary. But in any conspiratorial organization, *mutual trust* and *absolute loyalty* are indispensable. Maniadakis concentrated his efforts on destroying both.

In spite of 'Communist vigilance', the Security Police had
succeeded in planting undercover agents in the party ranks even
before the establishment of the dictatorship, and some of them
had moved up into higher party posts. As soon as the dictatorship was established, the Security Police moved swiftly, and,
using information supplied by the undercover agents, arrested
many of the leading party members. A wealth of information
was discovered in their hide-outs and put to effective use. In
October 1936 the police seized the archives of the KOA, the
Communist Organization of Athens, and in November the
archives of the Politbureau itself. Police agents, using the
appropriate 'signals and passwords' obtained from the archives,
established contacts with many party organizations in the
provinces and the armed forces, posing as representatives of the
party leadership. Through such contacts more information was
obtained; arrests were judiciously used to plant the seeds of
distrust among party members or to establish the 'loyalty' and
'reliability' of the agents while discrediting the really loyal
cadres. Soon, 'stool-pigeon phobia'—the fear that anyone
posing as a party member could be a police agent—completely
paralysed all party activity. A secret proclamation by the deci-
mated Politbureau gives a vivid picture of the distrust and
confusion generated by the success of police tactics. This is a
characteristic passage:

In addition to the other known methods used by the Security Police
in its anti-Communist drive, some new ones have been added lately,

taken from the Nazi Gestapo. For instance, they take arrested comrades and walk around the streets, visit the coffee shops, and arrest anyone who may talk to them or show signs of recognition. The Athens Security Police applied this method in the case of comrades Mytlas and Fykas. . . . Of course, the police agents take precautions so that the trap is not readily visible. Therefore, caution, and again caution![2]

When the above proclamation was issued in April 1937 Mytlas —a member of the Central Committee—was no longer a 'comrade'. He had been arrested six months earlier and immediately cut off from all contacts with the party. Completely isolated, deprived of 'advice' and moral comfort, he finally succumbed to psychological pressure and agreed to collaborate with the police. The party evidently knew nothing of his 'treachery' in April 1937.

Zachariades himself was arrested on 13 September 1936, by police agents assisted by Laios, another party member who collaborated with the police. Practically all the party leaders were discovered and arrested. Quite a few of them turned against their 'comrades' and gave the police valuable information. Several years later—in 1950—Vassilis Bartzotas[3] assessed the disintegration of the party in a report to the Third Party Conference:

In spite of the blows inflicted by the Dictatorship which succeeded in *beating down the KKE organizationally, liquidating its organizations*, the great majority of the KKE's leading members survived the blows and became the yeast for the reconstruction of the Party in 1940–41. During the Dictatorship, in contrast to the heroic leaders like Maltezos, Valianatos, and Maroukakis, cowards and traitors like Sklavainas, Nefeloudis, Tyrimos, Sitoconstantinou, Manoleas, etc. appeared.[4]

Sklavainas was the head of the parliamentary group of the Popular Front in 1936; Nefeloudis, the elected Secretary of the Central Committee, second only to Zachariades. Tyrimos and Manoleas were leading Communists. According to Bartzotas, they had 'climbed to the highest party posts *somewhat irregularly*', and 'they lost their courage and committed treason during

---

[2] Original in Maniadakis' archives.

[3] Also known as Phanis in the 1940s.

[4] Vassilis Bartzotas, *I Politiki Stelekhon tou KKE sta Teleutaia Dheka Khronia* (C.C. of KKE, 1950), pp. 20–21; hereinafter cited as *Politiki Stelekhon*; author's italics.

the difficult times under the Dictatorship'. In some other cases, Bartzotas asserted in his revealing report, 'unworthy elements sneaked into the high posts of the Party'. He mentioned:

the case of Andreas Tsipas who became an alternate member of the Central Committee only because he was a Slavo-Macedonian. Yet he was an adventurer and a hooligan. His appointment as leader of the prisoners in Akronauplia was a mistake. In the island of Anafi where most of the exiles were concentrated Siantos appointed the Trotskyist and police agent G. Dionysatos as leader.

In his report, Bartzotas denounced as police agents, traitors, and so on almost all the top leaders of the party—including such persons as G. Siantos, D. Partsalides, and K. Karayiorgis,[5] who played a leading role during the guerrilla war against the Germans. In 1950 the party, decisively beaten in its third attempt to seize power, was in need of scapegoats. This may explain in some measure the vehemence with which Bartzotas attacked the leaders, both living and dead. But his report, however exaggerated, does give a vivid description of the disintegration of the party machine during the Metaxas dictatorship.

Those leaders whom Bartzotas denounced so violently as traitors in 1950 had been promoted to the high posts they held in 1936 by Zachariades himself. Bartzotas realized, of course, the dark picture he was painting was nothing less than an indictment of Zachariades, who as leader had failed to avert the collapse of the party in 1936. As Bartzotas, too, owed his rapid climb to the party leadership in the post-war years to Zachariades, he took considerable pains to absolve him of any blame. In familiar fashion, he attacked those who 'because they do not understand anything about Marxism–Leninism or about our policy for the selection of party functionaries [*politiki stelekhon*] speak like star-gazers, and argue *ex post facto* that the Party should have foreseen the behaviour of the traitors'.[6] Ignoring the long array of 'traitors' he himself had named, Bartzotas concluded his report with the unsupported assertion that 'between 1931 and the German Occupation, the KKE had a correct *politiki stelekhon* for the first time in its history'. True, a nucleus of die-hards remained faithful and ready to resume revolutionary activity, but to a very large extent leading party members, most of them appointed by Zachariades, proved unable to withstand the pressure.

[5] See biographical note No. 3. [6] Bartzotas, op. cit., p. 21.

The 'declarations of repentance'

If police measures could by themselves wipe out the Communist challenge in any country, the Metaxas régime would have eliminated the movement for ever in Greece. Indeed, the success of the Greek authorities in causing the disintegration of the party was quite sensational. But to weaken and ultimately eliminate the appeal of Communist agitation in a given country takes a bold and concerted policy of removing the everyday and long-term causes of public disillusionment and discontent. Police measures can play a useful part only in certain critical circumstances. Whenever such forcible counteraction to Communist revolutionary agitation becomes necessary, the record of the Greek experience may provide some useful guidelines.

In dealing with the rank and file as well as with the party *apparatchiki*, Maniadakis used extensively a seemingly mild technique, that of 'declarations of repentance'. Any Communist, regardless of his position in the party hierarchy, was freed on signing a statement containing:

a chronological account of his Communist activities, with the names of those who initiated him in the Communist ideology, an account of all party meetings he had attended, the position he occupied in the party hierarchy, and any of his non-party activities such as participation in the 'Workers Assistance', the Communist Youth Organization OKNE, the trade union fractions, or the army fractions.[7]

A summary, including a signed denunciation of Communist ideology, was then published in the newspapers.

As an effective weapon for spreading mistrust and confusion in the Communist ranks, the 'declarations' surpassed the most optimistic expectations. Of course there were mistakes and excesses in the application of this unorthodox method of combating Communism. For instance, almost 45,000 such declarations were signed and published during the four years of the dictatorship—a number far exceeding the actual membership of the party at that time. Over-zealous local police officers often extracted 'declarations' from persons who were not party members but were for one reason or another regarded as sympathizers. Maniadakis repeatedly warned against naïve efforts by

[7] Maniadakis' archives.

police officials to obtain 'declarations' merely to appear active. When, for example, the newspaper *Tharos* of Trikkala published the statements of several individuals who denounced Communism while declaring that they had never been Communists, and expressed their devotion to Metaxas and the régime in a slavish manner, Maniadakis retorted immediately, calling the whole affair an 'indecency'. The Ministry, he wrote in his No. 9/118/15 Confidential Order of 8 February 1939, 'never asked for the publication of such declarations as "I have never been a Communist, nevertheless I denounce Communism and I recognize Metaxas as a great Premier of the Greek Kingdom" '. He added with anger:

Such declarations are not only idiotic . . . but they may give the Opposition the impression—and with good reason—that the system of declarations is actually a way of forcing people to declare their support of the Premier. Such an impression will be the logical consequence of the fact that individuals, without being Communists, are compelled to denounce Communism, and then, in order to have their statement accepted as true, they reach the point of unwillingly glorifying the Premier and pledging their support. . . .

. . . The Ministry has two objects in publishing the declarations of repentance of persons active in the Greek Communist movement or at least having sympathized in the past with the Communist ideology: (*a*) to give those individuals a chance to state publicly their present social ideology, and (*b*) to *shatter any confidence* the Communist party may have in those individuals, thus *making their further use* by the Party *inadvisable.*[8]

Despite the excesses of over-zealous officials, the impact of the 'declarations' on the cohesion of the party machine proved to be disastrous. In an attempt to minimize the impression created by the wholesale desertion of its ranks, the party divided the 'declarationists' into three main categories: Trotskyist and other untrustworthy individuals, expelled from the party long ago; persons of various political persuasions having only incidental contacts with the party, such as 'anti-Fascist or peace-loving individuals, or supporters of the Popular Front'; and persons who were members of the party or sympathizers but had denounced their ideology 'in a moment of cowardice'. The party was concerned only with those in the third category; addressing them, the hierarchy urged 'more heroism and self-sacrifice'.[9]

[8] Maniadakis' archives; author's italics.　　　　　　　　[9] Ibid.

K

Such was the effect of the declarations, especially those of
high-ranking party officials, that some ingenious members tried
to explain, in a whispering campaign, that the signing of the
declarations was actually a shrewd tactical manoeuvre used by
the party to obtain the release of as many members as possible.
To this a clandestine issue of *Rizospastis* gave an answer in 1938:

Alas, if we accept officially as a party the signing of the declarations,
then the entire party will disintegrate and we shall have no possibility of finding out who signed a declaration because of cowardice
and who made a fake declaration for tactical reasons. Our party is
a monolithic party and does not allow such tactics as the declarations which if sanctioned can disintegrate the party.[10]

On 19 June 1939, Maniadakis wrote in a confidential order:

The acceptance of declarations in which the Communists denounce
their principles has become one of the most important means of
combating Communism. . . . The acceptance of such declarations
aims not so much at the prosecution of the organized Communists,
as it does at the *smashing* of the party's *internal cohesion*. The declarations of repentance have spread so much confusion among the party
members that suspicion and mutual distrust prevail.[11]

Maniadakis was not exaggerating. The problem of the 'declarationists' remained for a long time the most thorny question
within the party. Zachariades himself, in 1952, still found it
necessary to denounce as

a basic mistake and a deviation from the bolshevik party principles
the fact that during the first occupation [1941–4] the party leadership 'solved' the question of the declarationists by accepting them
as 'collaborators in the National Liberation Front', thus mutilating
party morality by condoning submission to the enemy, capitulation,
and in many cases outright treason.[12]

In fact, as soon as Zachariades returned from a prison camp in
Germany in June 1945, the KKE took up an uncompromising
position on the question of the declarationists. The 12th
Plenum of the Central Committee, which met in June 1945,
violently condemned the party's practice of using 'declarationists' in responsible posts during the Occupation and ordered the
investigation of all declarationists who had re-entered the party

[10] *Rizospastis* (illegal), 15 December 1938.
[11] Maniadakis' archives; author's italics.
[12] Zachariades, *Provlimata Kathothigisis*, p. 232.

ranks between 1941 and 1944. The importance attached by the party leadership to the issue of the declarations was reflected in Article 4, Paragraph (*b*) of the Party Charter which was approved by the Seventh Congress of the KKE in 1945. The article provided that 'declarationists were not eligible to re-enter the KKE'.[13]

Zachariades, while assessing the issue of the 'declarationists' in his book *Provlimata Kathothigisis*, asserted that 'if the question of the declarations and the declarationists is examined in the light of bolshevik party obligations . . . we find that basically in every single case—and I mean the honest cases, of course —the petty-bourgeois prevailed over the militant'.[14] To some extent Zachariades was right. Most of the leaving party members came from the petty-bourgeois intelligentsia, which alone could provide a sufficient number of individuals with the necessary educational background to assume positions of responsibility in the party hierarchy. Many among them had joined the party in a spirit of desperation and protest against a social order which had frustrated their personal aspirations with its sterility. Some were mere careerists, seeking to climb swiftly in the political world outside the traditional political organizations, which were not willing to serve their personal designs. Few among them proved to be devout ideologues, ready to accept any sacrifice for the sake of their convictions. Due to the recurrent party crises, the constant fluidity of the membership, and the swift promotion of persons with questionable or uncertain motives to positions of responsibility, especially after 1931, the 'party age' of most party members in general averaged five to six years when the dictatorship was established. Presumably the party had not been given sufficient time to transform them into seasoned bolshevik militants. Whatever the reasons, the fact remains that too many high-ranking officials occupying key posts in the hierarchy showed an amazing eagerness to denounce their principles, desert the party, and even collaborate with the régime of the Fourth of August.

Maniadakis forms his own 'Communist Party'

Maniadakis was very subtle in his efforts to destroy the party machine and combat Communist subversion. He realized

---

[13] *Komep*, No. 39, July 1945.
[14] Zachariades, *Provlimata Kathothigisis*, p. 233.

that many Communists were not hardened militants but ordinary human beings, susceptible to reorientation. For this reason, the measures he adopted were far less harsh than is commonly believed, yet, or probably for that reason, quite effective. A characteristic excerpt from another confidential order gives some insight into his thinking:

From the reports submitted to the Ministry, concerning the exile to the Aegean Islands of individuals dangerous to public security because of Communist or other subversive activities, we observed that most police authorities complete the proceedings without the accused being present . . . without allowing him to defend himself. This practice, besides being a violation of the inalienable right of every person to defend himself against his accusers, has also another aspect concerning public security. The persons being considered for possible exile can either prove their innocence or they may confess their illegal activities in the past, and, repenting, they may occasionally reveal information by far surpassing the information already at hand; in such a case we must treat them with leniency. . . .

It must be fully understood by all that, in order to decide on the exile of a particular individual, it is not even enough to ascertain that a person has been involved in the past in Communist activities; it must be established that he is still an unrepentant and fanatical Communist whom it is advisable to isolate from the rest of the community.[15]

Taking into account that the Communist 'colonies' formed by the exiles in the various islands were very active in 'educational work', Maniadakis warned the local authorities that 'to exile a sympathizer or a young neophyte, without giving him an opportunity to repent and confess his past activity, is an error which helps the party to create new members where only sympathizers previously existed'.[16]

Maniadakis even tried to introduce some elements of social justice in his area of authority. Here is an excerpt from another confidential order addressed to the local agencies of the Ministry:

It is a matter of justice as well as of common sense to provide the repenting person with the means to obtain the necessities of life— once we accept his declaration of repentance as sincere. By removing all obstacles to his career, we prove that the Government is ready to

[15] Confidential Order dated 31 July 1939; original in Maniadakis' archives.
[16] Ibid.

welcome with affection, as citizens with equal rights, all those members of the national family who once went astray, then repented and came back. It would be absurd to ask a Communist to confess his past activities and denounce his principles on the one hand, and then deprive him of the ability to work and make a living on the other. Although we cannot help him to occupy key positions in the state, it would be unjust to hinder such a man from working and making a career in some of the other trades and professions.[17]

Through this ingenious combination of police repression, moral persuasion, common sense, and subtle psychological warfare, Maniadakis broke up the mechanism of the Greek Communist Party. His crowning achievement was the creation of his own Communist Party. Through renegades and police agents, he established contacts with the local party organizations and finally reached the point of forming his own Central Committee, known as 'Prosorini Dhiikisis' (Temporary Administration), which published its own *Rizospastis*. To create an impression of authenticity, this newspaper was subjected to the same persecution as all other Communist literature.

At the same time some party members, under the leadership of Vangelis Ktistakis, formed their own Central Committee as a continuation of the Central Committee elected by the Sixth Congress, publishing their own *Rizospastis*. In 1939–40 this Committee, which became known as the 'Old' Central Committee, followed a policy which was considered 'traitorous' even by Zachariades. Ktistakis was branded as 'traitor', 'fifth-columnist', and 'stool-pigeon' as late as 1943 by G. Siantos and the other Communist leaders who reconstructed the KKE after the German Occupation.

It seems useful to describe the methods used by Maniadakis in some detail, because he was able to break up the party organization—to a degree seldom duplicated—through a combination of ingenious methods of detection, understanding of the psychological problems facing a Greek Communist, leniency combined with toughness, exploitation of personal weaknesses, a masterful application of methods for spreading confusion and distrust among party members, and assistance to all those willing to denounce Communism. Many of his methods would not be acceptable under a democratic régime or in normal

---

[17] Confidential Order No. 18/106/7, 19 June 1939; original in Maniadakis' archives.

times. Maniadakis did not, of course, succeed in wiping out
Communism from the Greek political scene. However spectacular his achievements in the sphere of public security, his success
was only temporary. Under new and favourable circumstances,
Communism grew up again in Greece.

The Khania uprising of July 1938

The Communist Party has officially announced that its
records for the period of the Metaxas dictatorship have been
lost. This is partly true. Several important documents were
seized by the police, and some of the observations in this book
are based on their perusal. Others are of questionable origin and
therefore of limited usefulness. It is established, however, that
the 3rd Plenum of the Central Committee met secretly on
7 August 1936, three days after the establishment of the
dictatorship. As this writer was told by former party members
who have personal knowledge of what was said at the meeting,
the Plenum agreed on a wait-and-see policy. Since there is no
written proof available, their statements may be accepted as
valid in the light of the party's subsequent inactivity. The 4th
Plenum in February 1937—hardly a Plenum, since by then
several members of the Central Committee were either in
prison, in exile, or even collaborating with the police—decided,
according to the same sources of information, to co-operate with
republican elements contemplating an armed revolt against the
Metaxas Government. Reliable sources indicate that the meetings of September 1937 and June 1938 dealt with preparations
for the republican *coup* on the island of Crete, which finally took
place on 29 July 1938. Again, the fact that the Communists co-
operated, playing a leading role in the uprising, lends added
strength to the available evidence.[18]

Though several political elements contemplated uprisings
against the dictatorship, only this one *coup* materialized. In the
early hours of 29 July 1938 Cretan republicans, led by Venizelist
politicians A. Mitsotakis, E. Mountakis, Manousos Volou-
dakis, and General Emmanuel Mantakas, descended from the
mountains with a number of armed followers and, exploiting
the initial element of surprise, entered the city of Khania.
There they disarmed the 11th Regiment, broke into the arsenal,

[18] Confidential Order No. 18/106/7, 19 June 1939.

seized a considerable number of firearms, and, joined by other conspirators and a crowd of excited citizens, went on to the General Administration Building, occupied the premises, and placed the Chief Administrator, P. Sfakianakis, under arrest.

Prior to the uprising, the 'Old' Central Committee in Athens had been in touch with the republican conspirators through Vangelis Ktistakis, who happened to be a brother-in-law of General Mantakas. As its local emissary, the Central Committee selected a Communist by the name of Dimitrios Metaxas, who was an exile in the small island of Gavdos, off the south coast of Crete. Metaxas escaped from Gavdos and reached Khania in time to participate in the uprising. The uprising was, however, primarily a Venizelist affair.

The original plan provided for the overthrow of the government authorities, as a first step. Crete, the birthplace of Eleutherios Venizelos, had a long republican tradition and a strong undercurrent of anti-monarchical feeling. By establishing their control over Crete, the conspirators expected to induce the army units on the mainland to proclaim their solidarity with the revolutionaries and force King George to dismiss Metaxas and restore the constitution. The entire plan collapsed when the rest of Crete did not join the revolutionaries, while the people and the Army on the mainland remained indifferent. The revolutionaries found themselves completely isolated in the city of Khania. When a commercial aeroplane, dispatched by the Government, dropped leaflets calling the people to remain calm and asking the revolutionaries to reconsider their action and return to their villages, both leaders and followers of the uprising lost their nerve. The Communist Dimitrios Metaxas tried to provoke a revival of the revolutionary spirit, but it was too late. The whole affair turned out to be a pitiful fiasco. The *coup* was practically over, with no bloodshed, the same afternoon. The leaders escaped to the mountains, where they began to organize a second *coup* to take place in October of the same year. They found no response. Finally, General Mantakas asked for an amnesty. The Government ignored his request, but gave financial help to the other leaders of the uprising to enable them to 'escape' to the Dodecanese and then to Cyprus, after giving their word of honour that they would not participate in future revolutionary activities. Some of them apparently gave this promise gladly because they disliked being associated with the Communists.

The 5th Plenum and the Comintern

In February 1939 George Siantos, who had escaped from exile, presided over the 5th Plenum of the Central Committee. This was neither the 'Old' Central Committee under Ktistakis nor the Temporary Leadership, though several members of this Maniadakis creation participated in its deliberations. At that time the signs of approaching war in Europe were all too clear, and the attitude of the party to foreign and domestic affairs was discussed in detail. The gist of the decisions of the Plenum was as follows: 'Our Party defends, with all its forces, the independence and integrity of the country against the menace of the Axis; but the primary enemy of our independence and territorial integrity is Monarcho-Fascism. Without its overthrow, there is no way of defending the independence of Greece.'[19]

This resolution of the 5th Plenum was soon superseded by what appeared to be a new Comintern directive. The confusion surrounding this episode is indicative of the situation prevailing at the time within the party organization. Vangelis Ktistakis,[20] one of the leaders of the 'Old' Central Committee, revealed later that 'at the end of September or the beginning of October 1939 Comrade Papayiannis informed me that the Communist International had in July sent a directive (a) concerning the correction of the KKE's previous policies, and (b) setting its future political line'. As far as the new political line was concerned, Papayiannis intimated to Ktistakis that, according to the Comintern instructions, 'the formation of a peace-loving coalition in the Balkans with the support of the Soviet Union was the fundamental duty of the Party'. This version is supported by the fact that V. Potemkin, then Soviet Vice-Commissar for Foreign Affairs, visited several Balkan capitals in May

[19] From the Report of G. Siantos to the Pan-helladic Conference of the KKE in December 1942; see also *To 7o Synethrio tou KKE* (Athens, Edition of the Central Committee, 1945), Vol. II, pp. 30–31; cited as *To 7o Synethrio* (The 7th Congress).

[20] Ktistakis, after being denounced as a 'stool-pigeon' by Siantos for a time, was restored to party favour during the Occupation. In 1944 he was appointed by the Political Committee of National Liberation (PEEA) to be Chairman of the Administrative Committee of Crete. He was then arrested and executed by the Germans.

1939 and advocated the establishment of a 'neutral Balkan bloc'.[21]

The version of the Comintern directive which reached Siantos was entirely different. As he told the KKE conference in December 1942 and later, in 1945, the Seventh Congress of the KKE:

The Political Secretariat of the ECCI corrected the serious mistakes in the decisions of the 5th Plenum in the following manner: 'Your country is threatened by the Fascist Axis and particularly by Italian Fascism, which is very active in the Balkans. The first duty of the KKE is to defend the independence of the country. Since the Metaxas Government is fighting against the same danger, there is no reason for you to pursue its overthrow.[22]

To many Greek Communists, this Comintern policy towards Metaxas was incomprehensible, and Ktistakis and Papayiannis rejected it. With their doctrinaire approach to Communism, they were unable to realize that the Comintern had long been transformed into a mere instrument of the Soviet Commissariat of Foreign Affairs and that, in the calculations of the Soviet Government, any government determined to resist Italy's encroachments in the Balkans was a welcome ally regardless of its political colouring.

Siantos and Zachariades accepted the second version. To them, the Comintern directive was consistent with the overriding aim of safeguarding the interests of the Soviet Union. After the Italian occupation of Albania in April 1939 the Comintern directive could have only one meaning: that every effort should be made to block Italy's way in the Balkans. From that time on, Zachariades—still in prison—adopted the line that, in view of this extremely important objective of Soviet foreign policy, the party should temporarily suspend all activity against the Metaxas Government.

The signing of the Nazi–Soviet pact in August reinforced the position of the 'Old' Central Committee, who now argued that the policy of tolerating or even supporting Metaxas against Fascist Italy was out of step with the new Soviet policy of collaboration with the Axis. Zachariades remained unimpressed by the sudden turn in Soviet foreign policy, while

[21] D. G. Kousoulas, *The Price of Freedom, Greece in World Affairs, 1939–1953* (Syracuse, Syracuse University Press, 1953), pp. 40–42.

[22] *Dheka Khronia Agones*, p. 140; also *To 7o Synethrio*, pp. 30–31.

Ktistakis and his group continued their seemingly consistent policy until they unwittingly became organs of Axis propaganda.

Needless to say, the so-called 'Temporary Leadership' eagerly accepted the Siantos version of the Comintern directive and, through its own *Rizospastis*, emphasized the point that the party should concentrate on the external threat from Fascist Italy and refrain from any action undermining the position of the Metaxas Government. So by a complex twist of international intrigue, Maniadakis' brain-child became the mouthpiece of Moscow.

The KKE and the Greek–Italian war

When the Italian Ambassador presented Metaxas with an ultimatum at three o'clock in the morning of 28 October 1940,[23] Zachariades was in jail, practically forgotten by the Greek people. All the intrigues described in the preceding pages went on in the twilight of Greek political life, largely unnoticed except by a small circle of 'insiders'. For almost three years Zachariades had been kept on the island of Corfu. Shortly after the fall of France in June 1940 he ordered one of his fellow-inmates, a Communist named Michaelidis, to sign a declaration of repentance so that he could be released. The apparent purpose of this manoeuvre was for Michaelidis to go to Athens and take over the reorganization of the party machine. Michaelidis was released and did go to Athens. One of his first actions was to contact the 'Old' Central Committee. The *yiafka* on Syros Street in Athens was under the direction of one Koutsoyiannis, who was in fact an agent of the Security Police. Michaelidis and another Communist leader, N. Ploumbides,[24] a member of the 'Old' Central Committee, were arrested. Michaelidis, instead of reorganizing the party, collaborated with the Ministry of Security. Soon afterwards Zachariades was transferred to Athens and interned in the Security Building (police), where living conditions were decidedly superior to any ordinary jail. Ktistakis and Papayiannis inferred that a shady deal between Zachariades and Maniadakis had been effected through Michaelidis in this involved way in order to protect Zachariades' standing as the leader of the party.

---

[23] For more details see Kousoulas, op. cit., pp. 59–61.

[24] Ploumbides was executed in 1953 in Greece as a Communist spy, while simultaneously accused by Zachariades of having been a police agent all along.

Maniadakis told this writer that the reason for Zachariades' transfer to Athens was that Corfu was exposed to Italian invasion and the Government did not want Zachariades to fall into Italian hands. In any event, as soon as the Italians attacked Greece, Zachariades wrote a letter which was given to the press by Maniadakis.[25] In the letter, dated 20 October 1940, he wrote:

Mussolini's Fascism attacked Greece from behind, in a murderous, shameless way, with the sole aim of enslaving the Greek people. Today we are all fighting for our freedom, honour, and national independence. The struggle will be difficult and very harsh. But a nation that wants to survive must fight, disregarding the dangers and the sacrifices.

The people of Greece are today conducting a war of national liberation against Mussolini's Fascism. In addition to the main front, every rock, every ravine, every village from hut to hut, every town from house to house, must become a fortress for the struggle of national liberation. Every agent of Fascism must be exterminated without mercy. In this war, directed by the Metaxas Government, we shall all give every ounce of our strength without reserve. The prize for the workers and the reward for their present struggle must be a new Greece of work and freedom, relieved of any foreign imperialist dependence and exploitation, with a really democratic civilization.

All into the struggle, everyone at his post; the victory will belong to Greece and her people. The workers of all the world are standing by our side.[26]

The *Rizospastis* of the 'Old' Central Committee, in an article signed by N. Ploumbides and dated March 1941, denounced this letter as a forgery for the following reasons: (*a*) the letter was addressed to Maniadakis and 'it should have been addressed to the people', and (*b*) Zachariades had signed the letter as 'the Secretary of the Central Committee of the KKE', although 'he is the Secretary General and the Leader of the Party, and he knows his title very well; therefore, he would never have used the title which belongs to Comrade Nefeloudis'.[27] It seems to me that there can be only one plausible explanation for these 'errors': Zachariades wilfully planted them so that he, too, could denounce the letter as a forgery should it become expedient in the future. Be that as it may, Zachariades himself and the party have accepted the letter as genuine. In fact, immediately

[25] Maniadakis' archives.   [26] *Kathimerini*, 2 November 1940.
[27] *Rizospastis*, 17 June 1941.

after the liberation of Greece in October 1944 the party displayed a facsimile of this letter on huge posters—with only one phrase omitted, 'directed by the Metaxas Government'.

One month later, on 26 November 1940, Zachariades wrote a second letter; he had suddenly discovered that the defensive war against the Italians was 'an imperialist war'. 'Since the Italians have been expelled from Greek territory,' he argued, 'the war should be stopped and an armistice effected through the good offices of the Soviet Union.'[28] This letter, of course, was not published by Maniadakis.

What prompted this second letter? Apparently Zachariades felt that an advance by the Greek forces deep into Albania would actually mean the replacement of Italian influence over that country by that of the British. Once the danger of Italian expansion into Greece seemed to be averted, Zachariades saw no reason to support a policy which in his opinion served only British interests.

The fact that the 'Old' Central Committee issued a manifesto on 7 December 1940 declaring that 'the war was provoked by the King–Metaxas gang on orders from the English imperialists, and therefore cannot have any relation to the defence of our country', does not indicate a meeting of minds between Zachariades and the 'Old' Central Committee. The Ktistakis–Papayiannis–Ploumbides group was against the war from the beginning because the Axis was at that time 'co-operating' with the Soviet Union. It is characteristic that Ktistakis, as late as August 1943, argued in a letter to the Politbureau that 'at the time of the Greek–Italian war, since the Party implemented the instructions of the Comintern, which set up as the party's fundamental duty the struggle for the formation of a Balkan bloc with the support of the Soviet Union, the Central Committee, that is the 'Old' Central Committee, *had to take* a position against the war'.[29] An unspoken accusation was that the version of the Comintern directive on which Zachariades had based his entire policy since the summer of 1939 was nothing more than a gigantic hoax, a directive manufactured in the offices of the Ministry of Security.

A third letter was written by Zachariades on 17 January 1941,

---

[28] Maniadakis' archives.

[29] Y. Petsopoulos, *Ta Aitia tis Dhiagraphis mou apo to KKE* (Athens, 1946), p. 336. Hereinafter cited as *Ta Aitia*. Author's italics.

but it was published by the party only in July 1942. In this letter he explained the reasons for his first letter of 30 October 1940:

My letter which was published in the newspapers of 2 November 1940 [the first letter] had the following aims: (*a*) to give valid and united direction to the Communists of this country; (*b*) to mobilize the people in the anti-Fascist struggle for national liberation and independence; (*c*) to restore civil liberties, and an anti-plutocratic policy in the interior; (*d*) to make the war a national anti-Fascist, anti-imperialist war with the basic and sole object of securing our national independence, peace, and, our neutrality in the general imperialist war. This we could achieve only through a total orientation towards the Soviet Union and towards a true Balkan co-operation. Metaxas, from the outset, did the opposite. He waged a Fascist war of conquest. Once we threw the Italians out of Greece, our basic effort should have been to conclude a separate peace, without any concessions, which could have been accomplished only through the mediation of the Soviet Union; instead, the Monarcho-Fascist dictatorship continued the war for the benefit not of the Greek people but of the plutocracy and English imperialism. . . . Since Metaxas refuses to restore the liberties of the people and make peace, and since he wages a war of conquest, he remains the *main enemy* of the people and of the country. His overthrow is the most immediate and vital interest of the country. People and Army must take in their hands the administration of the country and of the war, with the purpose of restoring peace and national independence, and of establishing an anti-Fascist, anti-plutocratic, people's régime, in full co-operation with the Soviet Union, and a Balkan co-operation based on the peaceful solution of all intra-Balkan disputes. The position of the KKE and OKNE is this: the people of Greece are only defending their national independence. They are indifferent and unsympathetic towards the British-German war; they want separate peace through the good offices of the Soviet Union. They recognize the principle of self-determination, including separation, for all peoples. [They support] an alliance with the Soviet Union and a true Balkan entente. . . .[30]

This third letter explained in more detail what the second letter had already intimated. The Soviet Union saw with displeasure the possibility of a Greek, and thus a British, advance into Albania. Perhaps the Kremlin already contemplated Albania as a future Soviet satellite. Whether Zachariades kept surprisingly

[30] *Komep*, July 1942; also *Rizospastis*, 28 October 1945.

good contact with his superiors in Moscow, or whether he visualized the Soviet objectives through reasoning or intuition, the fact remains that he proclaimed the Greek stand against Fascist aggression as 'a war of conquest' and urged Greek soldiers and the Greek people, in the midst of war, to overthrow the Government.

At the same time the 'comrades' of the 'Old' Central Committee went even farther in their anti-war policy. On 18 March 1941 they called on the Greek people 'to follow the example of our heroic brethren in Bulgaria', who only a few weeks earlier had welcomed the Nazi motorized divisions 'with flowers and celebrations'.[31]

All this anti-war propaganda by the Greek Communists went completely unnoticed by the public. The Communist Party had long ceased to play any important role in Greek political life. The Communists themselves later admitted that:

The régime of the Fourth of August had succeeded in breaking up the forces of our Party, and in decapitating it, and, finally, it had almost accomplished its complete disintegration. . . . The Security Police had succeeded in creating a Central Committee composed of police agents, the so-called 'Temporary Administration', while there existed another Central Committee which followed a fifth-column policy during the Greek-Italian war [the 'Old' Central Committee]; in general those Communists who were not in prison had no connexion with each other but were dispersed here and there. . . .[32]

This is an authoritative and accurate description of the complete confusion which prevailed in the Communist ranks in 1941. When the German panzer divisions overran Greece, and the grey curtain of Nazi occupation descended along the Aegean shores, the KKE was practically non-existent as a political force. The party, represented by three factions—with two *Rizospastes* vying for the allegiance of the remaining party followers and spreading even more confusion with their conflicting and partly police-directed pronouncements, had lost all contact with the 'masses'. Yet this disjointed party of 1941 was able to pull itself together, take hold of the resistance movement, and, before the end of the Second World War, become a serious and dangerous contender for power in Greece. The tale of how this was accomplished will unfold in the pages that follow.

[31] G. J. Graf, *Wir marchieren gegen Griechenland* (Saarlautern, 1942), pp. 35–36.
[32] *To 7o Synethrio*, Introduction.

Part III

'TURNING THE IMPERIALIST
WAR INTO CIVIL WAR'

11. The Resistance Movement
Grows

Regrouping the scattered party ranks

On 27 April 1941 the first Nazi troops entered the city of Athens. They were met with silent hatred. In the first few weeks their only friends were some unrepentant Germanophiles and some misguided Communists; the former because they admired the Herrenvolk, the latter because they erroneously believed the Germans to be friends of the Soviet Union.

Politically, the Germans found an almost total vacuum. After the death of Metaxas in January 1941 the régime of the Fourth of August had begun to fall apart. With the appointment of Emmanuel Tsouderos to the premiership and the departure of the King and his Government for Crete, and then for Egypt,[1] the dictatorship was *de facto* terminated. The leaders of the old political parties, out of touch with the public for more than four years, confined their political activity to aimless discussions with their closest political friends. The Communist Party had virtually disintegrated. To quote a statement of the Central Committee, which met on 1 July 1941, 'The outbreak of the Greek–Italian war found the free party forces without leadership, dispersed into various groups, unable to organize a mass struggle because their leading organs had been infested with police agents and other untrustworthy elements.'[2] This assessment was quite

---

[1] For more details see Kousoulas, *The Price of Freedom*, pp. 72–78.
[2] *Dheka Khronia Agones*, p. 119.

accurate. One thousand of its most reliable *apparatchiki* were in prison or in exile. Other leading members had come to terms with the dictatorship; they were free, but useless to the party.

During the short period between 27 April and 22 June 1941 some of the Communist slogans circulated by the 'Old' Central Committee were defeatist, if not openly in favour of the Axis.[3] It was fortunate for the Greek Communists that the anomalous Soviet–Nazi 'collaboration' ended in the early hours of 22 June 1941, torn to shreds under the steel tracks of the German panzer divisions. Otherwise the Greek Communists might have committed disgraceful acts of collaboration with the occupation forces, instead of claiming a monopoly of patriotism, as they did in the war and the early post-war years.

With the collapse of Greece, many Communists escaped from their places of detention, while others were released from the Acronauplia prison under Order No. 621 of the *Geheim Feld Polizei*, on the suggestion—it was reported—of the Bulgarian Embassy in Athens.[4] Andreas Tzimas was one of those released at that time.

The party leaders who reached Athens in the early days of the Occupation had one overriding objective: to regroup the party's forces and reconstruct its organization. Eight days after the German attack on the Soviet Union, party leaders 'who had suffered in prison and in exile' met in Athens. They proclaimed their meeting to be the 6th Plenum of the Central Committee. In effect, this was a new Central Committee made up of leading members who had reliable credentials of loyalty. The new Central Committee, which claimed to be 'the only one authorized to represent and lead the Party', enjoyed several advantages over the other two 'leaderships', the 'Temporary Leadership' and the 'Old' Central Committee. The 'Temporary Leadership', being an instrument of the Ministry of Security, had lost its life-line after the collapse of the Greek state and had quickly disintegrated. The 'Old' Central Committee, on the other hand, had lost contact with the Comintern and had followed a policy of its own; during the Greek–Italian war its members, with their openly pro-Axis policy, had been guilty of outright treason. In contrast, the members of the new Central

---

[3] Th. Papakonstantinou, *I Anatomia tis Epanastaseos* (Athens, 1952), p. 152.

[4] *I Enantion tis Ellados Epivouli* (Athens, Ministry of Press and Information, 1947), p. 17.

Committee enjoyed the 'prestige' of having 'suffered in prison and in exile'. With Greece now under the domination of the Axis, the Communist leaders had every reason to disassociate themselves completely from the 'traitors' of the Old Central Committee.

The decisions of the 6th Plenum are indeed of particular interest. They centred on three main topics: (*a*) all party members, and particularly those connected with the other groups, were urged to desert 'the police agents and the other reactionary elements of these two groups' and to set aside their disagreements, 'thus sincerely contributing to the reconstruction of the Greek Communist Party'; (*b*) it was clearly stated that 'the *basic* duty of the Greek Communists was to organize the struggle *for the defence of the Soviet Union* and for the overthrow of the foreign Fascist yoke'; (*c*) it was further emphasized that 'while organizing the struggle against the everyday problems of the lower strata of the population, and also armed resistance against the Conquerors . . . the Communists must explain to the people that only a people's government of workers and peasants can for ever free the country from foreign dependence and exploitation'.[5] From the very first moment, the KKE viewed the resistance movement as a contribution to 'the defence of the Soviet Union', and a convenient method of preparing for the Communist take-over. The patriotic slogans, so abundantly used during the Occupation, were devised later to exploit the feelings of the Greek people and bring the resistance movement under Communist control. Nevertheless, as far as the Communists were concerned, the ultimate objective never changed. As G. Siantos said in December 1942 to the Pan-helladic Conference of the KKE, the object of the Resistance was 'to open up the way for the establishment of Socialism and the final liberation of the people from every political yoke and exploitation of man by man'.

Ethnikon Apeleutherotikon Metopon (EAM)

The Greek Communists soon discovered that, by following a strictly Communist line of propaganda and agitation, they jeopardized their chances of expanding the mass basis of the party and strengthening its control over the growing resistance movement. After four years of conditioning under the Metaxas

---

[5] *Dheka Khronia Agones*, pp. 120–1; author's italics.

régime the majority of the Greek people were more than ever distrustful of the Communists. Their record of perfidy, friction, and capitulation, skilfully exploited by the dictatorship, had left a strong residue of popular contempt and mistrust. The 7th Plenum of the Central Committee which met in September 1941 and, particularly, the 8th Plenum which convened early in January 1942 re-evaluated the party's policies and adopted a far more moderate and subtle line, consistent with the new element of co-operation between the Soviet Union and the Western Powers.

The 8th Plenum declared that 'although the Party is struggling for the establishment of a people's republic . . . we do not pose the acceptance of this objective as a prerequisite for the unity of all parties, of all the Greek people, within a common national liberation front'.[6] In other words, the 8th Plenum, which incidentally elected George Siantos[7] as the Secretary of the Central Committee, pushed the party's real objective into the background, as a necessary concession to the more immediate need to establish the party's control over the resistance movement. Siantos, speaking in 1945 at the Seventh Congress of the KKE, claimed that 'the meteoric rise of the Party immediately after the collapse of the Metaxas régime' proved that the KKE had 'deep roots among the people'.[8] This assertion was false on two points. First of all, the influence of the party did not have a 'meteoric' expansion till 1943, and secondly, it achieved this expansion not as the KKE but under the guise of EAM, the National Liberation Front. Siantos himself admitted at the Seventh Congress that the KKE, 'in taking the initiative to organize the resistance', refrained from any references to the proletarian revolution or even to a workers' and peasants' government; instead, it based its agitation and propaganda exclusively on the demand 'for a struggle for national survival and at the same time for our national liberation by every means including war'.

These two basic desires of the enslaved nation—survival and national liberation—offered the necessary ground for the formation of the United Front from below and from above, which had been prescribed by Moscow since 1934 and had been part of KKE policy ever since. The KKE prudently let Marxism—

---

[6] *Dheka Khronia Agones*, p. 127. [7] See biographical note No. 2.
[8] *To 70 Synethrio*, p. 13.

Leninism recede into the background. This was only a tactical manoeuvre. As Siantos openly stated in 1945, the party never ceased to view 'the struggle for national liberation as the first stage in the people's democratic revolution in our country'.[9] Clearly, with the collapse of the Greek state in 1941, the Communist Party felt that it was time to put into effect the ponderous resolutions of January 1934.

The Workers' National Liberation Front (EEAM) and the National Liberation Front (EAM) were the first two organizations created by the KKE. Even though 27 September 1941 was later claimed as the date for the establishment of EAM, the name of the organization did not appear on party documents till later. Probably the outline of such an organization was discussed at the 7th Plenum and some steps for putting it together were taken in the autumn of 1941 and the early winter months of 1942. It was a hard winter, that first winter of the Occupation. Yet famine, cold, destitution, and humiliation, instead of breaking the spirit of the people, generated a deep and resolute passion for survival and resistance. The first guerrilla bands appeared on the mountain ranges of Central Greece in the early summer of 1942. One of them was led by Colonel Napoleon Zervas, a pro-republican officer who represented a resistance organization known as the National Republican Greek Association (Ethnikos Dimokratikos Ellinikos Synthesmos, EDES). Another was commanded by Thanassis Klaras or Mizerias, a former member of the KKE, who had signed a 'declaration of repentance' during the dictatorship. Klaras had taken the imposing pseudonym Aris Velouchiotis. There were several other small groups, including the bands of Stelios Houtas, a doctor, operating in the Valtos area, and the group led by Andreas Mountrihas, or *Kapetan* Orestis, a former gendarmerie sergeant turned Communist, which had established itself late in 1942 in the vicinity of Athens. For several months the KKE leadership, uncertain as to what form the struggle should take, and thinking more in traditional forms of public demonstrations and political strikes, had shown marked reluctance to give its official blessing to either Aris or Orestis. In the case of Aris, the black mark of his 'declaration' was an added drawback. Finally, the KKE, faced with the fact that the guerrilla bands were already conducting operations against the enemy, set aside its reservations

[9] *To 70 Synethrio*, p. 15.

and accepted Aris Velouchiotis as the *Kapetanios* of the Roumeli bands. Later, in the spring of 1943, after a secret visit to Athens, Velouchiotis was elevated to the post of *Kapetanios* of the National Popular Liberation Army (ELAS, the name he had coined for the Communist-controlled guerrilla force of EAM). Furthermore, being in dire need of experienced members, the party issued a general ruling by which former 'declarationists' were accepted into EAM but not into the party.

Throughout 1942 the KKE made a vigorous effort to expand its influence under the cloak of EAM. In spite of the extensive and subtle use of patriotic slogans, 'by the end of the year EAM still had no mass support throughout the country, particularly in Macedonia, Thessaly, and Peloponnesus'.[10] This statement, taken from the minutes of the KKE's Pan-helladic Conference of December 1942, hardly bears out Siantos' later claim of a 'meteoric rise'. Yet it is only fair to say that among all resistance organizations which sprang up during that year, EAM was the most successful and could truthfully boast of having a larger following than any other.

EAM gains popular support

In 1942 and early 1943 the KKE, 'the principal leading and organizational force of EAM',[11] skilfully exploited the prevailing circumstances. What were these circumstances? One was the vacuum of leadership left after the departure of the Greek Government. The occupation forces filled the vacuum of authority but not that of leadership; neither they nor the puppet Government they installed could provide the leadership the prostrated nation so desperately needed. The old political leaders, whose names could perhaps have gained the confidence and the allegiance of the people, failed in general to grasp the significance of what was happening. They misinterpreted the collapse of Greece as the long-awaited moment for the resumption of the traditional Venizelist–Royalist feud, now centred around King George II, whom they held responsible for the establishment of the Metaxas dictatorship. Thus, in the midst of the Occupation, their first political move was not a call to resistance, not even an appeal for unity, perseverance, and courage in the face of mounting hardships, but a protocol (March

[10] *Dheka Khronia Agones*, p. 165.
[11] Article by N. Zachariades in *Ellino-Amerikanikon Vima*, 20 October 1950.

1942) by which they pledged themselves to work for the re-establishment of the republican form of government after the liberation.[12] The KKE did not, of course, object to any action which could impair the King's prestige in Greece and abroad; yet the constitutional issue was not given a central place in its propaganda. Instead, through EAM, it called on the Greek people to join the ranks of resistance against the foreign conquerors, while it fired the imagination of young and old alike with the vision of a free, prosperous, just, and progressive Greece. In the desperate hours of the Occupation the proclamations of EAM served as a brilliant beacon of hope piercing the darkness, bringing solace and courage to an enslaved nation.

The cruel and politically stupid actions of the occupation forces also contributed to EAM's success, for instead of terrifying the Greek people to the point of political inactivity, they strengthened their resistance. The quest for leadership in the struggle for survival, vengeance, and national liberation became universal. With every execution of innocent hostages, every burning of defenceless villages, every act of brutality, a deep and uncompromising hatred against the conquerors swelled into a mighty stream. EAM, guided by the KKE, fully exploited this 'revolutionary psychology'.

The breakdown of the social fabric also eased the task of the Communist leaders. Numbers of the former middle class stood in the same queue with the poor, patiently waiting for a bowl of soup. Destitution, like a gigantic bulldozer, had levelled the social distinctions of the past. The KKE was quick to realize that this meant an automatic expansion of its potential appeal. How to gain control over the people became the party's main preoccupation. The KKE, in accord with the specific instructions of its 8th Plenum (January 1942), meticulously avoided any open references to the class struggle, the proletarian revolution, Marxism, and the like. Instead, it concentrated on exploiting the strong nationalistic spirit which emerged from the appalling conditions of national humiliation and suffering. Svetozar Vukmanovic, or Tempo, Tito's emissary to EAM, in a pamphlet entitled *Le Parti communiste de Grèce dans la lutte de libération nationale*, criticized the KKE for its failure to win power in Greece at the end of the Occupation and revealed that 'Siantos

[12] E. I. Tsouderos, *Ellinikes Anomalies sti Messi Anatoli* (Athens, Aetos A. E., 1945), pp. 47-48.

and Yiannis Ioannides,[13] during a meeting with representatives of the Communist Parties of Yugoslavia and Albania in 1943, argued that because of the peculiar conditions in Greece, party members should not speak to the masses as members of the Communist Party but only in the name of EAM'. Tempo added: 'In general the Party concealed its identity from the broad masses of the Greek people.'

In contrast with other Greek political groups, the Communists had considerable experience of conspiratorial operations and underground organization. True, their illegal machinery had collapsed at least twice in the first two decades of its existence. This was partly because in the past the majority of Greeks had remained indifferent or even hostile to Communist underground operations. This time, however, the Communists were forging an underground organization which answered the deepest aspirations of the people in the best traditions of the Greek nation. Many thousands of patriotic Greeks supported EAM. Since 1934 and the notorious resolutions of the 6th Plenum the KKE had been prepared theoretically for the formidable task of 'turning the imperialist war into a civil war'. The formation of a United Front from below and from above had remained the focal point of Communist strategy since 1934. Initial doubts as to what form of sub-conventional warfare their action should take were resolved by the irresistible course of events and the call to guerrilla war advocated by the broadcasts of both Moscow Radio and the BBC.

For reasons of military expediency, the Western Allies, and especially the British, extended considerable aid to EAM and its military branch, ELAS.[14] In 1942 and 1943 Allied strategists wanted to foment resistance movements in occupied Europe, to harass the German lines of communication, and force the Wehrmacht to divert troops from the major fronts. Since the Communists appeared willing to fight the Germans, the British supported the Communist-controlled guerrilla bands without much regard to possible political complications in the future. Many independent bands operating in areas controlled by a strong EAM political organization joined ELAS because to remain 'independent' made little sense. The integration of

---

[13] See biographical note No. 4.
[14] Whenever reference is made to both the political (EAM) and the military branch (ELAS) the form EAM/ELAS is used in this text.

small, weak groups was advocated not only by EAM but also by the British emissaries who soon appeared in the Greek mountains. It must also be said that ELAS, with its initial daring attacks against enemy units, had fired the imagination of many patriotic Greeks, who saw in it a revival of the heroic traditions of 1821, the Greek War of Independence. The same was true for EDES. Small groups joined EDES or ELAS according to their locality rather than for any political considerations. At the beginning it was difficult to detect any serious differences between the aims of these two organizations. Only later did the KKE add to its arsenal two more techniques, forcible recruitment and provocation. When the occupation authorities adopted the principle of 'collective responsibility' for individual acts of violence against members of their forces, the Communists discovered an easy way of recruiting manpower for their bands. By ambushing a German soldier in the outskirts of a small town or a village, they could expect a rich harvest; the Germans would come the next day to kill and burn, and those who had time to escape would find refuge with the ELAS bands. It is only fair to say, however, that most of those who fought the Germans under the banners of ELAS had joined the resistance organization of their own accord.

The KKE defines its political objectives

Any party conference, being under KKE rules equivalent to a party congress, is important in our study of the party's history; but the Pan-helladic Conference of the KKE, which convened somewhere in Thessaly in the bleak winter month of December 1942, is of particular significance. Probably one of the most important gatherings in the history of the party, this conference outlined the policies and the objectives of the KKE not only for the period of foreign occupation but also for the day when the enemy would leave Greek soil. The chief figure in its deliberations was George Siantos, the former tobacco-worker, the erstwhile discredited participant in the 'struggle without principles', who was now the Secretary of the Central Committee. In his address to the conference, Siantos gave a clear and concise description of the party line:

The immediate objective of our Party today is the expulsion of the foreign conquerors. This is the immediate objective of the Communist Party of Greece. Yes; but do we forget the ultimate strategic objective of our Party, namely, the struggle for Socialism and the final liberation of our people from every political yoke and exploitation of man by man? Not only do we not forget this objective but, on the contrary, our present policy will open up the way for the realization of our ultimate strategic objectives.[15]

In accordance with the party's long-established tactical rules, Siantos emphasized the exploitation of the people's day-to-day problems and added: 'The daily, unceasing struggle for the everyday needs of life is the decisive link for the realization of the *political* objectives, and for the conquest, organization, and mobilization of the masses.'[16] For the sake of expediency, the well-known Communist clichés were temporarily shelved.

The conference further dealt with the problem of the 'declarationists'. To exclude all 45,000 of them from participating in the resistance movement would simply deprive the party of desperately needed support. The conference decided to take a fairly lenient stand on the subject. It found a way out by dividing the 'declarationists' into three categories: those 'who became stool-pigeons or dishonoured high posts'; those 'who went home and did not take part in political activities'; and those 'who repented and were willing to offer their services to the Party'. Those in the first category were to be tried by 'People's Courts' as soon as technically possible. Those in the second category were unworthy of consideration. But those in the third category should be allowed to fight 'as non-party members'. Later this decision was severely criticized by Zachariades, who held all 'declarationists' in an uncompromising contempt; but in 1942 Zachariades was a prisoner in German hands, while the party, struggling to establish its preeminence in the resistance movement, could not afford to be too selective.

[15] *Dheka Khronia Agones*, p. 146.   [16] Ibid., p. 170; author's italics.

12. Monopolizing the Resistance

The KKE and the British

In September 1942 Major I. Tsigantes, a well-known Greek officer, secretly entered Greece as an emissary of Allied GHQ, Middle East. His mission was to establish contact with political and military leaders in Athens and organize a resistance movement against the Germans under responsible leadership. Tsigantes, a daring but somewhat careless young man, failed to cover his presence with the necessary secrecy. Practically everyone knew that he was in Athens. His contacts with political and military personalities produced no results, partly because some of them were reluctant to become too involved in an enterprise which had already become too widely known, and partly because many of the military leaders, schooled as they were in conventional warfare, distrusted any suggestions for the organization of sub-conventional forms of warfare such as guerrilla bands. Many Greek officers fought in the Resistance, but only a few came from the highest ranks.

Tsigantes' mission came to a tragic end when an anonymous informer revealed his hide-out to the Italian authorities. In a desperate gun-fight with Italian carabinieri, Tsigantes was killed. One can only speculate whether the course of events would have been at all different had he successfully completed his assignment.

At about the same time, on 29 September 1942, a group of British officers and servicemen parachuted into Greece under the command of Brigadier E. C. W. Myers. Their mission was to cut off the line of supplies for Rommel's Afrika Korps. After several days of uncertainty the group established contact with the bands led by Aris Velouchiotis, which controlled most of the area where the prospective targets were located. To their request for military assistance, Aris replied that he was willing to contribute the necessary forces, but needed time to obtain the formal approval of his political organization in Athens. It seems, however, that this was only a pretext. The bridge of Gorgopotamos, which was selected as the most likely target, was heavily guarded and well fortified. Attacking such a target was not like ambushing a small enemy patrol. Strong resistance by the garrison could easily wipe out most of Aris' troops and so set back the development of his organization. To the British, the mission of a guerrilla force during the war was to harass the enemy's communications, immobilize large forces, and keep alive the spirit of resistance in the occupied areas. To the Communist leadership of EAM/ELAS the object of such operations was to prepare for the critical moment when the occupation forces would evacuate Greece, leaving behind a power vacuum to be filled by those prepared for the take-over. ELAS forces fought bravely several times during the Occupation with good results. But in the autumn of 1942, when the Aris forces were still in the making, the Gorgopotamos operation presented unacceptable risks. Aris changed his mind, however, when Myers turned to Zervas, who operated in Epirus, more than one hundred miles away. Success at Gorgopotamos meant prestige, which was indispensable to any organization aspiring for leadership in the resistance movement and made the risks involved politically worthwhile. The operation was carried out on the night of 25 November 1942, with complete success. A combined force of ninety ELAS and sixty EDES guerrillas wiped out the Italian garrison after a pitched battle, while a small group of British commandos demolished the vital bridge, thus cutting off Rommel's supply-line by rail through Greece for several critical weeks.

The original plan for the Myers group was to proceed to the Ionian coast and return to the Middle East by submarine. Instead, they were ordered to stay in Greece and establish a British Military Mission (BMM) to concentrate on organizing, training, and supplying guerrilla bands as an auxiliary military force.[1] Most of the costly mistakes of the following years stemmed from this basic approach. While the British were thinking almost exclusively along *military* lines, the Communist leadership of EAM/ELAS was primarily concerned with the *political* exploitation of the guerrilla movement 'for the realization of [the KKE's] ultimate strategic objectives', to quote Siantos' revealing statement at the Pan-helladic Conference of December 1942.

[1] E. C. W. Myers, *Greek Entanglement* (Rupert Hart-Davis, 1955), p. 122.

By April 1943, when Hitler and Mussolini met to discuss the situation in the Balkans, the guerrilla movement had spread throughout mainland Greece. In addition to EDES and ELAS, a third major organization had taken the field, the National and Social Liberation (EKKA), under the leadership of Colonel Dimitrios Psaros, an honest soldier with mildly left-wing ideas. With the withdrawal of the Italian garrisons from Grevena, Karthitsa, and Karpenision, a substantial area had come under guerrilla control. Throughout this period British supplies and British gold had played a key role in the expansion and growth of the bands. In addition to war material and supplies in general, EAM/ELAS, EDES, and other local resistance groups received one gold sovereign per month for every active and permanently enlisted guerrilla.[2] There is some evidence that ELAS handed over its share of gold sovereigns to EAM, which in turn passed most of it on to the KKE. The figures quoted range from 100,000 to 900,000 gold sovereigns for the entire period.

Up to the end of 1942 EAM/ELAS, still in the formative stage, refrained from any outright attacks against other non-Communist guerrilla groups; only in a few isolated cases, ELAS units forced small, newly-formed bands to integrate with the Communist-led organization or disarm and disperse. After the December 1942 Pan-helladic Conference of the KKE, which made it clear that the resistance movement was merely a preparatory step to the winning of power, this moderation was discarded. To prepare the ground for the moment of transition, the Communists worked out a set of tactical steps. The three most important were: (*a*) to monopolize the resistance movement by eliminating rival guerrilla groups; (*b*) to infiltrate the Greek armed forces which had escaped to Egypt and were being reorganized there by the Greek Government-in-exile; and (*c*) to undermine the prestige of King George II and his Government so that any opposition to Communist designs would be interpreted as the work of 'reactionary and undemocratic elements'.

Through these tactics the Communist leaders expected to eliminate, discredit, or at least weaken all possible rival forces so that, at the crucial moment of liberation, EAM/ELAS would have a free hand for the realization of the KKE's 'ultimate

[2] Cf. Myers, op. cit., pp. 222–3.

objective'. With this in mind, the KKE deployed its forces both in the mountains and in the towns so as to be able to seize power as soon as the withdrawal of the occupation forces created a vacuum. Siantos succinctly outlined these tactics in 1943:

The peculiarity in Greece is that the largest part of the population is concentrated in the towns; therefore whoever controls the towns, controls power. For this reason the KKE decided on the formation of military units in the towns, to seize power as soon as the conquerors departed. The guerrilla forces, composed mostly of villagers, should be near the towns to assist the town units to win power.[3]

With the seizure of power as their 'ultimate objective', the Communists made a conscious effort to preserve their guerrilla forces intact, as far as was technically feasible, for the final showdown. Kostas Karayiorgis, a former editor of *Rizospastis* and one of the leading Communists in that period, revealed in a 'personal note' he sent to Zachariades later (19 March 1948) that 'it was our general strategy always to withdraw in face of the enemy, not taking into consideration the ground lost, in order to conserve our forces unimpaired for our future objectives. This was how Siantos explained these tactics to me.'[4] These practices culminated in the notorious agreement of 1 September 1944, by which the ELAS forces guaranteed to refrain from harassing the withdrawing Germans on condition that the German forces surrendered the city of Salonika to ELAS.[5] In October 1944 many British officers were astonished to observe the ELAS guerrillas moving southwards while British units were pursuing the retreating Germans to the north. *Kapetan* Orestis, the legendary chief of the Second ELAS Division, told this writer in 1963 that at the time of the evacuation of Athens by the Germans his forces moved by night in small groups across the Thebes road in the direction of the capital, while during the day the German forces were left to move out unhindered. 'My orders', he said, 'were to avoid unnecessary losses.'[6]

From the moment when the first British commandos para-

[3] Quoted by S. Vukmanovic (Tempo) in *How and Why the People's Liberation Struggle of Greece met with Defeat*.

[4] Original captured by the Greek authorities in August 1949.

[5] *I Enantion tis Ellados Epivouli*, pp. 15–16.

[6] See also Richard Capell, *Simiomata; a Greek Note Book, 1944–1945* (Macdonald; 1946), p. 45; also C. M. Woodhouse, *Apple of Discord* (Hutchinson, 1951), p. 208.

chuted into Greece in the autumn of 1942 the Communists saw
that their plans were liable to be upset. How to deal with the
British became one of the KKE's major preoccupations. Ever
since the time of the celebrated resolution of the 6th Plenum in
1934, the 'liberation' of the Greek people from 'foreign exploitation'—primarily British in Communist eyes—had been seen as
one of the party's major tasks. Now, by the fortunes of war,
Britain had become an ally of the Soviet Union. Besides, by
being primarily responsible for the conduct of the war in the
Mediterranean, the British had a legitimate reason for assuming
a leading role in Greek affairs, including the resistance movement. Communist strategists could clearly see that British
intervention at the crucial moment of transition could easily
offset all the gains that EAM/ELAS might have achieved
throughout the 'preparatory' stage. Later, in 1952, Zachariades
criticized the leadership of the KKE during the Occupation for

straying away from the general line of the 6th Plenum (1934),
which had defined the country's considerable dependence on foreign
capital as a major peculiarity in its economico-political development.
The KKE leadership failed to realize that as a result of EAM's
movement . . . a clash with British imperialism, then the main
foreign oppressor in Greece, was inevitable.[7]

The criticism was unwarranted. The wartime leaders of the
KKE fully understood that a clash with the British was to be
expected. They, too, considered the British to be 'the main
oppressor', even though Greece was under Axis domination.
Their problem throughout the difficult years of the Occupation
was how to delay an open clash with the British until the KKE
had strengthened its control over Greece. On this issue two
major trends of thought developed within the Communist
leadership. One group, usually identified with Yiannis Ioannides and Aris Velouchiotis, favoured an aggressive policy of
eliminating all potential Greek rivals so that the British would
be faced with an accomplished fact. The other, represented by
George Siantos, advocated subtler tactics, to allay British
suspicions for as long as possible, while building up the party-
controlled forces for the seizure of power at the crucial moment
of transition, before the British had time to intervene effectively.
From a tactical point of view, the application of an 'aggres-

[7] Zachariades, *Provlimata Kathothigisis*, p. 26.

sive' policy depended on the country's early liberation; should the Axis Occupation continue long after the exposure of the KKE's real objectives, the British would have ample time to take counter-measures and block further Communist advances. This was understood by both factions. As a result, whenever the course of the war gave the impression that the liberation of the country was fast approaching, the 'aggressives' were given a free hand and acts of violence against other Greek forces reached civil war proportions. As soon as the expectation of an early liberation proved to be premature, the 'moderates' were called on to restore British confidence and avert a disastrous rift, entailing the cutting-off of supplies. In fact there seems to have been a convenient distribution of roles rather than a genuine difference of opinion on a major question of strategy. Both methods were applied alternately with varying intensity during 1943 and 1944, causing a great deal of confusion among many of those who were responsible for the conduct of the war in Greece.

ELAS *clashes with other bands*

By 1943 there were unmistakable signs that the scales of war were being tipped slowly but surely in favour of the Allies. The British Eighth Army, after its initial success at El Alamein on 2 July 1942, had continued its advance along the North African coast, while a combined Anglo-American expeditionary force had successfully carried out the greatest invasion yet known by landing in French North Africa on 8 November 1942. The complete rout of Rommel's Afrika Korps appeared to be only a matter of time. By 31 January 1943 the German Sixth Army was destroyed at Stalingrad, while two weeks earlier the Red Army had broken the seventeen-month siege of Leningrad. On 16 February 1943 the Red Army had captured Kharkov in the heart of the Ukraine. Spirits were high at EAM/ELAS headquarters as many over-optimistic strategists boldly predicted the early liberation of Greece as the next logical step after the cleaning-up of North Africa. Those who advocated the swift elimination of all rival organizations, regardless of any British reaction, were given a free hand; after all, if Greece was to be liberated within the next few months, it mattered little whether or not the British were displeased with EAM/ELAS. The Communists expected that an early liberation would involve large Allied forces landing in Greece. It seemed likely that the British would join with the non-Communist groups and—together with the Greek Government-in-exile—try to thwart the Communist designs. The leaders of the KKE, fully aware of the intricacies of power, realized that their bargaining position would be immeasurably strengthened if they could claim to be the only significant military and political force representing the great majority of the Greek people. The decisive link in the chain, to use a familiar Communist term, was that the British should find EAM/ELAS the most powerful organization in Greece at the moment of the liberation.

With the Allied successes, the Greek Communists thought that the time for a showdown was fast approaching. They took action both in the Greek mountains and in Egypt, where the Greek military forces were stationed. On 23 February 1943 their agents in the Middle East, supported by EAM followers whose journey to Egypt had been facilitated by the fact that ELAS controlled the escape routes, instigated a mutiny in the Greek armed forces. Committees of soldiers assumed command of military and naval units, while anti-royalist officers who had made their way to the Middle East pressed the Premier, E. Tsouderos, to replace certain members of the Cabinet by republicans. It required little imagination to see that if Greece was liberated by the Allies the King and the Greek Government-in-exile would return to Greece and act as the legitimate spokesmen of the people. The mutiny was designed to disrupt the effectiveness of the Greek units in the crucial months ahead and at the same time to force the removal from positions of leadership of those who, if allowed to return to Greece with governmental authority, could conceivably block the Communist objectives.

On 14 March the King and the Premier flew from London to Cairo, where ten days later, under pressure from the mutineers, they reshuffled the Cabinet. Some of the new ministers were known to hold anti-royalist views, and in the following months, by ignorance or design, they played the Communist game. Many loyalist (pro-royalist) officers resigned their commissions in an ill-considered show of protest at the political activities in the armed forces in the midst of war; they were arrested by the British, and confined to a concentration camp at Merjeyum. These events put almost 200 loyal officers behind barbed wire, while the armed forces were infested by 'anti-Fascist' committees, with the real power in the hands of the most 'capable', regardless of rank.[8]

In Greece proper the Communists went ahead with their plan of monopolizing the resistance movement before the liberation of the country. A first, unsuccessful attempt to eliminate EDES had already been made in late December 1942, when Aris, with 350 guerrillas, almost his entire force at that time, penetrated the Valtos area and attacked the forces under the command of Dr. Stelios Houtas.

In the early months of 1943 ELAS' rivals who really mattered were Zervas, Psaros, and Colonel Stefanos Saraphis. The last was a newcomer to the field. In February he had joined the group led by Captain G. Kostopoulos, which had been operating in Thessaly since late 1942. Saraphis, a well-known pro-republican officer and a leading figure in the Venizelist *coup* of 1935, had joined this force with the aim of establishing, with British assistance, a large un-Communist-dominated resistance organization. In this he had been strongly encouraged by Tsigantes, who had promised him ample British aid. The ELAS command in Thessaly, led by Kostas Karayiorgis, a leading Communist, regarded the arrival of Saraphis with some anxiety. His military reputation, his political views, his persecution by the occupation authorities formed an impressive background for successful leadership. Without even waiting for approval from the Central Committee of the KKE, Karayiorgis gave the signal for the elimination of the rival force. His bands first attacked a small group associated with Kostopoulos, and captured some of its officers. When Kostopoulos moved into ELAS territory to seek his friends' release he was allowed to proceed unhindered. In the late afternoon of 1 March 1943 the group including Colonel Saraphis reached the village of Vounesi, where the prisoners were held. Saraphis and his companions were received by the ELAS guerrillas and the villagers with warm expressions of friendship. Tired after a long and arduous journey, and reassured by the attitude of the Elasites, Kostopoulos, Saraphis, and the other members of his group went to bed. At dawn they were wakened by ELAS guerrillas, disarmed at gun-point, and taken prisoner.

Saraphis was already disillusioned after his first few weeks in the mountains. Seeing that ELAS was an established power, he

[8] Tsouderos, op. cit., p. 33.

felt that it was hopeless to try to raise a rival force. Without any particular pressure, he told his captors that he was willing to join ELAS and offer his services. At first they could not believe their ears. To avoid the charge of having forced him to change sides, they escorted him secretly to Athens, where the leaders of EAM/ELAS formally offered him the post of military commander of ELAS. Thus one of the rival groups had been eliminated and ELAS had gained a reputable military expert who could also serve as a convenient political smoke-screen. That ELAS was in need of a military leader is shown by the fact that in December 1942 Aris had tried unsuccessfully to persuade Zervas to accept the post of military commander of ELAS.

Soon after the liquidation of Saraphis' band and his personal *volte face*, the ELAS forces turned against the second rival on their list. On 12 May 1943 *Kapetan* Orestis passed to Aris the information that the party favoured the elimination of all other guerrilla groups operating in areas where ELAS predominated. Early next morning ELAS troops opened an attack against the force led by Colonel Dimitrios Psaros, known either as 5/42 Regiment or by the name of its parent organization, EKKA. The Psaros group was dispersed, but soon afterwards, under British pressure, ELAS agreed to let Psaros take the field again.

Three days after the attack on Psaros, ELAS forces attempted to cross the Acheloos river into the area of Valtos controlled by the bands of Dr. Houtas. Their effort failed. Houtas and Zervas mobilized their forces in anticipation of further ELAS moves, but with the exception of some probing attacks on outlying posts, ELAS treated EDES this time with caution.

These provocative moves by EAM/ELAS strained its relations with the British Military Mission to the point where ELAS openly refused to join in the attack on the Asopos viaduct, on the main railway line to the north. With this target well within the area controlled by ELAS, then virtually at war with EDES, the British could not use EDES to force ELAS to co-operate, as in the Gorgopotamos operation. Now that a rival organization could not take credit for a major feat, the ELAS command refused to participate; in the end the Asopos viaduct was blown up on 20 June by a group of six British Commandos.

From the first signs of EAM/ELAS perfidy the British tried to arrest the dangerous drift towards civil conflict. They were not, of course, concerned with the political designs of the Communist-led organization. To them the guerrillas were strictly an auxiliary military force. In their view ELAS attacks on other groups hindered the war effort. To restore the military effectiveness of the Greek guerrilla movement, the BMM drafted a document in April 1943 calling on all guerrilla groups to respect each other's independence and obey orders from General Headquarters, Middle East. This was the beginning of what later became known as the 'National Bands Agreement'.

The National Bands Agreement

In the spring of 1943 EAM/ELAS largely ignored the British call for a live-and-let-live agreement with the other groups. Its political leaders still hoped that Greece would soon be liberated, and therefore monopolization of the resistance movement remained the first priority. Yet the British held a strong bargaining card: EAM/ELAS still depended heavily on their support for supplies and war material. That the Communists were willing to risk the loss of such support can only be explained by their conviction that the liberation was near and British support and friendship would then be determined by a political factor— EAM's pre-eminence as the most powerful organization in the country. These views had to be drastically reassessed in the early summer of 1943 because of two major developments. One was the realization that Greece would not be liberated in the foreseeable future. The second was the dissolution of the Comintern.

On 14 May 1943 the Presidium of the ECCI submitted to the various 'sections' a proposal for the dissolution of the Communist International as the central organ of the international Communist movement. This decision was long overdue. The Comintern, which had long since become a mere appendage of Soviet foreign policy, had lost even that limited function when leaders personally devoted to Stalin took over the reins in the various Communist parties. During the war the various 'sections' had broadened their popular base and had gained unprecedented prestige and influence, especially in those European countries under Axis domination. As the Communist parties grew in stature and experience, the significance of the Comintern as a co-ordinating agency diminished proportionately. On the other hand, its very existence poisoned the war-time co-

operation of the Western Powers with the Soviet Union. By
liquidating the Comintern, Stalin was merely writing the formal
obituary of an organization which had long outlived its usefulness; at the same time, he could point to this 'gesture' as a proof
of his goodwill, while the local Communist parties could now
claim to be genuinely national parties. One may recall that
many in the West hastened to salute the demise of the Comintern as heralding a radical change in the long-term objectives of
the international Communist movement. The leaders of the
Greek Communist Party were not among those enthusiasts. The
Central Committee of the KKE, which met on 2 June 1943 to
discuss 'a single topic, the proposal of the Presidium of the
ECCI for the dissolution of the Communist International', did
not see the ECCI's proposal as a departure from traditional
Communist objectives; instead, the Greek Communist leaders
resolved that 'the dissolution of the Communist International
underlines the passing of the Greek Communist Party (which
from now ceases to be a section of the CI) from its vigorous
twenty-five-year period of *preparation* to a new and more responsible stage which entails historic and creative duties'.[9] In
other words, the end of the Comintern was seen as a sign that
the Communist parties had reached maturity and a step forward to higher levels of responsibility. The long period of 'preparation' was past; the time had come for the realization of the
party's 'historic and creative' aims, that is, for the seizure of
power.

For the Greek Communist leaders the liquidation of the
Comintern had additional significance. It was apparently a
gesture of goodwill on the part of the Soviet Union. Since the
Soviet leaders felt it necessary to placate their allies, even with
an empty gesture, it was evident that the end of the war was not
yet in sight and that a moderate attitude was more in line with
Soviet policies. These considerations, together with the prospect
of being deprived of all British assistance should they continue
their aggressive policy, led EAM/ELAS to take a more 'constructive' line. But they made one more effort to strengthen
their position *vis-à-vis* that of the other groups. Before accepting
the agreement suggested by the British, they demanded that all
communications between the BMM and ELAS units in the field

---

[9] Resolution of the Central Committee of the KKE, dated 2 June 1943; author's
italics.

should be effected through the ELAS GHQ. This General Headquarters of ELAS had been established on 20 May 1943 with Aris Velouchiotis, Stefanos Saraphis, and Andreas Tzimas (or Evmaios) in command. Velouchiotis was the *Kapetanios*, the guerrilla chief who enjoyed the confidence of the party; Saraphis was the titular C.-in-C., confined to military matters; Tzimas was the *Politikos*, the political Commissar representing the Communist Party and enjoying considerable power. This combination of military-political, military, and party authority was repeated throughout the ELAS structure, down to company level.

According to the EAM/ELAS proposals, Allied GHQ, Middle East, was to send general directives to the ELAS GHQ; 'but the method of their execution and the selection of targets should be left to the discretion and decision of the new ELAS GHQ'.[10] This demand involved more than merely nationalistic pride. Its acceptance would amount to a virtual recognition of ELAS as an independent army, with far-reaching political consequences. The Special Operations Executive (SOE) in Cairo, the office responsible for the conduct of the war in Greece during the Occupation, rejected the Communist proposals and instructed Brigadier Myers, head of the BMM, to proceed on that basis. In the face of British firmness, the Communists modified their demands. Their purpose was not to break off relations—at least for the time being. In proposing the formal recognition of the ELAS GHQ, they had followed the classic pattern, pitching their initial demands high in order to have room to make 'concessions', yet still attain their original objectives. They apologized for their attacks on Psaros the previous May and put forward a modified 'National Bands Agreement'. The new EAM/ELAS plan called for a Joint GHQ with representatives from all guerrilla organizations 'in proportion to their strength', and including the Commander of the British Military Mission. This Joint GHQ, they said, should consist of six members: three from EAM/ELAS, one from EDES, one from EKKA, and the Commander of the BMM. It was still a very advantageous arrangement for the Communists. The British tried to water down this proposal. The 'tacit blackmail and counter-blackmail'[11] continued through June. The draft which was finally accepted still favoured EAM/ELAS and the BMM and SOE were forced to compromise on a number of important points. They had a good reason for doing so. The invasion of Sicily was approaching, and the Allied plan called for large-scale guerrilla operations in Greece to divert German attention towards the Balkans and create the false impression that the next Allied move would be directed against Greece. The non-Communist guerrilla leaders, who harboured serious misgivings as to the wisdom of accepting an agreement which patently boosted the prestige and the potential power of EAM/ELAS, were finally persuaded by the British to accept the bitter pill. One of the two arguments used to convince them was stated later by Brigadier Myers in his book: 'Although ELAS at that time possessed a large number of arms . . . the Movement was rapidly expanding and it would require a great number more. That being so, the Middle East Command, through my Mission, held what I thought at the time was a trump card. . . .'[12] In other words, the British thought that they would be able to keep a check on EAM/ELAS by threatening to cut off supplies and money. A second consideration which influenced the non-Communist leaders was based on the widespread belief that any concessions to EAM/ELAS would be of little consequence once large Allied forces had landed in Greece. Both assumptions were soon invalidated by events.

Under the terms of the agreement, which was signed during July by EAM/ELAS, EDES, EKKA, and some other minor organizations, all guerrilla bands were ostensibly united 'for military purposes' into the National Guerrilla Bands of Greece. In fact, the various organizations kept their own separate structures and territories, their animosities, and their individual objectives. The Joint GHQ, established by the agreement, followed in the main the EAM/ELAS proposal, with three top EAM/ELAS leaders participating. EDES and EKKA appointed to the Joint GHQ two of their top political personalities, Komnynos Pyromaglou for EDES and George Kartalis for EKKA, who were later replaced by minor staff officers. Considering that the location of the Joint GHQ was that of the ELAS GHQ, the reluctance of Zervas and Psaros to participate personally is understandable. The 'moderates' among the Communist strategists at the ELAS headquarters could now claim with justifiable pride that without any real concessions on

[12] Myers, op. cit., p. 187.

their part they had been able to re-establish normal relations with the British, while in addition, the agreement had established the pre-eminence of ELAS by giving it a majority in the Joint GHQ. That the site of this Joint GHQ was the same as that of the ELAS GHQ was a visible proof of their success. We may safely assume that the 'tough' strategists of the KKE were no less delighted. In the zig-zag tactics of their movement both 'factions' had a role to play. The British, on the other hand, concerned as they were with the military effectiveness of the guerrillas, could only welcome with relief the apparent end to internecine strife. It was to be a short-lived respite.

13. The Conflict Deepens

The decision is left to an army pilot

When the Commander of the BMM, Brigadier Myers, discovered that Greece was not to be liberated in the summer of 1943 he signalled the Special Operations Executive in Cairo that, in view of all the problems he faced, it was necessary for him to go to Egypt and discuss the future with his superiors. His suggestion was approved provided the trip could be made by air—his original idea of going by caïque being rejected as much too dangerous. The construction of a landing-strip near Neraida in Thessaly was completed at the beginning of August, and Myers made arrangements for an aircraft to land there on the night of 9 August 1943.

Shortly before the end of July Brigadier Myers mentioned to Andreas Tzimas, the ELAS *Politikos*, that he planned to visit Cairo in the near future. Immediately Tzimas suggested that he should go too. Cairo approved this suggestion. Soon Komnynos Pyromaglou and George Kartalis, representatives respectively of EDES and EKKA at the Joint GHQ, learned about the proposed trip and also asked to join the party. Cairo again approved. Presumably the British wished to see the apparent consolidation of the guerrilla forces consummated by further agreements between the Greeks of the mountains and the Greeks of the Middle East. The SOE authorities in Cairo were little concerned with the post-war political implications of their actions. In fact, their view was that 'post-war considerations should not be allowed to prejudice the success of future operations, for which the maximum effort would be required'.[1] But if the British authorities were deliberately ignoring the political problems, the Communists were thinking of nothing else. On the evening of 8 August, the day before the aircraft was scheduled to land at Neraida, Tzimas arrived there accompanied by G. Siantos, Secretary of the KKE Central Committee, Elias Tsirimokos, then the leader of a small Socialist party known as the Popular Democratic Union (Enosis Laikis Dimokratias,

---

[1] Myers, op. cit., p. 230.

ELD), and two other known Communists, Petros Roussos and
Constantine Despotopoulos, all members of the Central Committee of EAM. Siantos decided that not only Tzimas but also
Roussos, Despotopoulos, and Tsirimokos should fly with Myers
to Cairo. He insisted that a signal he had received from Myers'
headquarters indicated that the Central Committee of EAM
was invited to send as many representatives to Cairo as it
wished. He even produced the signal, which was indeed phrased
in such a way that with a great deal of imagination it could have
been read to mean what Siantos suggested. To Myers' objection
that it would be impossible for him to take Tsirimokos, Roussos,
and Despotopoulos, Siantos replied that in that case he would
not allow Tzimas to go to Egypt alone. As a seasoned tactician,
he realized that to send Tzimas as just one of three representatives of the resistance organizations would jeopardize the image
of EAM/ELAS pre-eminence, only recently established under
the 'National Bands Agreement'. He was also fully aware of the
areas of disagreement on which Pyromaglou and Kartalis could
easily side with the Greeks of the Middle East against Tzimas.
The Central Committee of the party had decided what its
representatives should do once they reached Egypt; and this
could not be accomplished by Tzimas alone. On the other hand,
he realized that a deputation from the resistance would not
amount to much without EAM/ELAS participation. His little
blackmail succeeded. After considerable wrangling, Myers gave
in and agreed that, if the pilot of the plane had no objection, he
would take all four EAM/ELAS delegates to Egypt.[2] Thus a
decision of major political importance was left to the discretion
of an army pilot, deciding on purely technical grounds.

The talks in Cairo

The next morning, 9 August, Myers had a long talk with
Siantos. The Communist leader agreed that the resistance
representatives should tackle the various problems along the
lines of a plan worked out by the BMM. This plan, which had
previously been discussed in meetings with Pyromaglou and
Kartalis, provided for the discussions to be conducted in three
stages. During the first stage the negotiations would deal with
the recognition of the guerrillas as an integral part of the Greek
armed forces. Such integration would include the exchange of

[2] Myers, op. cit., p. 242.

liaison officers between the regular forces and the guerrilla units. The second stage would deal with the more delicate subject of civil relations in those areas under guerrilla control. The guerrillas living among civilian populations in the liberated districts could not avoid getting involved in administrative and even legislative matters. In the view of the British such duties should be discharged in accordance with Greek civil law as far as was technically possible. The third stage was the most significant from a long-term point of view. It dealt with the establishment of a more representative government.

It was not difficult to see that the British plan, whether inspired by military or by political considerations, would establish a system of checks and controls over EAM/ELAS which could, at the crucial moment of transition, frustrate Communist plans for the seizure of power. The Central Committee of the party, already informed about this plan, had discussed its implications before Siantos left for Neraida. When in the morning of 9 August Siantos agreed to the British plan, he already knew that the Communist representatives had specific instructions to disregard it when they got to Egypt.

At dawn on 10 August 1943 the aircraft carrying the resistance representatives landed at an aerodrome near Cairo. Only then did the Greek Government learn that six of them had come.

Up to that time EAM/ELAS had not particularly stressed the 'constitutional issue'. This was abruptly changed in Cairo. The question of the King's return was the one issue on which the Communists could expect full support from the other resistance representatives. On the first two stages of the British plan they could easily foresee a more or less solid alignment of the EKKA and EDES representatives with most members of the Greek Government and the British. As soon as the talks got under way, Tzimas startled his non-Communist companions and the British by brushing aside the first two stages and launching a violent attack against the King and his Government. By a master stroke he had singled out the one issue on which he could expect support from Pyromaglou and Kartalis and possibly from many pro-republican politicians and officers in Egypt. He not only received the expected support of the other resistance representatives, but he was joined by Panayiotis Kanellopoulos, who had resigned from his post as Vice-Premier and Minister of

Army, Navy, and Air Force after the March mutiny and apparently wanted to prove his republicanism; and by G. Exindaris, who by a strange coincidence had arrived in Egypt shortly before the resistance delegates, bringing the views of pro-republican political leaders from Athens. These eight individuals signed a protocol addressed to Premier Tsouderos in which they declared that 'for the sake of national unity' the King should formally state 'that he will not return to Greece before the people decide on the constitutional issue'.[3] The Communists had chosen their ground well. On 19 August 1943 the Council of Ministers themselves signed a statement to the effect that 'it is the wish of the overwhelming majority of the Greek people that the King should not return to Greece before a Plebiscite'.[4] They then authorized the Premier to present this document to the King.

Two months earlier several political leaders in Greece, including Sofoulis, Kafandaris, Gonatas, Papandreou, and others, had suggested that only an official declaration by the King, agreeing to settle the constitutional question through a free election, 'could unite the people'. The King, on advice from his Government, had accepted the suggestion and on 4 July, in a broadcast to Greece, he formally declared his intention of submitting the fate of his throne to the free verdict of the Greek people. The determination of the constitutional question was to be effected through the election of a Constituent Assembly within six months after the liberation of the country.

Reports from Greece at the time had indicated that the royal declaration had been received with satisfaction. The Communists were understandably disturbed. Should the constitutional issue be deferred till after the liberation and cease to be a constant irritant poisoning the relations between the pro-royalist and the pro-republican factions, the Greek Communists could easily find themselves isolated, faced with a solid front of all the nationally-minded political leaders. Tzimas' unexpected move rekindled the controversy. Once he had opened the subject, he let the republican politicians carry on the attack. They played their role with amazing vigour and equally unbelievable blindness. Their demand that the King should not return to Greece before a plebiscite had decided the issue went a long way beyond what the King had implied in his declara-

---

[3] Tsouderos, op. cit., p. 64.   [4] Ibid., p. 65.

tion of 4 July. He turned for advice to Roosevelt and Churchill, who were then conferring at Quebec. Both answered his query, Churchill on 26 August, Roosevelt on 7 September. Both agreed that the King should return to Greece as soon as the country was free from enemy troops, and then submit the constitutional question to the people along the lines suggested in his declaration. Churchill even offered to instruct the British agents operating with Greek guerrilla groups 'to refrain from encouraging those elements to put forward political claims at this time as to the future form of government'. Brigadier Myers was replaced by Colonel C. M. Woodhouse, who had served as his second-in-command since November 1942. There is much evidence that Woodhouse was more inclined than his predecessor to think of post-war political repercussions. Yet to blame Brigadier Myers for the costly political blunders of the period would be unfair to say the least. He was sent to Greece to organize a resistance movement against the Germans. He was constantly reminded by his superiors that his actions should be determined by military considerations. If seasoned Greek politicians fell into the trap set by the Communists, how could anyone expect a British officer, with only limited acquaintance with the personalities and the politics of a foreign country, to avoid the innumerable pitfalls?

The King, encouraged by the warm support extended to him by Churchill and Roosevelt, refused to yield to the demands of the Greek politicians. The representatives of the resistance stayed on till the middle of September. Finally, they returned to the mountains by air, practically empty-handed.

Full-scale civil war

Even before the return of the resistance representatives from Egypt, the 'aggressives' among the Communist leaders had begun to press for more decisive action against rival organizations. Hopes of an early liberation were high. On 8 September 1943 Italy had surrendered unconditionally to the Allies. All over the Greek mainland large quantities of Italian weapons passed into the hands of EAM/ELAS. In Thessaly the Pinerolo Division under General Infante agreed to surrender to the BMM as the representative of the Allies in Greece. Under the Instrument of Surrender, signed on 12 September, this division became the first actively co-belligerent Italian formation in

Europe. The Italian units came over with all their equipment to the ELAS territory, which happened to be the closest to the areas occupied by the division. The EAM/ELAS leaders, although they had participated in the surrender agreement, had no intention of letting all these weapons and military supplies slip through their fingers; under various pretexts, they broke up the Italian division into scattered units, then disarmed them gradually and appropriated their weapons. By the end of September the division existed only on paper.[5] The weapons and material which fell into the hands of EAM/ELAS far exceeded anything they could expect from the British in the most favourable circumstances. Thus the BMM lost its most important trump card.

We have seen that in July 1943 two major considerations led EAM/ELAS to sign the 'National Bands Agreement': their dependence on British supplies, and the belief that the Occupation would continue for some time. By September the first consideration was no longer relevant; EAM/ELAS had become self-sufficient after the windfall of Italian weapons. The second consideration was being rapidly overtaken by events. North Africa had been cleared of all Axis troops; Sicily had been successfully invaded and occupied; Mussolini had been deposed and imprisoned; King Boris of Bulgaria had died mysteriously; Italy had been invaded and Badoglio had capitulated. On the Russian front the Red Army was advancing steadily. Much nearer home, the Allies had reoccupied some of the Aegean Islands. On 29 September Cairo ordered the Joint GHQ to prepare for operations against six major airfields in Greece. Correlating this order with the apparent withdrawal of the Germans towards the north—actually a skilful redeployment of their forces after the Italian surrender—EAM/ELAS concluded that the Allied forces were about to return to Greece with King George leading the invasion. Once again the 'aggressives' were given a free hand. Less than three months after the signing of the 'National Bands Agreement', ELAS reopened its drive to eliminate all other resistance organizations and strengthen its bargaining position at the time of liberation. In the process, some of the smaller resistance organizations were driven to a position where they had either to disband, join ELAS, or quit the mountains and join the Security Battalions which were

[5] Woodhouse, op. cit., p. 163.

being organized by the puppet government of Ioannis Rallis in the larger towns. Many Greek officers, without any pro-German sympathies, collaborated with the German-sponsored Battalions in the last year of the Occupation when the defeat of Germany was already in sight. The apparent paradox has its explanation. Most of those who served in the Battalions did not do so to help the Germans. They fought against the danger of a Communist take-over. Not only the volunteers but even those who were conscripted found a moral justification for their actions in the belief that they were fighting Communism. Inevitably, many irresponsible individuals wormed their way into the Battalions and under the pretext of anti-Communism committed outrageous excesses and despicable crimes. But excesses were common at that time. Human life had become very cheap indeed. Denounced by the Greek Government-in-exile and the British, the Battalions failed to avert a Communist take-over of the towns they held at the moment of liberation—the objective which was the only acceptable justification for their existence.

On 8 October 1943, after rushing the mountain artillery of the Pinerolo Division across the Pindus range,[6] ELAS attacked EDES. Two days later the fighting spread, as ELAS attacked all the other groups except EKKA.

The support given to King George by the Allied leaders and the prospect of his return to Greece with strong Allied forces gave the arguments for the elimination of all rival organizations an added urgency. Still, the attacks had to be justified. The Communist leadership resorted to outright falsehood. In strongly-worded public announcements, EAM/ELAS shamelessly asserted that the British had ordered them to attack the other resistance organizations because they were 'guilty of collaboration with the Germans'. They assumed that by the time the British had a chance to issue a denial the operation would be over.

This time the Communists were fooled. The Germans were not leaving. Having successfully baffled the intelligence systems of every guerrilla organization, they redeployed their forces and then took to the mountains, attacking both EDES and ELAS. In the clashes that followed it seemed doubtful that any of the guerrilla organizations could survive. The smaller groups,

[6] Woodhouse, op. cit., p. 78.

pressed by both the Germans and ELAS, left the field. But the large organizations were not destroyed. After some initial successes the Germans returned to the plains, and the guerrillas of ELAS, EDES, and EKKA re-emerged in the unoccupied regions.

The Plaka Agreement

The Communist attacks on the other resistance organizations and their loud claims that all those not willing to accept EAM/ELAS tutelage were 'traitors'[7] brought a painful awakening to many well-meaning patriots of liberal persuasion who had joined EAM/ELAS after the dissolution of the Comintern and the signing of the National Bands Agreement. There is a basic fallacy in the argument that more patriotic elements should have joined EAM *before* it fell under the domination of the KKE: there was no such period, simply because EAM *was created* by the KKE. On the other hand, those liberal officers and politicians who joined EAM/ELAS in the summer of 1943, hoping to gain the confidence of the Communists and influence them to move in another direction, soon found out that theirs was a very naïve expectation. The Communists never showed any intention of meeting them half-way. Their plan, drafted long ago, was to turn 'the imperialist war into a civil war' for the seizure of power. Any temporary concessions were only tactical manoeuvres in line with the old Leninist zig-zag policies. Some of those liberals and republicans withdrew in time; others stayed on longer, only to find out with dismay that when EAM/ELAS revolted in December 1944 against the British and the Government of National Unity they were totally unable to influence the decisions of the Communists.

When it became clear once again that the liberation of the country was not in sight the Communists realized that they had moved too soon. After two months of carnage in the Greek countryside EAM/ELAS expressed their willingness to make peace. By then most secondary organizations had been liquidated, while EDES had been driven into a small area in Epirus. The Communists needed time to consolidate their gains and wipe out the impressions generated in the public mind by their perfidy and by the open denunciation of their organization by the British. On 19 December 1943 they asked the Allied Military

---

[7] *Dheka Khronia Agones*, p. 209.

Mission, which after the arrival of the Americans in September had replaced the BMM, to mediate in negotiating a new agreement with Zervas.[8]

The Tsouderos Government in Egypt decided to make an effort to assist the cause of peace and reconciliation on the Greek mainland. On 21 December Tsouderos broadcast a message to the people. In it the Premier suggested that those guilty of collaboration should be expelled from the resistance organizations, and that if the guerrillas could not make peace among themselves they should disband and go home. The first point was designed to placate EAM/ELAS. The second suggestion seemed unbelievably naïve. The Government-in-exile had no effective control over the resistance organizations. How could it even suggest that the guerrillas should lay down their arms and go home? In their comments the resistance leaders criticized those parts of the Premier's speech which seemed to be directed against their particular interests. Zervas was displeased with the apparent acceptance by Tsouderos of the Communist claim that the other organizations harboured collaborators and traitors. The Communists were infuriated—and perhaps also amused—by Tsouderos' demand that the guerrillas should either make peace with each other or disband.

Shortly afterwards Zervas made a last effort to recover the territory he had lost to ELAS during October and November. His gains were negligible; but the operation gave EAM/ELAS a pretext to launch another attack. The ELAS attack which came three weeks later was coupled with a set of proposals for a 'permanent' truce. Under these proposals each organization was to retain the position it occupied at the time of the ceasefire; Zervas was to denounce all members of EDES who were accused by ELAS of collaborating with the Germans; and negotiations were to begin at once to form a united guerrilla army. All three conditions were clearly to the advantage of ELAS; yet Zervas, hard-pressed militarily by ELAS and politically by the British, accepted them all. Aris Velouchiotis delayed the ceasefire under various pretexts until he had driven the remnants of

---

[8] At about the same time the 10th Plenum (January 1944) reiterated that 'the immediate political objective of the Party is the national liberation and a people's solution of the domestic problems along the inspired lines which were established by our Party in 1934 [6th Plenum] under the leadership of N. Zachariades' (Report by Yiannis Zevgos, in *Dheka Khronia Agones, 1935–1945,* p. 184).

EDES back to a restricted area in Epirus. The truce took effect finally on 4 February 1944.

Once the fighting between ELAS and EDES had stopped, long and tortuous negotiations began at Plaka, Epirus, with the mediation of the Allied Military Mission. The British were definitely interested in a unified guerrilla army, provided that it could be effectively controlled. For the Communists, genuine unification had little attraction. What they wanted was to absorb EDES and EKKA within the ELAS framework. All their proposals and counter-proposals during the arduous talks were shrewdly calculated to achieve this end. This time the British, who were no longer deceived by the democratic pretensions of EAM, showed no intention of fitting in with Communist designs. Next, the Communists proposed the setting up of a 'preparatory governmental committee' to negotiate with the Greek Government in Egypt to form a coalition government. This proposal, which was evidently inspired by Tito's 'provisional government', was blocked by GHQ, Middle East; they insisted that the conference at Plaka should confine itself strictly to military matters. This was, of course, an artificial limitation, since the whole dispute was political rather than military.

Once the two main Communist objectives—the monopolization of the resistance and the infiltration of the Greek Government—were blocked at the conference table, the negotiations broke up. An agreement was signed, however, which practically amounted to an indefinite continuation of the truce. This was the so-called Plaka Agreement, signed at the end of February at the Plaka bridge which spanned the Acheloos river dividing EDES from ELAS territory. The only point of seemingly practical significance was a promise by EAM/ELAS to facilitate the return of Allied troops to Greece.

This promise met with severe criticism at Communist headquarters. Those who had made it argued—and with good reason—that at any rate ELAS could not prevent the Allied forces from entering Greece; the seeming concession was nothing more than a recognition of reality. They did not know then, of course, that the British were interested in obtaining this pledge because after the Teheran Conference of the Big Three there was no prospect of large-scale operations in the Balkans. Only token forces would enter Greece at the moment of liberation.

The establishment of the PEEA

In January 1944 the 10th Plenum of the Central Committee of the KKE had resolved that 'the ruthless suppression of all enemy agents and of the puppet government, and the isolation of all those who undermine the national unity, are indispensable prerequisites for the realization of our Party's political objectives . . .'.[9] Those familiar with the Communist jargon during the Occupation can easily identify the real meaning of these words: all resistance organizations, all individuals who refused to accept Communist tutelage and be incorporated into EAM/ELAS were 'undermining the national unity' and should be suppressed 'without mercy'. This was an 'indispensable prerequisite'.

No exceptional powers of imagination or political acumen were needed to realize that the final outcome of the struggle hinged on the ability of EAM/ELAS to present the Allied authorities, upon the liberation of the country, with the choice between two alternatives: co-operation with EAM/ELAS as the only effective politico-military force in Greece, or a clash which could easily be presented to a misinformed world as a sinister plot by incorrigible 'imperialists' against the 'genuine' representatives of the Greek people. That such an interpretation was possible was amply proved by the attitude of many well-intentioned but wholly duped people in Western countries even as late as December 1944.

The KKE set out to create the 'objective circumstances' needed to confront the Allies with the choice between co-operation and open conflict. The first preoccupation of the Communist leaders was to wipe out the impressions left by the actions of EAM/ELAS in the dark months of civil strife; the second, to eliminate any remaining rivals of potential significance at the crucial moment of liberation.

In the spring of 1944 the Communist control over EAM, so carefully concealed for almost two years, had been fully unmasked, and the KKE faced the danger of seeing itself isolated and the conflict transformed from the convenient context of a dispute between royalists and republicans into a struggle between all patriotic Greeks, on one side, and Communists trying to impose their rule by force or subversion on the other.

[9] *Dheka Khronia Agones*, p. 209.

N

Hitherto, the KKE had successfully used EAM as a device to gain wide support from the rank-and-file of the nation for generally acceptable nationalistic and progressive ideas. The wartime need for secrecy ruled out the disclosure of the names of those in the highest councils of the organization. For this reason, the fact that the Central Committee of EAM was made up largely of Communists and political nonentities made little difference. But in the spring of 1944 the KKE needed reputable names, people from the leading national circles, the professional groups, the younger generation of republican politicians, if it was to restore the movement's tarnished prestige.

At about the same time several well-known individuals of the republican persuasion felt that EAM/ELAS, with its augmented strength, should not be left under the exclusive control of the Communists. Professor Alexandros Svolos, a highly-respected authority on constitutional law, was one of those who believed that if there were patriotic liberals and social-democrats in the leading posts of the movement they could exercise a restraining influence and avert Communist-inspired revolutionary adventures. His hopes and fears were shared by several other prominent people, among them General Mantakas, one of the leaders of the 1938 revolt against the Metaxas dictatorship, Angelos Angelopoulos, another university professor and a well-known politician, Dimitrios Stratis, a Socialist, and General Euripides Bakirtzis, who became one of the leaders of EKKA on his return from the Middle East in September 1943 on the aircraft that carried the resistance representatives back to the mountains. To the invitations to co-operation addressed to Greek politicians by the KKE and EAM[10] in December 1943, these well-meaning individuals answered that their co-operation depended on the early termination of ELAS attacks on other guerrilla organizations. Another tacit condition was that such co-operation should begin shortly before the liberation of the country. It appears that in their view the truce and the signing of the Plaka Agreement answered the first requirement—and had about the same effect as the 'National Bands Agreement', which had brought several democratic individuals to the ranks of EAM/ELAS the previous summer. The information that the Allied authorities envisaged the liberation of the country in

[10] G. Papandreou, *I Apeleutherosis tis Ellados* (Athens, Elliniki Ekthotiki Etairia, 1945), pp. 13–23.

April satisfactorily fulfilled their second condition. There was another consideration behind their decision to co-operate with the Communists. They hoped that they could somehow split the 'moderate' Communists from the 'extremists'. There was, after all, unmistakable evidence of two factions among the Communist leaders. But this proved to be wishful thinking. They apparently did not know that the 10th Plenum of the Central Committee of the KKE had stated bluntly and unanimously in January 1944 that 'the political objectives of the Party still follow the same long-range political line which was drawn up by our Party under the leadership of N. Zachariades since 1935'.[11] What they mistook for two warring factions were two groups with different roles, amicably pursuing the objectives outlined by their imprisoned leader almost a decade earlier.

On 26 March 1944 a broadcast from the Greek mountains announced that a Political Committee of National Liberation (known by its Greek initials as the PEEA) had been established there with General Bakirtzis as its temporary chairman till the arrival of Svolos from Athens. It was apparently similar to the 'preparatory governmental committee' proposed by EAM/ ELAS at the Plaka talks and rejected by the British, except that this committee had a more imposing title and was formed without the participation of EDES or EKKA. Bakirtzis, till then associated with EKKA, was immediately repudiated by his organization.

The KKE had once again succeeded in forming a front-organization. It was more than that. Obviously imitating Tito's provisional government, the KKE had created its own governmental agency as a challenge to the authority of the Greek Government in Cairo. The time for this operation appeared to be well chosen; and good timing was of the essence. For entirely different reasons, the Communists agreed with the republican personalities that their co-operation should become effective shortly before the liberation, so that the maximum psychological benefit could be derived from their presence in the leadership of the movement. It seems that the decision on this and the other important moves in the spring of 1944 was influenced by a confidential order sent by SOE to the Allied Military Mission on the Greek mountains. That order, which became known to the

[11] *Dheka Khronia Agones*, p. 184.

Communist leaders shortly before the end of February, implied that the liberation of Greece could be expected before May and that only a small Allied force would accompany the Greek armed forces returning to their homeland. This confidential order was not the KKE's only guide in calculating the probable date of the German withdrawal. April was a most likely time; it was the first month after the winter in which the Germans could carry out large-scale movements of troops and concentrate them in a more compact front for the defence of Central Europe from the advancing Red Army. The Red Army had already reached the borders of Rumania. A mere glance at the map could convince even armchair strategists that a Soviet thrust westward would cut off all German forces in the Balkans. The puppet régimes in the area were tottering. Pavelitch in Zagreb and Neditch in Belgrade had both handed in their resignations and were both forced by the Germans to stay in office; Bozhilov in Sofia had received a letter signed by Georgiev and Bagrianov, warning the Bulgarian Premier to change his policies while there was still time. As April thus appeared to be the most probable time for the German withdrawal and the return of the Allies, the Communists acted in March. The establishment of the PEEA was the curtain-raiser.

The mutiny in the Middle East

The Communist strategists had many reasons for self-congratulation. Politically, they had set up a governmental agency strengthened by the presence of many democratic personalities under the chairmanship of Professor Svolos. Although the Communists were in a distinct minority, the PEEA was for them a valuable instrument, most effective abroad where lack of information led to faulty judgement. Militarily, they now controlled the greater part of the Greek countryside. EDES was no longer a dangerous rival; cornered in a small area in Epirus, far away from all important cities and all major lines of transport and communication, it was virtually isolated. EKKA still controlled an area in Roumeli, close to the Athens–Salonika highway, but it could easily be wiped out at the right moment. ELAS had little influence in Crete and in Western Thrace, but both were outlying regions of marginal significance in the approaching showdown. In the major towns the Security Battalions, which could have presented an obstacle at the moment of transition, were severely compromised by their association with the occupation authorities.

In the eyes of the Communist strategists the only serious challenge could come from the British and the Greek armed forces in the Middle East. The importance of these forces became even greater when the Communists learned in late February that only token Allied troops were to accompany the Greek Government.[12] Zachariades, referring to these Greek forces, said at the Seventh Party Congress in October 1945 that 'their organization was broadly popular, purely democratic in its political and mass context'. In simpler language this meant that EAM had infiltrated into these forces to such an extent that they could be considered as friendly to the Communists. Zachariades expressed this view in 1945. Similar views were voiced at the Communist headquarters in the spring of 1944. There was some ground for such an assessment. However, some Communist leaders argued that this evaluation was over-optimistic. They pointed out, too, that it would be immeasurably safer for the Communist Party if there were no such forces at all to accompany the returning Greek Government. Soldiers were known to have obeyed orders running counter to their own political beliefs. They reminded their colleagues that the mutiny of March 1943 was intended not so much to change the complexion of those forces as to remove them from the scene at a time when everyone thought the liberation of the country was near. True, some units of the First Brigade had large numbers of Communists and sympathizers in their ranks, sometimes as many as 70 per cent. of their total strength. The Brigade had a secret three-member committee made up of one captain and two soldiers, with one of the two soldiers as its chairman. The Second Brigade was even more infested with EAM agents and other 'democratic elements'. Yet, with power within their grasp, the Communists could not take any chances. After all, the Greek Government under Tsouderos was the legitimate Government, and if the support extended to King George by Churchill and Roosevelt the previous autumn was any indication of Allied sentiments, only incurable optimists could expect anything but the triumphant return of the King and his Government with the blessings of the Allies. The view which

[12] Myers, op. cit., p. 259; also Woodhouse, op. cit., p. 185; also author's conversation with Orestis.

had prevailed the year before prevailed once again. It would be safer not to have any rival Greek forces from the Middle East to cope with.

On 9 March Brigadier F. Beaumont-Nesbitt, chief liaison officer with the Allied armies, informed the Greek General Staff that increased activity by persons involved in the mutiny of the previous year had been reported to the GHQ, Middle East. He warned the Greek authorities that a repetition of the events of that time would be disastrous. To this, the Greek Minister of the Army, V. Karapanayiotis, replied that all fears were without foundation and that discipline was assured in the Greek units of the Middle East.[13] Shortly afterwards the First Brigade was moved from the vicinity of Tel Aviv to Bourk-el-Arem, a few miles south of Alexandria, to receive supplies and equipment before leaving for the Italian theatre of war. The implication was clear. From Italy the Brigade would most probably land in Epirus in the area controlled by Zervas and then fan out towards Athens and Salonika.

The Communists decided to move swiftly. Yet it is extremely important to understand that all the machinations of the extreme left would have come to nought had it not been for the gullibility of many republican politicians and officers and, to a minor degree, the shortsightedness of some pro-royalist officers who obstinately refused to co-operate with the Government after the events of February–March 1943.

On the morning of 31 March 1944 a group of officers purporting to represent a 'Committee of National Unity of the Greek Armed Forces' visited the Premier and handed him a 'memorandum' in which they demanded the establishment of a new government 'based on the Political Committee of National Liberation (PEEA)'.[14] Most of these officers were not even Communist sympathizers. They were so immersed, however, in the atmosphere of political intrigue and so blinded by their republicanism that they played the Communist game with an effectiveness that by far surpassed the most optimistic Communist expectations.

Tsouderos, instead of placing them immediately under arrest for mutiny in time of war, accepted their memorandum and discussed it with the other Ministers in Council. To force the hand of the Government, mutinies broke out in several military

[13] Tsouderos, op. cit., pp. 125–7.   [14] Ibid., p. 132.

units, with soldiers' committees taking over command. The rebels declared allegiance to the PEEA and refused to obey the orders of their superior officers. Soon the revolt spread to the First Brigade and to the Greek naval units stationed in the port of Alexandria. The Second Brigade declared its loyalty to the PEEA. On 2 April Sophocles Venizelos, the son of the Cretan statesman, who was Minister of Merchant Marine in the Tsouderos Cabinet, spoke of the necessity of reaching a political understanding with 'the mountains'. In a hastily convened Council of the Cabinet at the house of Admiral Voulgaris, Venizelos asked Tsouderos to resign and, supported by some Cabinet members, suggested that he himself should replace Tsouderos in the premiership. The next day Tsouderos submitted his resignation to the King, who was in London, and suggested to the sovereign that Sophocles Venizelos should be given the mandate to form a new government. At the same time it became known that the PEEA and Tito's Committee of National Liberation had agreed to exchange representatives.

On 6 April a committee of naval officers visited the Ministry of Foreign Affairs and told the ministers who assembled there that the 'democratic elements' in the armed forces did not like the idea of having Venizelos as the new Premier and demanded a broad coalition government based on EAM and the PEEA. While the Ministers were discussing these new proposals a report came in that the crew of one of the naval units had arrested their officers and thrown them overboard. The entire structure of the Greek Government in the Middle East, the only remaining serious challenge to the Communists in Greece, was rapidly collapsing in an avalanche of blunders committed by otherwise patriotic Greeks.

Venizelos was sworn in as Premier on 13 April by the King, who had flown in from London on the 10th. This did not put an end to the mutiny. In the Navy, the Air Force, the Second Brigade, and the First Brigade, which was scheduled to leave for Italy on the 12th, the mutineers ruled with their soldiers' committees.

The British, under the impact of these events, felt that there was only one way out of the crisis: to have a government of 'national unity' with 'the mountains' taking part. With this in mind they proposed that representatives of EDES, EAM/ELAS, and EKKA come to Cairo. In Greece the AMM called a conference of guerrilla representatives at Koutsaina in West Thessaly. The conference was to convene on 17 April. On the 14th Siantos is said to have dispatched the following message to Despotopoulos:

14.4.44. Urgent. Dear Kosta, We have talked many times about Psaros, and I cannot understand why you ask for an order to liquidate his organization. If he does not accept our terms, then we have to clear up the situation by force and swiftly, without any delays. On this point, I draw your attention to the fact that you must take the necessary military steps for such a case; you must give an order, i.e., free the hands of Rizos, to clear up the situation as soon as Psaros rejects our terms or even one of them. . . . Sgd. Geros.

Geros' was the underground pseudonym of G. Siantos. This document is said to have been captured later during the December revolution. Its authenticity has been disputed by the Communists, but whether it was genuine or not makes little difference. During the night of 16–17 April Psaros' force was attacked by the Fifth Brigade of ELAS. It was outnumbered and broken up; Psaros himself was captured. On his way to the ELAS headquarters he was met by Major Euthimios Zoulas, a Communist of long standing, with whom he had an old personal quarrel. On seeing Psaros, Major Zoulas brought up the old dispute and began to threaten and vilify him, working himself up into a rage. When Psaros calmly reminded him that now was his chance to settle the old account, Zoulas drew his pistol and shot Psaros. This brutal murder was probably not officially planned. But after it the conference at Koutsaina, which was expected to complete the Plaka Agreement and define the boundaries of ELAS, EDES, and EKKA territories, served no purpose.

In Egypt Venizelos' efforts to put an end to the mutiny failed, and in the end the British authorities had to step in and disarm the mutineers. In the First Brigade the leaders of the mutiny destroyed all the new equipment that had been given 'to the Brigade in anticipation of its departure for the front.[15] The mutiny in the Navy was finally put down by Greek units under the command of Admiral Voulgaris. The Second Brigade was easily disarmed and broken up. In the opinion of some knowledgeable participants this demise of the Greek forces was wel-

---

[15] Thrasyvoulos I. Tsakalotos, *40 Khronia Stratiotis tis Ellados* (Athens, Akropolis 1960), Vol. I, p. 422; also p. 432.

comed, if not instigated, by the British, who were justifiably concerned at the infiltration of these forces by the Communists. In any event, by 23 April 1944, the Greek armed forces in the Middle East were a thing of the past. The end of April found EAM/ELAS almost without rivals—but not quite.

The jubilation of the Communist leaders proved premature. The whole Communist strategy had been based on the assumption that the country was to be liberated by the end of April or the beginning of May at the latest. To their discomfiture, the evacuation of Greece did not take place until the following October.

After his return to Greece, in 1945, Zachariades denounced the mutiny as having served what were, 'objectively speaking, anti-democratic aims', while he claimed that 'foreign forces played a decisive role in the outbreak of the mutiny and also its method and timing'. He implied, in other words, that the British had deliberately instigated the mutiny in order to break up the 'democratic forces'. If this is what really happened, then the Communists had unwittingly played the British game. For the mutiny was in fact planned and instigated by the Communists as part of their overall strategy for monopolizing power. It had been timed to coincide with the moment of liberation, and as the liberation did not take place in April, the plan misfired. Its outcome really depended on who had the best information.

[16] *Rizospastis*, 3 October 1945.

14. The 'Bloodless' Liberation

The Lebanon Agreement

The mutiny had a catalytic effect on the thinking of those who directed the affairs of the Greek nation, whether publicly or behind the scenes. A fresh start was needed, without illusions, without self-deception. Sophocles Venizelos was replaced in the premiership by a newcomer to the Middle East, a veteran Liberal political leader, George Papandreou, a man of tremendous political skill, determination, and foresight. The new Premier was faced with a disheartening task. The Greek Government had lost its military arm in the Middle East, while in Greece EAM/ELAS was now, for all practical purposes, the only political and military force of any significance. In the circumstances there was a very real danger that the PEEA might proclaim itself the only Government representing the Greek nation and deny the King and his Government the right to return to Greece after the liberation of the country. Should this happen, open British intervention in support of the 'lawfully constituted Greek Government' could be denounced by a mis-informed Western public opinion as an 'imperialist' action against the independence of an Allied nation. Whatever time remained till the liberation should, then, be used to establish some form of control over the Communist-led camp, to guarantee the peaceful return of the legitimate Government to Greece. The suggestion first made by the British and Tsouderos during the mutiny was revived and representatives of the political parties, the resistance organization, and the PEEA were invited to Egypt.

At the conference which opened in the Lebanon on 17 May 1944, under the chairmanship of Papandreou, there were twenty-five individuals representing seventeen political parties and resistance organizations. The PEEA was represented by Alexandros Svolos, Angelos Angelopoulos, and Nikolaos Askoutsis; EAM by Miltiades Porphyrogennis and Dimitrios Stratis; ELAS by General S. Saraphis; the KKE by Petros Roussos. Of the twenty-five delegates only two, Porphyrogennis

and Roussos, were Communists. Svolos thought of himself as a
mediator between 'right' and 'left', and as an architect of the
much-needed national unity. His was a thankless task, because
the Communists had not given up their 'ultimate objectives'.
As Vassilis Bartzotas, the Communist leader, revealed in 1950,
'the First Army Corps of ELAS had worked out a plan of
operations for the seizure of power in the autumn of 1943 and
again in the spring of 1944'.[1] Both times the plan had failed only
because the occupation troops did not leave when the Communists expected them to.

Even before the departure of the PEEA, EAM/ELAS, and
KKE delegates for the Middle East, some Communists had
voiced misgivings. What was the sense, they asked, of participating in a conference which, if successful, would only restrict
the power of their movement and give a new lease of life to the
'bourgeois politicians'? Yet this time the Communists were
caught in their own web. To refuse to take part in the conference would put an early end to the PEEA and leave the party
completely isolated.

Those Communists who had expressed doubts were soon
justified. At the Lebanon Conference the Communists, for the
first time since the beginning of the war, came face to face with
a solid front of opposition. Even the non-Communist members
of the PEEA delegation were more concerned with unity and
accommodation than with the promotion of the Communist
objectives. In the person of George Papandreou, the representatives of the extreme left met a skilful, determined, and resourceful opponent. Karayiorgis, the Communist leader, referring
later to the Lebanon Conference in a 'personal note' he sent to
Zachariades on 18 March 1948, condemned both the participation of the Communists in the conference and the agreement
which was reached there. He termed them 'a terrible tactical
mistake, one of the most stupid actions in the history of our
party'. He added: 'If our representatives had left the Lebanon
nothing could have changed for the worse. On the contrary, we
would not have been thrown so stupidly into Papandreou's bag,
hanging from Svolos' coat-tails.'[2] This was a fairly accurate
description of what took place at the Lebanon Conference.

What is known as the Lebanon Agreement was signed on 20
May 1944 by all the delegates, including the Communists. The

---

[1] Bartzotas, *Politiki Stelekhon*, p. 49. [2] Ibid.

most important points called for in it were: (1) the reorganization of the Greek armed forces in the Middle East; (2) the unification of all guerrilla forces under the command of the Greek Government of National Unity; (3) the establishment of conditions of liberty and order after the liberation, so that the Greek people could have a free choice of political and social régime; (4) the immediate end of terrorism; (5) the dispatch of food and pharmaceutical supplies to Greece.

The Communist headquarters in the Greek mountains received the news of the agreement with mixed feelings. Some leaders argued that it opened up the way for the infiltration of the Greek Government by the KKE. In the proposed Government of National Unity, they maintained, the Communists would have the only real levers of power in their hands, since there was no longer an army loyal to the 'reactionary circles', while ELAS, in Greece, was stronger than ever. Others—and those included some of the most powerful figures in the Communist camp—voiced the opinion that by subscribing to Papandreou's programme, the Communist representatives at the conference had made unnecessary concessions to the 'reactionaries'. Again, the British factor loomed large in the background. As these Communist leaders pointed out, the 'reactionary' members of the anticipated Government of National Unity would not be as powerless as the other group suggested. General Constantine Ventiris, a tough professional soldier, had already been placed at the head of the Greek General Staff in Cairo and was busy—they argued—clearing the ground for the reconstruction of the Greek armed forces with the loyal remnants of the two dissolved Brigades.[3] Even without Greek forces at its disposal, the Greek Government 'could draw on the might of the British Empire'. Besides, the Communist members of the Government of National Unity, being in the minority, would have 'their hands tied behind their backs', and could be forced into disadvantageous and compromising positions. In their view the 'surrender' of the Communist representatives in the Lebanon should serve as a warning.

Soon there were unmistakable signs that the PEEA delegates, under evident pressure from 'the mountains', had no intention of accepting the five ministerial posts reserved for their group in the new Government of National Unity which was formed on

[3] Tsakalotos, op. cit., pp. 483–501.

24 May 1944 under the premiership of George Papandreou. To a letter by Papandreou dated 4 June, Svolos, Porphyrogennis, and Roussos, on behalf of the PEEA, EAM, and the KKE respectively, replied that 'the necessary discussions [with 'the mountains'] have not as yet reached the conclusion we all desire', and that they had to wait 'hopefully'.[4] Finally, General Saraphis and, a few days later, Porphyrogennis decided to return to Greece, presumably to speed up 'the necessary discussions'. When they reached 'the mountains' they found a hardened mood at the ELAS headquarters.

The British–Soviet Agreement on the Balkans

The British, well aware that they could extend only limited armed support to the 'lawfully constituted Greek Government' should the Communists repudiate the Lebanon Agreement, made serious efforts to reach a broader understanding with the Soviet Government. On 30 May 1944 Lord Halifax, then British Ambassador to Washington, handed a communication to Secretary of State Cordell Hull, inquiring whether the United States had any objection to an understanding between the Soviet Government and the United Kingdom whereby Rumanian affairs would be dealt with by the Russians and Greek affairs by the British. A few days earlier the Soviet Government had agreed to such a proposal in principle, provided the United States raised no objection.

Cordell Hull, who was 'flatly opposed to any division of Europe or sections of Europe into spheres of influence',[5] rejected the British suggestion. Finally, after an exchange of communications between Churchill and Roosevelt, the American President by-passed the State Department and personally approved the proposed agreement 'on a three-month trial basis'. In the meantime the British–Soviet understanding had been expanded to include Bulgaria in the area under Soviet responsibility, with Yugoslavia under combined Soviet–British influence.[6]

This preliminary understanding with the Soviets had no immediate effect on the attitude of the Greek Communists; for one thing, they were completely unaware that their cherished

[4] Papandreou, op. cit., p. 73.
[5] Cordell Hull, *Memoirs* (New York, Macmillan, 1948), p. 1452.
[6] See more details in Kousoulas, *The Price of Freedom*, pp. 108–9.

'fatherland' had abandoned them. Disregarding the signing of the Lebanon Agreement by their own representatives, they continued to obstruct the completion of the Government of National Unity by refusing to accept the ministerial posts offered to them. On 6 July 1944 Premier Papandreou announced to the Cabinet that the Communists had presented new demands in two telegrams, one signed by Saraphis and Porphyrogennis, the military and the political chiefs of ELAS respectively, and the other by the PEEA. In these telegrams they demanded that 'the present organization of ELAS be continued until the liberation', this obviously implying the retention of the political commissars and the other elements of Communist control over ELAS. They further demanded that 'the Supreme Commander of all the guerrillas be an ELAS senior officer', that 'out of fifteen ministerial posts, the Ministries of the Interior, Justice, Education, Agriculture, Labour, and Public Welfare and the Under-Secretaryship of the Army be given to the PEEA', and that 'a branch of the Government be sent immediately to Free Greece'.[7] It was clear that the heads of the ministries claimed by the PEEA should, because of their functions, be among the first to leave for 'Free Greece'. Papandreou rejected the Communist terms without hesitation and declared that if these terms were accepted the subjugation of Greece by EAM would become a real possibility. He was merely stating a fact: with ELAS already the only significant military force in Greece, the KKE could easily establish effective control over the country should the Communist-controlled ministers set up a seemingly legitimate administration in Greece.

Papandreou received full support from the British. On 27 July and 2 August 1944 Eden and Churchill respectively blasted EAM for bearing 'the responsibility for the failure to bring about unity in Greek politics at this ultimate moment of the common struggle'.[8] Even this open denunciation might have been totally ineffectual had it not been for the Soviet instructions finally relayed to the KKE.

Up to this time the KKE kept in touch with Moscow through Tito's headquarters in Yugoslavia. In the summer of 1943, after the dissolution of the Comintern, several leading European

---

[7] Kousoulas, op. cit., pp. 112–13.

[8] See full text in *British Speeches of the Day* (New York, British Information Services), September 1944, Vol. II, No. 9, p. 14.

Communists who had been living in the Soviet Union were sent back to their native countries. Dimitrios Sakarelos was sent to Greece. Originally a school-teacher in the village of Krokylion in Central Greece, he had escaped in 1934 from the Aegina prison, where he was serving a sentence for the murder of a Marxist opponent of the KKE named Georgopapadatos. After his escape Sakarelos was sent to the Soviet Union, where he completed his political education. He fought in the Spanish Civil War and later became a member of the Western European Bureau of the Comintern in France. He left France with Maurice Thorez and stayed in the Soviet Union until the summer of 1943, when he was dispatched to Greece to establish direct contact between Moscow and the KKE. He never reached Greece. According to some reports, his plane crashed while trying to land at a small air-strip in Yugoslavia. Sakarelos and his pilot were killed. As a result, the KKE continued to communicate with the USSR through Tito's headquarters. But in the summer of 1944 Moscow again felt it necessary to establish direct contact with the KKE. On 25 July 1944 a Russian aeroplane took off from an Allied base in Italy on a flight authorized for training purposes. During the night it flew to Yugoslavia, landed near Tito's GHQ, picked up ten members of the Soviet military mission, and took them to Greece. Two of them parachuted into Macedonia; the plane landed with the rest on the mountain air-strip in Neraida, Thessaly. On the morning of the 26th the Russians, under Colonel Gregory Popov, reached the ELAS headquarters. Up to this moment the Allied Mission in Greece knew nothing of this operation.

Popov's instructions to the Communist leaders had an immediate and decisive effect. Colonel Woodhouse, who was with the Greek guerrillas at the time, described the change in these words:

As if by a magic wand, the angry, anxious, bewildered obstinacy of the early summer was translated into good will. Almost for the first time PEEA was really unanimous. The anger of the apostles of direct action, the anxiety of the apostles of political infiltration, the bewilderment of the apostles of conciliation, melted back into harmony.[9]

Similar instructions were given by the First Counsellor of the Soviet Embassy to the EAM representatives in Cairo. As a

[9] Woodhouse, op. cit., p. 199.

result, on 2 August 1944 the EAM/ELAS leaders retracted their
previous demands and agreed to take up their Cabinet posts.
They only asked that Papandreou be removed from the
premiership. Apparently they had been alarmed by his successful handling of Greek affairs and, particularly, by his effective
methods of exposing the Communist objectives to Greek public
opinion.

The other members of the Cabinet rejected this last Communist demand. So did the British. Finally, without pressing the
point further, six representatives of EAM were sworn in as
members of the Greek Government of National Unity on 2
September 1944. However, reliable reports from Greece
pointed out that 'EAM terrorism in the capital continued to
increase', that 'the people were afraid of ruthless massacres', and
that 'the leaders of EAM had made it clear that they were
determined to occupy Athens immediately after the departure
of the Germans'.[10] These alarming reports were not unfounded.
As V. Bartzotas—the secretary of the KOA—revealed in 1952,
'the KOA [Communist Organization of Athens] dealt, in early
August, with the practical aspects of seizing power; we transferred all the party *apparatchiki* to ELAS; and the EP of the
KOA [the Town Committee of KOA] decided on armed
insurrection in two meetings at the beginning of September'.[11]
In other words, while the KK, Ein conformity with Popov's
instructions, was joining the Government of National Unity, the
Communist organization of the Greek capital was planning to
seize power by force.

One of the major provisions of the Lebanon Agreement was
that all guerrilla organizations should come under the command
of the Government of National Unity. Now that this Government had become a reality, Papandreou made a further effort
to bring ELAS under government control. On 26 September he
summoned General Zervas, Chief of EDES, and General
Saraphis, the military head of ELAS, to Caserta, in Italy. The
Communist representatives who accompanied General Saraphis
tried to limit the commitments of ELAS, but finally they
accepted all the terms. Under the provisions of the agreement
which was signed on the 26th by the guerrilla representatives, as
well as by G. Papandreou, General Maitland Wilson, and Mr.
Harold Macmillan, the then British Resident Minister, all

[10] Papandreou, op. cit., p. 121.   [11] Bartzotas, op. cit., p. 48.

guerrilla forces were placed under the command of the Greek Government, which in turn transferred this authority to the British officer commanding the Allied Forces for the liberation of Greece. Lieutenant-General R. M. Scobie had been appointed to this post, with an American Brigadier-General as his second-in-command.

Karayiorgis was right when he called the Caserta Agreement the 'military Lebanon' of the KKE.[12] The Communists had taken a second big step on the road to 'co-operation'. Although Yiannis Zevgos,[13] the Communist representative at Caserta, is usually blamed for this 'mistake', there is little doubt that the Caserta Agreement was in accord with the instructions brought to the KKE by Popov. But of course it would be highly irreverent to accuse the Soviet Union of making a 'mistake'.

In spite of the agreements Papandreou knew well that only the presence of considerable Allied forces in Greece could provide an effective barrier to a Communist attempt to seize power at the crucial moment of liberation. On 8 October 1944 he met Churchill and Eden, as they stopped in Italy on their way to Moscow. He emphasized that only the presence of British forces in Greece and the early formation of a national Greek Army based on general conscription would enable the Government to withstand Communist pressure. The two British leaders, having in mind their impending formal understanding with the Soviet Government on the division of responsibility in the Balkans, assured Papandreou that the whole matter would be settled in the near future. A few days later, during their stay in Moscow, the original understanding of the previous May was broadened and put into an unusually precise form. Churchill, we are told, wrote on a piece of paper the percentages of the respective responsibilities of Britain and the USSR in the Danubian–Balkan region. Stalin merely wrote on the paper a mark of approval. According to the agreement, the Soviet Union would have a 75 per cent. predominance in Bulgaria, Hungary, and Rumania; Britain would have a 100 per cent. predominance in Greece, while the two Powers would share equal responsibilities in Yugoslavia.

This agreement, at least on the part of the British, was in fact a realistic recognition of the existing situation. On 30 August

---

[12] Personal note to Zachariades, dated 18 March 1948.
[13] Zevgos was assassinated by a Communist in Salonika in 1947.

the Red Army had captured Ploesti; they entered Bucharest the
next day. The same day, Bagrianov, the Premier of Bulgaria,
resigned and was replaced by Muraviev, who severed relations
with Germany. By 5 September the Germans were evacuating
Bulgaria, while the Soviet Union was declaring war on that
country. Within twenty-four hours Muraviev asked for an
armistice. The next day the Red Army reached the Danube at
Kladovo, and two days later it crossed the Yugoslav frontier.
Muraviev declared war on Germany and resigned on the 8th;
he was succeeded by a government of the pro-Communist
'Fatherland Front' under Kimon Georgiev. The Red Army was
welcomed tumultuously in Sofia, just as the Wehrmacht had
been three years earlier. In other words, by the time of the
signing of the Soviet–British agreement the Red Army had
already gained effective control over the areas 'assigned' to the
Soviet Union.

The Soviet–British agreement meant that the KKE's ambitious plans for seizure of power would be shelved—at least
temporarily. In the post-war years the Greek Communists have
never mentioned this agreement; to do so would involve an
outright accusation that their 'Socialist Fatherland' had sold
them down the river for the sake of its own broader objectives
at the time. Instead, they blamed Siantos and the party leadership of that period. Here is a characteristic—and revealing—
passage from Bartzotas' report to the Third Party Conference of
October 1950:

On October 12, 1944 we could easily have seized power with the
forces of the First Army Corps of ELAS alone (that is, the 20,000
Elasites of Athens and Piraeus). We did not seize power because we
did not have a correct line, because we all vacillated, including me.
. . . Thus, although we had decided on armed insurrection, beginning in September 1944, instead of going ahead, instead of organizing the struggle for power, instead of seizing power, we capitulated
and kept order![14]

In other words, the Communists co-operated in the 'bloodless
liberation' in spite of themselves. Admittedly, their best opportunity for seizing absolute power in Athens was during the
few days in mid-October when the Germans were evacuating
Greece and only token British units had appeared in the streets
of Athens. For two years they had planned every move with one

[14] Bartzotas, op. cit., p. 49.

ultimate objective: to exploit this 'weak point' of the transition and 'seize power'. Yet, when the crucial moment came, they 'kept order' and welcomed 'the brave children of Great Britain, our freedom-loving Ally'.[15] Only the British–Soviet agreement can account for this radical change.

On 18 October 1944 the Greek Government of National Unity arrived in Athens. Hundreds of thousands of people, from all walks of life, had gathered on the beaches, on the rooftops, along the streets, wherever they could see and cheer the Government of National Unity. The nightmare of slavery was over; even more important, the threat of a Communist *coup*, which had for days darkened the anticipation of the approaching liberation, seemed to have been finally averted. In accord with the general spirit, the Politbureau of the Central Committee officially praised Bartzotas for keeping 'exemplary order in Athens'[16]—a commendation which Bartzotas considered later as 'a badge of shame'.

The 'sudden and inexplicable' decision to revolt

It seems that very few people knew about the British–Soviet understanding. Orestis, the *Kapetanios* of the II Division of ELAS, which had the primary responsibility for military operations in Athens during the December Revolution, told me that he learned about the agreement for the first time when he read the Greek edition of my book *The Price of Freedom* in 1955. George Siantos must have been among the very few, if not the only one, who knew about it. Zachariades wrote later in his book *Provlimata Kathothigisis* (Problems of Leadership):

The strategy of the KKE's leadership during that period was the strategy of Siantos, that is, the strategy of capitulation to the English, the strategy which did not serve or speed up the victory of the people's revolution in Greece, the strategy which delayed and finally shattered the revolution, the strategy which promoted the plans of the British, the restoration of the bourgeois-feudal power, the return to the régime of foreign dependence.[17]

Though Siantos implemented the policy of co-operation with the British which had been ordered by the Kremlin almost single-handed, he was not the originator, and could hardly

---

[15] Decision of the Politbureau of the C.C. of the KKE, dated 17 October 1944.
[16] *Dheka Khronia Agones*, p. 230.
[17] Zachariades, *Provlimata Kathothigisis*, p. 80.

be blamed for this 'strategy of capitulation to the British'. In fact, Zachariades should rather have blamed the Soviet Government for the fact that

in the extremely advantageous conditions of the Second World War, the leadership of the KKE went astray from the line of the 6th Plenum (1934), in spite of the fact that the Party gathered under its banner for the struggle against the Conqueror the great majority of the people. . . . While fighting the Hitlero-Fascist Conqueror, we should have been prepared to direct our basic blow against the British who pretended to be the 'saviours' of Greece; we should have prepared at the same time, politically, militarily, and organizationally, the people's revolutionary forces for the inevitable conflict with British imperialism.[18]

It is only fair to acknowledge that the KKE's leadership during the Occupation had done just that; only, at the last moment, superior orders from Moscow had forced the party to adopt this policy of 'capitulation' to the British. Therefore one cannot agree with Zachariades that 'all the evidence leads to the conclusion that, because of the inefficiency of the party's political and military leadership during the *first armed struggle* of the Greek people *for power*',[19] the party had failed 'to exploit the extremely advantageous conditions created in Greece by the smashing of Hitlerism by the Soviet Army'.[20] Zachariades was merely searching for scapegoats in order to avoid mentioning the true culprit for the party's 'capitulation' to the British.

This period of 'capitulation' lasted until the night of 27–28 November 1944. On that night Siantos and Ioannides—the 'moderate' and the 'aggressive'—decided to give the signal for revolution. What prompted this decision?

Ever since the return of the Government of National Unity to Athens Papandreou's main preoccupation had been the disarming of ELAS and the organization of a National Army based on general conscription. He realized that as long as ELAS maintained its strength and organization, no effort of the Greek Government to extend its effective control beyond the area of the capital could succeed. In fact, EAM had established its own

---

[18] Zachariades, *Provlimata Kathothigisis*, p. 79.

[19] This was an interesting admission by Zachariades himself; in the past the standard contention was that the 'heroic people of Athens had taken up arms to defend themselves against the Greek bourgeoisie and the British interventionists' (author's italics).

[20] Zachariades, *Provlimata Kathothigisis*.

authority—*de facto* if not *de jure*—over the larger part of the
country.

On the other hand, the KKE leadership was well aware that,
however strong the EAM following might have been, the disarmament of ELAS would leave the Communists in a political
minority—a poor substitute for the absolute power they had
been seeking. During the six weeks between the liberation and
the outbreak of revolution the KKE's main concern was to
minimize the impact of ELAS' disarmament. For weeks plans
were proposed and withdrawn daily. Finally, Papandreou
invited the PEEA ministers to draft in any form they wished the
decree for the demobilization of the guerrilla forces. In the
afternoon of 27 November, Alexandros Svolos, Elias Tsirimokos,
and Yiannis Zevgos visited the Premier at his home and
handed in the requested draft. It was the product of long, stren-
uous efforts on the part of all those who were striving to find a
generally acceptable solution. Under the terms of the proposed
decree the guerrilla forces of EDES and ELAS, as well as the
Greek military units in the Middle East, were to demobilize on
10 December 1944; a National Army was to be organized in
which the Mountain Brigade, the Sacred Battalion,[21] an EDES
unit, and an ELAS Brigade were to be incorporated; the ELAS
Brigade was to equal in men and armaments the combined
force of the other three units. Papandreou immediately
accepted the draft and, before the left-wing ministers departed,
he drafted two directives, one from the Premier to the Minister
of War—who incidentally was a member of EAM—to take the
necessary steps so that 'the ELAS Brigade, which shall be
formed after the demobilization of the guerrilla forces, will have
power equal to the combined forces of the Mountain Brigade,
the Sacred Battalion, and EDES'. The second directive, from
the Minister of War to the GHQ of the Greek Armed Forces,
read as follows:

Two Brigades are formed. The first shall be composed of the III
Mountain Brigade, the Sacred Battalion, and a military unit of

---

[21] The III Mountain Brigade under Gen. Th. Tsakalotos had been formed by
the Papandreou Government in the Middle East, after the mutiny, from the
remnants of the Greek armed forces. It was considered by the Communists as one
of the mainstays of 'reaction'. The Brigade was also known as the Rimini Brigade
because of its victory at the Battle of Rimini, in Italy. The Sacred Battalion was a
special military unit composed of army officers.

EDES. The second Brigade, which shall bear the name ELAS, shall be formed of units from the military organization ELAS, and shall have equal power to that of the first Brigade.[22]

The next day Papandreou announced to the press that the agreement had been approved by the other members of the Cabinet, and that he was confident that it would be signed by them within the day. It seemed like reaching a safe harbour after a long journey through rough and dangerous seas.

Papandreou's announcement proved to be premature. When Zevgos came back from the Premier's residence in the evening of 27 November and announced that their draft had been enthusiastically accepted by Papandreou, Siantos left for the EAM headquarters; there he went to a quiet, secluded office on the top floor and began an article for *Rizospastis*. Suddenly he was called to the KKE headquarters; there he had a long discussion with Ioannides. Probably no one will ever learn what transpired at this fateful meeting of the two top Communist leaders; Siantos is dead, while Ioannides was denounced by Zachariades some time ago and is now somewhere behind the Iron Curtain. When Siantos returned to the EAM headquarters a few hours later he was a different man. From that moment on, Siantos and Ioannides had the same objective: the seizure of power through armed action.[23]

What had caused this 'sudden and inexplicable' change, as Svolos termed it on 29 November? As far as he knew, nothing had happened since the three PEEA ministers had received congratulations and exchanged pleasantries with the Greek Premier; nothing, at least, that could be traced to the actions of Papandreou or the British. Nor can we accept that Siantos was finally convinced by Ioannides' revolutionary arguments; similar discussions had taken place before between these two men without any dramatic results. The KKE had reversed its aggressive policies and had entered the Government of National Unity only *after* the arrival of Popov's mission to the ELAS headquarters. In the middle of October the Communists had discarded their original plans and had let pass their best opportunity of seizing the capital. This they did under instructions received by Siantos from the Soviet mission. The top Communist leaders—those who knew about them—had

---

[22] *Athinaiki*, 5 July 1955.   [23] As Orestis told the author in 1955.

accepted those instructions rather reluctantly, and, according to Orestis, they had turned to Tito for advice. They pointed out that the British forces in Greece were far less powerful than they had originally anticipated. This being so, they asked Tito whether they should try, on their own, to take the capital, since the rest of Greece, with the exception of a few areas, was already under their control, and also whether they could count on his moral support. According to Orestis, Tito's answer came on the evening of 27 November; it was affirmative on both points. It is not known whether the Greek Communist leaders sought the approval of the Soviet representatives in Greece. Orestis believes that they did and that they were given a free hand on the understanding that they should not expect open support from the Soviet Government.[24] True, there is no documentary proof available. But after all, such documents, if they exist, seldom reach the light.

The December Revolution

The next morning, 28 November, *Rizospastis* did not carry the article Siantos had been preparing just before he was called to the KKE headquarters. Instead, it had as its leading editorial an attack against Zervas, whom it called 'a mercenary'. In the afternoon Zevgos visited the Premier at his home and, discarding altogether the previous day's agreement, demanded the disarmament of the III Mountain Brigade and of the Sacred Battalion. Papandreou refused to yield and asserted that the Government would abide by what had been agreed. The conversation was stormy, and finally Zevgos left the Premier's home without even saying good-bye.

A few hours later, in the evening of 28 November, the leaders of ELD—the second largest political organization within EAM —met to review the rapidly-developing situation. Elias Tsirimokos, the Secretary of ELD, stated that the KKE's change of policy and the resulting danger of civil war made it imperative for ELD to disengage itself from EAM. It was a dramatic moment for this man who had for so long honestly sought to channel Communist objectives into a truly democratic and constructive path. His efforts had failed. The gathering unanimously agreed that Tsirimokos should resign from his post

[24] According to Orestis.

in the Government of National Unity, and should ask the other non-Communist PEEA ministers—Alexandros Svolos, Nikolaos Askoutsis, and Angelos Angelopoulos—to do the same. Hurriedly, Tsirimokos wrote out the text of the decision to be published, with its accompanying story, the next morning in ELD's newspaper *Machi*. By 12.30 a.m. the newspaper was ready for printing. The headlines spoke of a 'Communist ultimatum' to the Greek Government, and of the 'break-up' of the EAM coalition. At this crucial moment, on the eve of civil war, the KKE could not afford a 'break-up' of EAM. It must be remembered that the KKE's theme during that period was that the Greek people, 'united under the banner of EAM, were fighting for their legitimate right to decide their domestic issues for themselves'. A 'break-up' of EAM at that point would have exposed the Communist nature of the revolutionary agitation, thus depriving the Communists of the moral support they expected from misinformed Western circles. One can only speculate as to what effect the dissolution of EAM would have had on the Communists, as the 'break-up' never materialized. Shortly before the newspaper went to press Tsirimokos called Stratis Someritis, the editor of *Machi*, and ordered the replacement of the entire first page by another in which there was no mention of ELD's decision to withdraw from EAM, nor of any charges against the Communists. Tsirimokos told me that he reversed his position on the advice of Svolos, who felt that the resignation of the non-Communist PEEA ministers could only help the Communists by forcing the dissolution of the Government of National Unity.

Next morning, 29 November, the Central Committee of EAM met in extraordinary session. Siantos himself was present, but not Tsirimokos. The representative of ELD at the meeting —a secondary leader named Stavros Kanellopoulos—spoke on the basis of the previous decision of his party and asked EAM to abide by its original plan providing for the formation of two brigades, as presented to Papandreou by the EAM representatives.

Siantos, angry and excited, interrupted the speech of the ELD representative on the grounds that 'he was expressing his personal views and not the views of his party'. He assured the other members of the Central Committee of EAM that he had spoken to both Tsirimokos and Svolos, and neither of them had expressed disagreement with the KKE policies.[25] Finally, he asked for a postponement of the discussion so that Tsirimokos and Svolos could be present.

At the second conference of the Central Committee of EAM, which took place on 30 November, Siantos had the situation well under control. In this large body, composed of several organizations, there were quite a few 'moderates' who loathed the possibility of civil war and were willing to do everything in their power to find a solution. These men placed their hopes on Tsirimokos. Svolos was not present, although he had been invited; but in view of their close relationship, no one doubted that Tsirimokos spoke for Svolos as well as himself. In his speech Tsirimokos pointed out the terrible consequences of civil war and asked that every effort be made to avert such a calamity. Dimitrios Stratis and Kalomiris, the two non-Communist labour leaders of EEAM, spoke in the same vein. But Siantos was not inclined to let the situation slip through his fingers. He asked for a vote on the main issue: that the draft agreement for the disarmament of ELAS and the formation of a national army be discarded if Papandreou refused to agree to the demobilization of the Mountain Brigade and the Sacred Battalion. The composition of the Central Committee was such that Siantos and Partsalides, the Secretary of the Central Committee of EAM, could tip the scales as they wished. On this particular point, Orestis has made this revealing observation:

In this large body which is called the Central Committee of EAM, the docile admirers of the KKE prevailed. These were the so-called '*zitotzithes*' [a term similar to that of 'yes-men']—those who only knew how to shout '*zito*' [hurrah]. Their following, their power, and even the title of the organization they represented was immaterial; in fact, the smaller and weaker their organization, or the more moderate their title, the more extremism and absolute devotion to the KKE— the largest party of the coalition—they showed.[26]

Siantos arranged the voting procedure in such a way that ELD would vote last. Before the end of the voting Tsirimokos interrupted and stated that since the majority favoured the position

[25] The next day, 30 November, in the afternoon, Svolos visited Papandreou and deplored the actions of the Communists. Papandreou asked him to stay in the Government, disassociate himself from the Communists, and thus 'deprive them of the democratic mask'. Svolos answered that 'because of his ties with EAM, his position was difficult'. Papandreou, op. cit., p. 212.

[26] Orestis' archives.

of the KKE, it was unnecessary to continue. Stratis and Kalomiris and some other moderates expected Tsirimokos to express his disagreement with the KKE policy, thus giving the signal for the dissolution of EAM. Instead, Tsirimokos declared that 'the decision of the majority must always be respected by all'.[27]

Siantos, having secured the solidarity of EAM, visited Papandreou on the same day, 30 November, accompanied by Partsalides, the Communist Secretary of the Central Committee of EAM. For the last time they asked the Premier to accept their terms and demobilize the Mountain Brigade and the Sacred Battalion. Papandreou finally had to show them a telegram from Churchill himself advising against the disarmament of these two military units. This failed to impress the two Communist leaders. Yet it was a noteworthy indication that the British Government would not remain indifferent to what happened in Greece. The interest shown by the British Premier in even secondary issues should have dispelled any Communist illusions that a conflict would be confined to ELAS and the meagre forces of the Papandreou Government. In 1946 Partsalides stated apologetically, in an article on 'The Fifth Anniversary of EAM', that 'no one thought that the British would occupy Greece, whose people had stood by England at a difficult moment of the war'.[28] In other words, the Communists did not expect the British to make any active intervention; on the other hand, they counted on the moral support of the other two Allied Powers, the Soviet Union and the United States.[29]

The following day, 1 December 1944, General Scobie issued a statement. His aim—as he explained to the journalists—was to clarify the intentions of the British Government. In his proclamation the British general stated that he was determined to

---

[27] Orestis' archives.   [28] *Komep*, 1 October 1946.

[29] Because of misinformation, American circles in Athens as well as in Washington viewed EAM as a genuine democratic coalition representing the noblest aspirations of the Greek people. It is characteristic that Admiral King ordered Admiral Hewitt, the United States Commander of the Mediterranean Fleet, to forbid the use of any American LSTs to transport supplies to the British forces in Greece. This order was withdrawn only after strong British protests. Lincoln MacVeagh, the United States Ambassador in Athens, declared that 'the American policy is to stay clear and take no part in Greek politics'. This hands-off policy clearly favoured EAM. See the *New York Times*, 6 December 1944, p. 13; also W. D. Leahy, *I Was There* (New York, Whittlesey House, McGraw-Hill, 1950), p. 285.

support the constitutional Government and protect the Greek people against any act of force. Because of a rather unfortunate translation which conveyed an irritating air of arrogance, the proclamation served as excellent material for arousing the *'filotimo'*[30] of the rank and file of ELAS. The Communist agitators took care that full use was made of it.

During the same day the Cabinet met without the left-wing ministers. The atmosphere was heavy; still, there was no intention of capitulating to the Communist demands. With the British solidly behind the constitutional Government the Cabinet—implementing a previous agreement—issued a 'decision' which authorized the newly-formed units of the National Guard to replace the EP of ELAS (the ELAS militia) in safeguarding public order. This 'decision' was sent to the left-wing ministers for their signature, on the understanding that failure to sign the document would be tantamount to resignation from the Government. The left-wing ministers refused to sign. Siantos had already dispatched his orders for mobilization to ELAS headquarters.

When General Saraphis insisted on knowing more about the intentions of ELAS' political leadership, Siantos decided to resurrect the Central Committee of ELAS—an organ which had been liquidated in March 1944 when the PEEA was established. Though the reorganization of the Central Committee was publicly announced on 3 December 1944, it actually took place two days earlier, on 1 December.[31] From then on, Siantos controlled not only the political activities of EAM but also the military actions of ELAS. In the words of Zachariades, 'Siantos exercised a monopoly control over the December Revolution; without consulting anyone, he arbitrarily abolished the ELAS GHQ and established the Central Committee of ELAS, in which he was the absolute master.'[32] For this 'unacceptable and incomprehensible mistake' Zachariades later held the whole Politbureau responsible.

Although Zachariades repeatedly accused Siantos of deciding on and directing the December Revolution single-handed, he also denounced him as a British agent. In his article 'Dheka Khronia Palis; Symperasmata, Didagmata, Kathikonta' (Ten

---

[30] The Greek word for pride, sensitivity, honour.   [31] Orestis' archives.

[32] Zachariades, *Provlimata Kathothigisis*, p. 17; see also his article in the *Ellino-Amerikanikon Vima*, 20 October 1950.

Years of Struggle; Conclusions, Lessons, Duties), which was published in the Communist Review *Neos Kosmos* behind the Iron Curtain in August 1950, Zachariades 'revealed' that in December 1944 the party was 'politically, organizationally, ideologically, and militarily unprepared'. He added:

It must be revealed now that the pro-British (so to speak) forgery of the KKE's policies, with all its tragic consequences for our movement, began in 1937 when the leadership of the KKE, composed at that time of Partsalides, Nefeloudis, Sklavainas, and Siantos, erroneously underestimated the British influence on Greek political and economic life, and thus weakened and emasculated the struggle waged by the people against British imperialist policy in our country.[33]

In his final speech to the Third Conference of the KKE (October 1950), Zachariades was more explicit. He said: 'This is the picture which emerges from the facts. You place in line one, two, three, many data and you have a picture which spells out that SIANTOS WAS A STOOL PIGEON, a suspect character.'[34] In his book *Provlimata Kathothigisis*, Zachariades went even further: 'In the sector of revolutionary vigilance, the criminal blindness and complacency of the leadership allowed Siantos, who was an agent of the class enemy, to carry out his treacherous deeds, to sell out and destroy the revolution.'[35] There is an apparent contradiction between the two major arguments; on the one hand, Siantos is denounced as a 'traitor' and a 'British agent', and on the other, he is accused of deciding on and conducting the December Revolution single-handed—an action, of course, which can hardly pass as a pro-British undertaking. Yet the implication is that the British had reasons for wanting a Communist revolt, and that they used Siantos to bring it about. This fiendish reasoning is, obviously, an *ex post facto* attempt to explain away the disaster. There is no doubt that the defeat of the Communists in the streets of Athens turned the clock back for them; but is this proof that Siantos instigated the revolt on behalf of the British? Besides, 'during the five weeks which intervened before EAM/ELAS admitted defeat, General Scobie's forces nearly succumbed'.[36] Five years later, in August 1949, another revolt, instigated and directed by Zachariades

[33] *Neos Kosmos*, No. 8, August 1950, p. 16.
[34] *Neos Kosmos*, Nos. 11–12, November–December 1950, p. 818.
[35] Zachariades, *Provlimata Kathothigisis*, p. 27.   [36] Woodhouse, op. cit., p. 218.

himself, met with an even more disastrous defeat. Should one, by the same reasoning, consider Zachariades as an American agent? To be sure he was denounced just as violently by those who threw him out of the party in 1956.

The bloody incidents which took place on Sunday morning, 3 December 1944, have long been regarded as a convenient starting-point for the December Revolution. Yet the revolution was not provoked by those incidents; it had been decided on by Siantos and Ioannides at least five days before the pavement of Constitution Square was made red by the blood of the demonstrators who fell—according to some accounts—under the bullets of one unidentified person dressed in military uniform and carrying a light machine-gun. The Government had initially given permission for the demonstration. This permission was later withdrawn when mounting evidence showed that the KKE was bent on revolution. The Government ordered its police to use only blank cartridges should the demonstrators become too unruly. This may explain why no one was hurt by the heavy shooting—except for the twelve or fifteen people who were felled in the first few minutes by the unidentified assailant. Other eyewitness accounts claim that some of the demonstrators made use of hand grenades and firearms. Whatever the truth, it is immaterial from an historical point of view. If these particular incidents had not occurred some others could have served just as well. What matters is that five days earlier the Communist leadership had decided to plunge the country into civil war.

Two days before the bloodshed in Constitution Square ELAS forces, by order of the resurrected Central Committee of ELAS, began to converge towards the capital to join the 20,000 reserve Elasites in Athens—that is, the units composed of Communist-led inhabitants of the city and the suburbs.[37]

A paragraph of Operational Order No. 791 of the II Division of ELAS under Orestis gives the impression that many ELAS leaders still entertained the hope that the conflict could be confined to ELAS and the 'Fascist' forces under Papandreou. In this Operational Order the Command of the II Division instructed its units that in the event of interference by British

[37] The following orders were dispatched on 1 and 2 December 1944: Secret Order No. 25/1 Dec. 1944, of the First Army Corps of ELAS; Operational Order No. 791/2 Dec. 1944, of the II Division of ELAS; Secret Order No. 52/3 Dec. 1944, from the First Army Corps to the II Division of ELAS.

motorized forces they should 'avoid any provocation and try to persuade the British to stay out of the conflict'. However, in the event of 'forcible intervention' on the part of the British the ELAS troops were ordered 'to defend themselves by all means, upholding their military honour by the use of arms'.

The decision to attack the capital did not come as a surprise to the ELAS troops. The psychological preparation of the rank and file had been carried on unceasingly by party agitators while the Communist leaders were participating in the Government of National Unity and ostensibly co-operating in the solution of the pressing political, military, and economic problems. Here is an interesting excerpt from the diary of *Kapetan* Orestis: 'Even the low cadres of KOA [the Communist Organization of Athens] were not surprised by the beginning of the revolt; because, even during the days when nothing foreshadowed a change in party policy, the revolutionary agitation went on.'[38] According to the available information, the party line during that period was that in France and Belgium, and possibly Italy, the people's resistance forces were facing similar problems and that revolutionary developments were quite possible. Likewise, the 'resistance forces of the Greek people should be prepared for any eventuality'.[39]

There is no longer any doubt that the December Revolution was prepared, decided on, and launched by the KKE. Even Zachariades himself did not deny it. For him, it was Siantos who directed the revolt—presumably on behalf of the British. Yet a closer look at the party records reveals that all the top leaders of the KKE took part in the preparation and the launching of the revolt in one way or another.

Why the revolution failed

Since 1945 Zachariades has denounced Siantos and most of the other leaders who played an important role in the December Revolution. The long list includes such names as Siantos, Ioannides, Partsalides, Karayiorgis, Zevgos, Aris Velouchiotis, and Orestis.[40] Was it because they plunged the country into civil war? Of course not. After all, Lenin himself wrote that: 'A Marxist can under no circumstances consider civil war to be

---

[38] Orestis' archives.   [39] Ibid.

[40] Subsequently Zachariades and Bartzotas joined this long list of 'traitors', denounced in 1956 by the group of Apostolos Grozos and Kostas Koliyiannis.

abnormal or demoralizing. A Marxist stands on the ground of the class struggle, not of social peace. . . . No moral condemnation of civil war can be allowed from the standpoint of Marxism.'[41] Their crime was not that they launched the revolution but that they lost the battle.

From a Marxist point of view, the responsibility of Siantos and the other leaders can be determined by examining two basic points of theory and practice. Was the time ripe for a revolution in December 1944? And if so, why did the Communist bid for power fail?

According to Lenin, the time is ripe for revolution when: (a) the forces hostile to the Communists are weakened by conflicts among themselves; (b) the petty-bourgeoisie and the petty-bourgeois democrats have lost the confidence of the workers; and (c) the proletariat is determined to support the Communist Party in the struggle for power. Stalin's tactical instructions had been very explicit:

Never *play* with insurrection, but when beginning it firmly realize that *you must go to the end*; you must concentrate *a great superiority of forces* at the decisive point, at the decisive moment. . . . Once the insurrection has begun, you must act with the greatest *determination* and, by all means, without fail, take the offensive; 'the defensive is the death of every armed rising'; you must try to take the enemy by surprise and seize the moment when his forces are scattered. You must strive for *daily* successes, even if small (one might say hourly, if it is the case of one town) and at all costs retain 'moral ascendancy'. The selection of the moment for the decisive blow, of the moment for starting the insurrection, must be so timed as to coincide with the moment when the crisis has reached its climax, when it is fully apparent that the vanguard is prepared to fight to the end, the reserves are prepared to support the vanguard, and maximum consternation reigns in the ranks of the enemy.[42]

Lenin had voiced a note of warning: 'The history of insurrection teaches that the oppressed masses have never won in a fight to the death without being reduced to despair by long sufferings and acute crises of every kind.'[43] All the above conditions in fact existed on the eve of the December Revolution.

[41] Lenin, *Selected Works*, Vol. X, p. 85.
[42] Stalin, *Problems of Leninism* (Moscow, Foreign Languages Publishing House, 1947), pp. 72–73; author's italics.
[43] I. V. Lenin, *Preparing for Revolt* (London, Modern Books Library, 1929), p. 289.

With almost the whole of Greece under the actual domination of EAM, the Communists could 'concentrate a great superiority of forces at the decisive point', namely, the Greek capital. On the other hand, the forces of the 'enemy' were weak and 'scattered'. The forces that could be counted as loyal to the Papandreou Government were the police and the gendarmerie, scattered in their various precincts all over Athens; Zervas' EDES in Epirus, isolated more than 300 miles away from the capital; the small force of Tsaous Andon in Eastern Macedonia; the Sacred Battalion, in the Aegean Islands; and the Mountain Brigade, which was stationed in Athens. Finally, there was also the small British force under General Scobie. This force was dispersed all over Greece, in the major towns and the capital, 'in a manner which suited the administrative task for which they had come to Greece, and was not adapted to fighting. . . . The prevalent assumption of the British military authorities . . . was that EAM/ELAS did not intend to precipitate a fight.'[44]

Another necessary condition for the beginning of a revolution is the neutralization of the middle segments of the population. This also had been achieved. Some of the most vocal and energetic elements had been forced by the ELAS attacks during the Occupation to join the German-sponsored Security Battalions, thus being discredited in the eyes of the Allies; after the liberation they had been imprisoned, in most areas by EAM/ELAS with the approval of the Government of National Unity. Most of the people, being under the armed control of EAM/ELAS, could not assist the constitutional Government in any practical manner. Moreover, the 'bourgeois' politicians had been at loggerheads till very recently over the constitutional question. A major crisis could easily bring the old animosities to the foreground once again, thus precipitating an inner conflict within the anti-Communist camp.

During the weeks before the Revolution the mass demonstrations of EAM had made it 'clear that the vanguard was prepared to fight to the end, and that the reserves were prepared to support the vanguard'. The last bloody demonstration of 3 December had served as the 'acute crisis' which was expected to have 'reduced the masses to despair'.

[44] Woodhouse, op. cit., p. 211.

The Communists entered the civil war with most of the odds in their favour. From a Marxist–Leninist stand-point the time was ripe for revolution.

The Communist leadership also followed the tactical advice in the pursuit of 'daily' successes. They concentrated their first blows against the outlying police units and other small strong-holds of resistance. One after the other the peripheral police stations were wiped out or forced to surrender. This provided the Communists with the prescribed 'daily' successes, but at the same time it resulted in an unnecessary waste of time and forces. They made another, even more serious, mistake. Anyone familiar with modern Greek history should know that whoever controls Athens has the best chance to gain control over the rest of Greece. Orestis pointed this out in a strained conversation with Zevgos when he learned that strong ELAS units had been ordered by Siantos to attack the isolated force of Zervas in Epirus, instead of being sent to join those engaged in the difficult battle for the capital. Orestis repeated his objections to Siantos himself when they met a few days later. He received the cryptic reply that some day he would fully endorse this decision. Siantos gave him a full explanation later, in February 1945, when it was all over. According to Orestis, Siantos, anxious to avert an intervention by Tito's troops in Northern Greece under the pretext of eliminating a potential rival to ELAS, had ordered Saraphis and Aris Velouchiotis to move north and attack EDES. The implication is that Siantos acted as a good patriot interested more in safeguarding the territorial integrity of his country than in promoting the ultimate success of his party. Tempo, Tito's lieutenant, who was presumably waiting across the border ready to move in, has not replied to a written query on this point.

Whatever the real motives of Siantos' strange move, the ELAS forces under Saraphis and Aris attacked EDES between 18 and 30 December. Under heavy pressure by superior forces the EDES guerrillas were finally evacuated by British naval units to the island of Corfu. Another ELAS force wiped out the units of Tsaous Andon. By the end of December the legitimate authorities had been driven out of every part of the Greek mainland with the exception of a small area in the centre of Athens. In the cities of Salonika and Patras ELAS forces lived side by side with the British in a strange sort of uneasy

P

co-existence. Some of the Aegean islands were still held by
the Germans, others by loyal Greek forces.

The Communists had accomplished a great many 'daily'
successes. Yet this was exactly what led to their final defeat.
Their fatal mistake was that instead of storming without delay
the small area in the centre of Athens where the seat of government and the British headquarters were located, they dispersed
their forces, attacking peripheral opponents who would have
been easy prey once the centre of power in Athens had fallen
into Communist hands. This gave the British enough time to
send in reinforcements.

At the beginning of the conflict EAM/ELAS was in a strong
position, not only militarily but also politically. The debate in
the House of Commons, on 5 and 8 December, had revealed
that the Labour Party was taking a critical view of the actions
of the British Government in Greece. Even the course of the
war helped the Greek Communists politically. The Battle of the
Bulge in the Ardennes underlined the fact that, when British
troops were needed to fight against the Germans, they were
engaged in military operations 'against the Greeks', one of the
Allied nations. The American Secretary of State was proclaim-
ing a 'hands-off' policy, while American high-ranking authorities refused to permit the transportation of British troops and
supplies on American LSTs. The Allied Press, with the London
Times in the lead, was denouncing the British intervention
'against the wishes of the Greek people'.[45]

On 17 December the Communists, playing the familiar game
of 'negotiations plus pressure', sent Porphyrogennis to General
Scobie with new proposals. They overlooked the 'British idio-
syncrasy of regarding all terms as unreasonable when they are
in danger of defeat'.[46] General Scobie rejected the EAM/ELAS
terms. Nevertheless, the exchange of communications continued,
till the dramatic arrival of Prime Minister Churchill and
Foreign Secretary Eden in Athens on Christmas Day shifted the
negotiations to a higher level.

In the meantime the fighting went on. So did the reinforcement of the British. This reinforcement had been speeded up
after the visit to Athens of Resident Minister Harold Macmillan

---

[45] See more details in Kousoulas, op. cit., pp. 119–21, and Woodhouse, op. cit.,
p. 220.

[46] Woodhouse, op. cit., p. 222.

and Field-Marshal Alexander, the Supreme Commander of the Mediterranean theatre of war.

The Communists had missed their chance of storming and winning the capital early in December when the British forces were still weak and dispersed. Now, with the constant build-up of British forces and the strengthening of the loyal Greek troops with volunteers and recruits, the danger of an imminent Communist victory had passed. The visit of the British Prime Minister offered the Communists an excellent opportunity for a compromise. Yet at this point they overlooked a relevant warning by Stalin:

Manoeuvre the reserves with a view to effecting a proper retreat when the enemy is strong, when retreat is inevitable, when to accept battle forced upon us by the enemy is obviously disadvantageous, when with the given alignment of forces retreat becomes the only way to ward off a blow against the vanguard and to keep the reserves intact.[47]

Lenin also had said: 'The Communists have to realize that the knowledge of attack is not enough. They must also learn "how to retreat properly".'[48]

At the conference which took place on 26 December the British were represented by Churchill, Eden, Macmillan, Leeper—the British Ambassador to Athens, Field-Marshal Alexander, and General Scobie; EAM/ELAS by Siantos, Partsalides, and Mantakas; the other Allies by the United States Ambassador and Colonel Popov of the Soviet mission; other participants from Greek political circles included Themistokles Sofoulis, George Kafandaris, and General Nikolaos Plastiras, who had been brought from Cannes to Athens by the British on 13 December 1944. The fact that the Soviet and the American representatives attended the conference and did not dispute Churchill's statement that he had come to Greece 'with the knowledge and approval of President Roosevelt and Marshal Stalin' was dramatic evidence that the KKE/EAM had been abandoned by those who could provide political support.

Siantos failed to read the signs. Instead of grasping the chance of a 'proper retreat' which could leave his reserves 'intact', he presented conditions which were made deliberately unacceptable. He demanded half the seats in the Cabinet, including such

---

[47] Stalin, op. cit., p. 74.   [48] Lenin, *Selected Works*, X, p. 66.

key posts as the Ministries of the Interior and of Justice and the Under-Secretaryships of War and Foreign Affairs; the demobilization of the gendarmerie, the Mountain Brigade, the Sacred Battalion, and the newly-formed National Guard; a plebiscite on the constitutional issue in February and elections for a Constituent Assembly in April. If he intended to provoke the immediate rejection of his proposals he was completely successful. The only point on which there was some agreement was the establishment of a Regency—a proposal which had been discussed on and off for several months and more intently after the outbreak of the revolution. Damaskinos, the Archbishop of Athens, under whose presidency the two sessions of the conference took place, had long been considered for the post. He took the oath as Regent on 31 December, after the King had acquiesced on the previous day. At the same time he accepted Papandreou's resignation, and on 3 January General Nikolaos Plastiras took office as Prime Minister.

The day before the appointment of the Regent, Vyshinsky summoned Politis, the Greek Ambassador to Moscow, and announced the appointment of Sergeyev as Soviet Ambassador to Athens. This Soviet gesture, coming at the moment when the Greek Government was engaged in an armed struggle with the Greek Communists, was interpreted as showing open disapproval of the Communist revolt. When the news reached the ELAS ranks it caused a great deal of distress and confusion, as this writer was able to witness personally, being then a prisoner at the HQ of the XIII ELAS Reserve Division in Lamia.

When the conference of 26 and 27 December failed to put an end to the fighting, the British units, having been methodically reinforced in the preceding few weeks, began their counter-offensive. By 5 January most of Piraeus and Athens had been cleared of ELAS troops. New terms, slightly different from those presented by Siantos, were now offered by a delegation headed by Zevgos. To accept these terms now that the military situation had been altered in favour of the anti-Communist forces would have been utterly unrealistic.

On 3 January 1945 'even the spineless military advisers of Siantos declared that the fighting could not go on much longer'.[49] General Matsoukas, the Military Commander of the OMS, the group of ELAS divisions in Central Greece, took the initiative

[49] Orestis' archives.

and ordered the retreat of the XIII Division. By 6 January the Central Committee of ELAS gave the order for a general retreat. It was too late, even militarily. Instead of an orderly retreat, it turned into a stampede of bewildered Elasites trying to reach their villages and Athenian members of ELAS leaving their homes in the capital in search of refuge behind the lines of the EAM 'state'. Only a few units of the II Division offered some resistance to the advancing British troops.

Before their withdrawal from the Athens perimeter the Communist leaders ordered the abduction of thousands of people as hostages. This action, together with the excesses committed by the Communists during the revolution, generated a volcanic reaction against them. As to the abduction of hostages, the 6th Conference of the Communist Organization of Athens (KOA), which met on 17 August 1945, resolved that this was one of the major mistakes: 'The abduction of hostages was a mistake as a decision because it was ordered at an inopportune time—24 December; and the manner of its execution was a mistake.'[50]

Speeding towards the northern town of Trikkala, Siantos ordered Theodoros Makrides,[51] the so-called 'military brain' of the KKE, to ask for a truce. Makrides, who could have signalled in time for a retreat, had been sent with Saraphis and Velouchiotis against Zervas—probably in order to leave the field open for Siantos to be in absolute control. Now he was asked to seek an armistice. Zevgos and Partsalides were sent along 'to keep an eye on him', as Orestis told me in 1955.

On 10 January the two KKE political leaders and their military expert reached General Scobie's headquarters, and the next day a truce was signed whereby the cessation of hostilities was to be effected at one minute past midnight on 15 January 1945. Immediately after the truce the ELAS troops were to withdraw behind a line roughly to the west of the Athens–Salonika highway.

[50] *Report* of the 6th Conference of KOA.
[51] Theodoros Makrides was a former major in the Greek Army. He had been a member of the KKE for many years and the party's foremost military expert. In 1947-9 he refused to participate in the Third Round. Finally, he was allowed by the Greek Government to emigrate abroad.

The Varkiza Agreement

With the Yalta Conference approaching, the British were extremely anxious to reach a final settlement in Greece. This may explain the moderation shown by them during the talks which took place at Varkiza, near Athens. One of the most difficult issues was the question of an amnesty. The representatives of the Greek Government were very reluctant to agree to a general amnesty, while on the other side Siantos refused to conclude an agreement as long as the question of a general amnesty remained unsettled. ELAS forces still occupied most of the country, while as a last lever of extortion the Communists held the hostages they had abducted shortly before their withdrawal from Athens.

Yet Siantos was not genuinely interested in securing a general amnesty for his men. In fact, he had reasons of his own for opposing such an amnesty. Should the ELAS men return to their towns and villages, free from persecution, they would automatically begin to search for the causes of the disaster. This could make the position of Siantos, Ioannides, and the other top leaders who had played a central role in the revolution very difficult indeed. On the other hand, persecution of the rank and file would force them to close ranks around their leadership as the only means of survival. Ioannis Sofianopoulos, the leader of the Peasant Party, who in 1936 had signed the Popular Front agreement with the Communists and who, because of his friendly relations with EAM, had been appointed Foreign Minister of the Plastiras Government in January 1945, revealed in 1950 that as a member of the government delegation to the Varzika Conference he had refused to agree to a general amnesty, while two other members of the government delegation, the 'rightists' Petros Rallis and M. Makropoulos, had accepted the British suggestion that such an amnesty should be granted. The implication of Sofianopoulos' statement was that he had been 'plus royaliste que le roi'. Yet a more intimate study of the available information shows that he was actually playing Siantos' game. Siantos finally 'gave in' and 'accepted' Sofianopoulos' suggestion of a partial amnesty which included only those high-ranking Communist officials accused of political crimes, while it left the EAM/ELAS rank and file unprotected. To quote *Kapetan* Theseus, 'it is difficult to find in history a similar example of a leadership which abandoned its followers while it took care to protect itself completely against persecution'.[52] Other provisions of the Varzika Agreement were clearly advantageous to the Communist Party. They allowed the Communists, in effect, to carry on their subversive activities under the cloak of legitimacy, and freely prepare the so-called 'third round', their third attempt to seize power. Much later, in October 1949, the 6th Plenum of the Central Committee of KKE under Zachariades stated that, 'following the military defeat in December 1944, the Varkiza Agreement became a necessary manoeuvre for the regrouping of the people's democratic forces'. As such, the Varkiza Agreement was not the end of the Communist drive for power; it was merely the termination of the 'second round' and 'a respite for the regrouping of the popular democratic forces, in view of the new decisive confrontation which is inevitably coming'.[53] In the evening of 11 February 1945, the day before the signing of the Varkiza Pact, Siantos invited the correspondents to a press conference at the Greek Foreign Ministry. Replying to one of the questions, he said: 'Since the Allies have decided that it is useful for the British army to be in Greece, then it is beneficial. The fact that the British were in conflict with ELAS we consider to have been the result of an unfortunate misunderstanding which we hope will be forgotten.'[54]

The defeat of the Greek Communists in the streets of Athens showed that the classic concepts of proletarian revolution were no longer valid. With the development of modern weapons, the old form of popular revolution with the familiar features of street barricades, sharpshooters, revolutionary songs, and individual heroism is largely a thing of the past.[55] There has been another, further transformation: to the traditional two protagonists in the class struggle, the 'proletariat' and the State, a third factor was added: foreign assistance to either of the two. In December 1944 the 'proletariat' in Greece launched its drive for the seizure of power while the 'State' was feebly armed and the middle segments of the people were neutralized in the iron

---

[52] *Kapetan* Theseus (real name Takis Sarris).

[53] Zachariades, *Provlimata Kathothigisis*, p. 19; see also Vukmanovic, op. cit., p. 46.

[54] Capell, op. cit., p. 200.

[55] This operates both ways. In October 1956 the Hungarian revolution was similarly crushed by the superior Soviet military machine.

grip of the 'proletarian' forces. According to the classic outlines of Leninist revolutionary theory, the Greek 'proletariat' should have won the battle, even with all the various tactical mistakes committed during the course of the conflict. But there was a third factor which tipped the scales: the British military forces. By adding these forces to the side of the 'State', the 'proletariat' lost its original supremacy and, forced to face the overwhelming power of modern weapons, it suffered a crushing defeat.

On the other hand, 'proletarian' régimes were imposed on various Eastern European countries not as a result of 'proletarian revolutions', but by the open intervention of the Red Army, that is, of another *external* factor.

The Greek Communists failed to heed the lessons of the December 1944 débâcle, and they tried again. This 'third round', as they themselves called it, ended in disaster. Its story is the subject of the next chapter.

Part IV

THE THIRD ROUND

15. 'Regrouping the Communist Forces'

The return of the leader

On the morning of 30 May 1945 an RAF transport plane landed at the Eleusis airport near Athens and out stepped Nikos Zachariades, the acknowledged leader of the Greek Communist Party. He had been found a month earlier by Allied troops among the inmates of Dachau concentration camp. The next day *Rizospastis* triumphantly carried the first statements on Greek soil of the long-eclipsed *Archigos*. 'There is no other solution,' Zachariades insisted. 'Either we go back somehow to the régime of the Monarcho-Fascist dictatorship of the Fourth of August, in a form more severe than ever, or EAM's struggle for national liberation will find its completion in the establishment of a People's Democracy in Greece.'[1] At the time few were familiar with the real meaning of the term 'people's democracy'. To Zachariades, however, it meant 'a form of power which fulfils the functions of the dictatorship of the proletariat'.[2] Yet, in keeping with the spirit of the moment, he asserted that he envisaged the establishment of a People's Democracy in Greece only as the result of free and genuine elections.

In 1945 an electoral victory for the extreme Left, as the KKE and its fellow-travellers were then popularly called, was most unlikely. The disintegration of EAM, which had started during the December Revolution, was carried a long step further when Svolos, Tsirimokos, Askoutsis, and Stratis, the former leaders of

---

[1] *Rizospastis*, 31 May 1945.
[2] Zachariades, *Provlimata Kathothigisis*, p. 87.

the PEEA experiment, announced on 18 April that they had
formed a new political party known as ELD/SKE (Popular
Democratic Union/Socialist Party of Greece). To some extent
this was their answer to a call by the 11th Plenum of the KKE's
Central Committee (5–10 April 1945) 'to all democrats to join
the front of democracy . . . for a democratic rebirth, for a
People's Democracy'.[3] While the forces of the Left were breaking up, the anti-Communist forces were gaining ground, as
many who in the past had refused to identify the royal issue
with that of anti-Communism were rapidly turning their
revulsion against Communism and its methods into an almost
passionate support for the King. The British, then a dominant
factor in Greek politics, had placed their hopes on the Regent,
the capable Archbishop of Athens; at the same time they had
embarked on a deliberate effort to promote to positions of
power personalities from the pro-republican Liberal centre. In
the opinion of a great number of ordinary Greeks—traditionally distinguished by their not so ordinary political acumen—
this British policy had little chance of success; it reminded them
too much of the discredited wartime policies, which in their
view had ultimately led to the December Revolution. This
British experiment with the pro-republican centre came to an
end with the overwhelming success of the pro-royalist parties in
the elections of March 1946. In the intervening months Greece
went through a succession of caretaker Cabinets, starting with
the one Plastiras formed on 3 January 1945. Although these
Cabinets included some of the most capable personalities on
the Greek political scene, they largely failed to solve the mounting problems of economic recovery, while inflation swiftly wiped
out the modest gains that were made. The extreme Right,
seconded heartily by the extreme Left, manipulated the cur-
rency without restraint, sending prices spiralling upwards and
undermining all efforts to restore financial sanity.

In the midst of political and economic instability the political
forces in the country were clearly divided by the so-called
'constitutional issue', i.e. whether King George should be
allowed to return to his throne or a Republic should replace the

[3] As a token of its peaceful intentions, the 11th Plenum denounced Aris
Velouchiotis, who had refused to accept the Varkiza Pact and had remained in
the mountains with a small band of die-hards. Shortly afterwards his hide-out was
betrayed and he was killed.

Vassilevomeni Dimokratia. But in the minds of many ordinary citizens this was not a contest between a Republic and a royal form of government; to them it was a struggle between a democratic and a Communist state. This writer lived through those turbulent months and can truthfully say that a strong majority, even among traditionally pro-republican circles, was turning towards the King, not as an alternative to the Republic, but as a guarantee against the Communist challenge. In this they were pushed by the Communists themselves, who, being unable to force a three-way choice between King, Republic, and a People's Democracy, had made the cause of the Republic their own, practically drowning the voices of the genuine pro-republicans. For all these reasons the Communists could not realistically expect to establish a People's Democracy through genuine elections in 1945. Zachariades' statement notwithstanding, the Greek Communists were not thinking of electoral victories, but dreaming of a new armed confrontation. In fact, they were more than just dreaming. To quote Zachariades himself:

What was the strategy of the KKE in the post-Varkiza period? It was the strategy which has as its objective 'to gain time, to undermine the opponent, and to gather forces, to pass, then, to the attack' (Stalin). It was the strategy of retreat-manoeuvring to preserve and regroup the main forces and the reserves, to pass to the new attack.[4]

This strategy of 'retreat-manoeuvring' to gain time required subtlety and a measure of deception. In the nationalistic atmosphere of the early post-war months, when the Greek people were rightly or wrongly anticipating the fulfilment of long-cherished aspirations expressed in the expansion of Greek rule over areas held to be Greek, such as Cyprus, the Dodecanese, or Northern Epirus, the Communists could not afford to appear less patriotic than their opponents or even their reluctant friends. As far as Cyprus or the Dodecanese were concerned, the Communists faced no ideological or political dilemma. The Greek claims on Cyprus, a British crown colony, and the Dodecanese, a possession of defeated Italy, received the unqualified support of the KKE. Northern Epirus, however, was a different case altogether. This Greek claim was directed, in effect, against Albania, a country already on its way to becoming a People's Democracy. Should the KKE take a stand against the Greek claim on

---

[4] Zachariades, loc. cit.

Northern Epirus? This question came up on 1 June 1945 at the first meeting of the Politbureau which Zachariades attended. In line with the strategy of 'retreat-manoeuvring', the Polit-bureau went so far as to say that 'if the majority of the democrats decide in favour of an immediate military occupation of Northern Epirus by the Greek Army, the KKE will state its objections but will go along (*tha pitharchisi*)'.[5] Later, in 1950, Zachariades was to pronounce this statement 'a monstrous error, product of the nationalistic heritage of the first occu-pation'.[6]

Macedonia, the old familiar bone of contention, was no longer an issue. Since 1935 the KKE had switched to the sup-port of 'complete equality for the minorities'. In August 1945 Zachariades, in a much-publicized visit to Macedonia, de-clared in Salonika that 'Macedonia is and will remain Greek'. Clearly, in the months which followed the 'tactical retreat' of Varkiza, the party was forced by the prevailing wind of nation-alism to make a deliberate effort to cleanse its image from the stain left by the revolution.

On the labour front the Communist leadership, following a policy of 'United Front from below only', established a separate labour organization known as Ergatikos Antifasistikos Synaspismos (ERGAS); their success was at first limited, but gradually their influence increased, and by March 1946 a new directorate of the General Confederation emerged, through free elections, which was predominantly left-wing and largely under the influence of ERGAS. The Secretary-General was the Communist Paparighas. Nevertheless strikes, instigated with the all too clear object of obstructing or delaying the painful efforts towards economic recovery, never attained the scope the Communists intended. The Politbureau blamed the lack of complete success on the Communist 'fractions' and called on them to intensify their efforts to instigate a concerted strike campaign. Finally, the Greek Government, taking advantage of a technicality, annulled the election of the pro-Communist administration of the GSEE and appointed in its place a 'Provisional Executive Committee'. The ERGAS representa-

[5] *Rizospastis*, 2 June 1945.

[6] Zachariades, *Dheka Khronia Palis* (a collection of articles originally published in the periodical *Neos Kosmos*, August–September 1950, reprinted in book form by the Central Committee of the KKE somewhere in Eastern Europe in November 1950), p. 25.

tives refused to participate as a minority in the 'Provisional Executive Committee' and remained outside the GSEE. In the following months the influence of ERGAS began to decline, and with the outbreak of the Communist rebellion the leaders of the organization went underground and finally emerged at the headquarters of the Communist guerrillas.

Preparing for the Third Round

In justifying his policy during the late forties, Zachariades asserted in 1950 that 'during the national liberation struggle under the first Occupation, social movements had taken place which had decisively changed the correlation of class forces in our country in favour of the Revolution'.[7] Prior to the rebellion of 1947–9, speaking at the 12th Plenum of the Central Committee which met in Athens from 25 to 27 June 1945—the first he attended since his arrest on 13 September 1936—Zachariades discarded his own theory of a 'bourgeois-democratic stage'. This stage, he said, had been left behind. 'The approaching revolution will be socialist in nature, and will simultaneously solve the bourgeois-democratic problems which still remain, such as foreign domination, lands, etc.' To assume that Greece was ripe for a 'socialist' revolution proved a fatal miscalculation in the following years. At the same time Zachariades candidly acknowledged at the Plenum the importance of the 'British factor' in Greek politics.

Greece [he said] is located in one of the strategic, most sensitive and significant points on one of the most vital communication arteries of the British Empire. As long as there is a British Empire, this artery will remain, and England will do everything in her power to preserve it. A realistic foreign policy cannot ignore this fact. . . . A correct [Greek] foreign policy must move between two poles, that of the European–Balkans with its centre in Soviet Russia, and that of the Mediterranean with England as its centre.[8]

The Stalin–Churchill understanding of October 1944 had placed Greece unconditionally within the British sphere of interest. At Yalta, in February 1945, Stalin had made it clear that he continued to abide by the agreement. When he asked Churchill 'what was going on in Greece' he hastened to add that 'he was not criticizing the British in Greece but merely seeking

---

[7] Zachariades, *Provlimata Kathothigisis*, p. 81.
[8] The minutes of the 12th Plenum; mimeographed copy.

information'.[9] The 12th Plenum, by accepting Zachariades' statement, was actually moving away from the Soviet–British understanding, taking the position that Greece, between two major centres of power, should accord equal importance to both.

While acknowledging the importance, though not the predominance, of British interests in Greece, the party was directed to regroup and prepare for a new confrontation. There was an evident inconsistency in the positions taken by the 12th Plenum. If Greece was admittedly so important to a vital lifeline of the British Empire, why should anyone expect that the British would allow in 1946 or 1947 what they had prevented by use of force in December 1944? Zachariades later provided an explanation. 'The existence of the Soviet Union and the People's Democracies in the Balkans and Eastern Europe', he wrote in 1950, 'constituted an extremely favourable, decisive factor for our passing into the Socialist revolution.'[10] It was to prove to be another fateful miscalculation. Milovan Djilas, in his book *Conversations with Stalin*, relates that in a dramatic meeting with Yugoslav and Bulgarian Communists on 10 February 1948, Stalin said firmly: 'The uprising in Greece must be stopped, and as quickly as possible.' According to Djilas, Stalin had come to the conclusion that the Greek Communists had 'no prospect of success at all'. 'What do you think?' he is reported to have said. 'That Great Britain and the United States—the United States, the most powerful state in the world—will permit you to break their line of communications in the Mediterranean Sea? Nonsense. And we have no navy.'[11]

A sober analysis of the 'existing correlation of forces' would have discouraged the Communist leadership from attempting a new armed confrontation. If there were any such wise counsels they were silenced before they reached the surface. In fact, the preparation of the Third Round, as the Communists themselves named their 'approaching socialist revolution', had started even before the curtain of defeat fell behind the retreating hordes of bewildered Elasites in January 1945. On 15 January, the same day that the cease-fire came into effect, the organization of EAM in Salonika, for example, where Markos Vafiades,

---

[9] Edward R. Stettinius Jr., *Roosevelt and the Russians; the Yalta Conference* (New York, Doubleday, 1949), p. 217.

[10] Zachariades, *Provlimata Kathothigisis*, p. 81.

[11] Milovan Djilas, *Conversations with Stalin* (New York, Harcourt, Brace and World, Inc., 1962), p. 182.

the future leader of the Communist guerrilla army, was the leading figure, laid out in revealing detail the tasks of the members:

(*a*) to develop mass activity by fighting for the economic demands of the people;

(*b*) to concentrate attention on developing the Reserve ELAS, purging the timid and vacillating elements, securing weapons; all EAM members must as one man help ELAS to transport all war material to where it is needed;

(*c*) to create a strong illegal machinery with military staff precision.

There was a noteworthy addendum: 'The City Council agrees that the *armed conflict* has stopped only *temporarily*.'[12]

The decision to conceal the best weapons of ELAS was put into effect the moment the failure of the December Revolution became clear. This writer, at that time a prisoner-interpreter at the HQ of the XIII ELAS Reserve Division in Lamia, witnessed the packing and later the transportation of automatic and other selected weapons to mountain hide-outs in the area of Roumeli. Numerically ELAS surrendered more rifles than were required by the terms of the Varkiza Pact. But these were mostly obsolete, often worthless Italian carbines.

In the post-Varkiza period of regrouping and preparation for the Third Round the KKE turned its propaganda guns first against the Greek Right and, before the end of the year, against the British, who were allegedly blocking 'a normal democratic development in Greece'. The 12th Plenum,[13] setting the stage, decided on 'mass popular self-defence', and called on 'democratic citizens to defend their lives, and confront a Fascist *coup* with every means, starting with the general Pan-helladic strike'. After the 12th Plenum a series of Politbureau decisions (4 July, 12 July, 1 August, and 6 September) deplored 'the conditions of terrorism imposed by the black front of Monarcho-Fascist reaction'. *Rizospastis* and *Eleutheri Ellada*, the two Communist-controlled dailies, blasted the alleged repressions of the Right against 'innocent democratic citizens' without respite—and

---

[12] EAM pamphlet; author's italics.
[13] The 12th Plenum elected to a six-member Politbureau N. Zachariades, G. Siantos, Y. Ioannides, D. Partsalides, V. Bartzotas, and Khryssa Khatzivassiliou. The Secretariat of the Central Committee consisted of the same individuals with the exception of V. Bartzotas and Khryssa Khatzivassiliou. N. Zachariades remained Secretary-General.

without hindrance. The picture painted by the Communist press was, of course, exaggerated. Yet there were incidents in which irresponsible excesses by Rightist elements were often inspired by personal vendettas or an ill-considered anti-Communist fanaticism. The central Government in Athens, working with painful and agonizing slowness to reassemble the administrative machinery destroyed by war, occupation, and revolution, sometimes could not effectively curb these excesses.

Behind the façade of republican pre-eminence, many elements of the extreme Right took advantage of the strong anti-Communist feelings generated by the Communist excesses during the December Revolution to make their way back into positions of power. Furthermore, the Communist attempt to brand the stigma of collaboration with the Axis on to any real or imagined opponent gave those who had actually collaborated the opportunity to claim that they, too, were falsely accused.

On the other hand, the prisons were bulging with thousands of former Elasites suspected of common crimes against life or property. Many were probably innocent, but in the wake of the revolution guilt or innocence could not easily be established.

This convenient set of circumstances was fully exploited by the Communist leadership. On 24 August 1945 Zachariades, while visiting Salonika, once again denounced 'the attacks of the Monarcho-Fascists against the defenceless democratic citizens of Greece', and gave a public warning that

if the situation is not soon and drastically turned towards a normal democratic development, we will reply to Monarcho-Fascism in the towns, the mountains, and the villages with the same means. . . . And if the supreme interests of the People demand it, the glorious marching-song *'Empros ELAS gia tin Ellada'* will sound again in the ravines and on the mountain-tops.[14]

The familiar Stalinist advice 'to veil offensive operations under the guise of defence in order that the undecided and vacillating elements may more easily be swept into the whirlpool of revolution'[15] was once again applied by the KKE.

Zachariades added an aside against the British:

If Mr. Bevin is not able to impose order in Greece with his occupation forces, let him withdraw them from our country. Then, the

[14] *Rizospastis*, 25 August 1945.   [15] See supra, p. 139.

Greek People, in spite of the unilateral application of our Peace Agreement [the Varkiza Pact], will be ready to restore order and quiet in the country by their own unaided efforts.

'*The British must go*'

Zachariades, who in May had declared that he anticipated the establishment of a People's Democracy in Greece only through the ballot, soon changed his mind—if he ever really believed in such a possibility. When Dimitrios Partsalides, speaking at the Seventh Party Congress which met in Athens in the first week of October 1945, referred to 'the peaceful transition to Socialism', Zachariades took exception to this. In his speech he criticized 'the tendency of certain comrades to present the issue one-sidedly when they speak of a peaceful transition. It must be stressed right away that there is a *possibility* of a peaceful transition but not a certainty . . . a possibility which recedes with every day that passes.'[16]

The Seventh Congress, the first in the history of the party to convene openly and attract nation-wide interest, met in the Titania Theatre, in the centre of Athens, with the full protection of the Greek authorities. The spacious meeting-hall was decorated with Greek flags, red banners, and revolutionary slogans, while two huge portraits of Stalin and Zachariades over the speaker's platform looked benignly down on the delegates.

Behind the exultation and the camaraderie, the two familiar trends, the moderate and the aggressive, made themselves felt, the first timidly, the second quite boldly. While most speakers blasted 'the British occupation' and the 'Monarcho-Fascist lackeys of imperialist reaction', some used moderate phraseology, and one of them, Leonidas Stringos, went so far as to praise 'the American way of developing agriculture, which has led to a broad domestic market on which the dramatic expansion of American industry in the last decades has been based'.[17] Favourable references to the United States were not unusual among Greek Communists at that time. Even during the December Revolution and its aftermath they made a sharp distinction between the British and the Americans; one would have had to look hard in 1945 to find any hostile remarks about the American President and the United States.

Whatever mild differences of approach could be detected in

[16] *To 7o Synethrio*, p. 7; author's italics.   [17] Ibid., p. 8.

Q

the deliberations of the Congress, there was no evidence of any crisis. Apart from anything else, the composition of the Congress ruled out any open rift. Yiannis Petsopoulos, the veteran Communist, provided revealing glimpses into the workings of Democratic Centralism in a pamphlet he published after his final withdrawal from the party in 1946.

The Central Committee [he wrote] does not merely suggest topics for discussion but decides in advance and with finality the agenda of the Congress. Even the number of delegates and the manner of their election is determined by the Central Committee, not by the local organizations. The secret ballot, that exceptionally democratic institution, is not established by the Charter, but the manner of voting is left to the Central Committee. Finally the Congress does not meet to check the record of the Central Committee but merely to hear and accept its report.[18]

The Congress approved a new party programme which, compared to that of 1935, offered little that was new or different. The only significant change was that it set up as the party's immediate objective 'the victory of the People's Democracy in Greece' and for its ultimate target 'the construction of a Socialist-Communist society'.[19] Those interested in the nuances of Communist theory and strategy should note that the 1945 party programme formally discarded the 'bourgeois-democratic stage' in the revolutionary process as being already left behind in Greece, and adopted the establishment of a People's Democracy as the prelude to a Socialist transformation.

Even more important from a practical point of view, the KKE opened a fierce drive for the withdrawal of British forces from Greece,[20] discarding all pretence and reluctant or veiled accusations. The daily recriminations against British interference in the domestic affairs of Greece culminated on 8 December in a vitriolic article signed by Zachariades. In it the leader of the KKE attacked 'the British occupation which for a whole year now has been the only obstacle to the recovery of the country', and asserted that 'the first national demand at this moment is that the British must go'.[21] He combined this demand with a thinly-veiled threat that 'the Greek People who

[18] Petsopoulos, op. cit., p. 289. [19] *To 7o Synethrio*, p. 51.
[20] Only one week after the 12th Plenum, the 4 July 1945 decision of the Politbureau includes for the first time a reference to the British political and military authorities of *occupation*. See N. Zachariades, *Dheka Khronia Palis*, p. 143.
[21] *Rizospastis*, 8 December 1945.

have faced so many storms and have made so many sacrifices in the past ten years for their freedom will not lay down their arms till they secure the peace and the future of their country in the way they themselves wish'.[22]

Zachariades was largely correct in saying that the British presented 'the only obstacle' to a new Communist drive. By their presence alone, the British troops, however limited in number, formed a shield behind which the political and economic reconstruction of the country could proceed. Even more ominous from the Communist point of view was the fact that the British were in the process of organizing a reliable Greek Army. In February 1945, at the time of the Varkiza Pact, the total strength of the Greek armed forces, including the III Mountain Brigade, the Sacred Battalion, and the hastily organized National Guard units, amounted to approximately 30,000 men. In the first six months of 1945 the Greek Government, with British assistance, expanded the III Brigade into the II Division, and with the officers of the Sacred Battalion it staffed two more Divisions (IX and XI) by the end of the year. By December 1945 the total strength of the Greek armed forces had reached 75,000.[23]

The Communist drive against the British presence in Greece took some time to develop. A first indication that Soviet 'disinterestedness' in Greece was nearing its end appeared in a speech by Marshal Tito on 8 July 1945. Soon thereafter, at Potsdam, the Soviet Government questioned the presence of British troops in Greece. There were other signs that the climate was changing. In August Mikhail Kalinin, then Chairman of the Supreme Soviet Presidium, said in an address to rural CPSU secretaries:

But even now, after the greatest victory known to history, we cannot for one minute forget the basic fact that our country remains the one Socialist state in the world. Only the most concrete, most immediate danger which threatened us from Hitlerite Germany has disappeared. In order that the danger of war may really disappear for a long time, it is necessary to consolidate our victory.[24]

Another development was that as early as 19 March 1945 the Soviet Government had notified Turkey that it did not

[22] The word 'People', when used with a capital P, is in effect a code word for 'the Communist Party'.   [23] Tsakalotos, op. cit., Vol. II, p. 27.
[24] Quoted from *Propaganda i Agitatsia*, Leningrad, No. 18, 1945, p. 3.

intend to renew its 1925 treaty of friendship, which was to expire the following November. This was the prelude to a Soviet demand that the Turks should cede to the Soviet Republics of Armenia and Georgia the frontier provinces of Kars and Ardahan, agree to Soviet military bases in the Straits of the Bosporus and the Dardanelles, and be willing to revise the Montreux Convention. By the middle of December 1945 a Soviet drive towards the Iranian province of Azerbaijan was clearly visible. In Eastern Europe and in Greece's Balkan neighbours pro-Communist 'coalition' governments—in some cases with the overt support of the Soviet armed forces—were setting the stage for the establishment of People's Democracies.

The Greek Communist leaders needed no special directives from Moscow to sense the meaning of all these political moves. The wartime alliance between the 'Capitalist' and the 'Socialist' camps was becoming a thing of the past, a historical freak which was rapidly shrivelling away, being replaced by a new phase in the struggle for a world Communist society. More precisely, the Soviet Union was obviously opening the new drive by applying pressure in the direction of the Mediterranean and the Persian Gulf. The KKE had a task to perform.

Using the familiar tactical device of concealing an attack behind the guise of defence, the Communist agitators brought their charges against the Greek authorities and the British to a hysterical crescendo. Zachariades himself, addressing the Plenum of the party activists (*activ*) of Macedonia and Thrace in late December 1945, openly declared that Greece had become the staging-point for armed attacks against the People's Democracies of Albania, Bulgaria, and Yugoslavia. 'In conclusion,' he said, 'we [Greece] are threatening international peace.'[25] In the first week of 1946, strikes instigated by the Communist-led ERGAS were launched in Athens and other Greek cities to protest against 'the persecution of innocent democratic citizens by the Monarcho-Fascist thugs'. On 13 January *Rizospastis* published a leading article under the title 'The Savage Persecution of the Slavo-Macedonian People'. It accused the 'tyrannical Greek–British régime of Athens' of carrying out an 'unimaginable terroristic oppression against the Slavo-Macedonian minority'. Finally, on 21 January, the Central Committee of the KKE released a manifesto in which it

[25] *Rizospastis*, 1 January 1946.

charged 'the British occupation forces with the principal and major responsibility for the situation in Greece' and listed a series of allegations against British troops, and particularly against British instructors with the Greek Army. The manifesto further included a demand for 'the immediate withdrawal of British troops from Greece', and a call for the organization of 'a voluntary corps consisting of faithful democrats, tested in the national resistance, who will clean up the Monarcho-Fascist dirt from the country and remove this threat to peace . . .'. On the very same day the acting chief of the Soviet delegation to the United Nations addressed a letter to the Security Council asking for a discussion of the situation in Greece, under Article 35 of the Charter. In his letter he declared:

. . . the presence of British troops in Greece after the termination of the war is not called for now, in the interests of protecting the communications of the British troops stationed in the defeated countries. On the other hand, the presence of British troops in Greece has been turned into a means of bringing pressure . . . which has not infrequently been used by reactionary elements against the democratic forces of the country. Such a situation . . . has given rise to extreme tension fraught with the possibility of serious consequences both for the Greek people and for the maintenance of peace and security.[26]

The similarity in timing and argument between the Soviet letter and the KKE manifesto seemed too exact to be entirely accidental.

After this, events began to move fast. Three weeks later, on the first anniversary of the Varkiza Pact, the 2nd Plenum of the Central Committee elected by the Seventh Congress met in Athens. 'After weighing the domestic factors, and the Balkan and international situation, the Plenum decided *to go ahead with the organization of the new armed struggle* against the Monarcho–Fascist orgy.' Zachariades, who repeated this statement in 1950 in a brochure entitled *Kenourghia Katastasi, Kenourghia Kathikonta,* added: 'Tito and his clique promised us the most substantial aid. This played a decisive role in our decision because in Yugoslavia, the main factor in the Balkans at that time, our new revolutionary move did not have an opponent who could

---

[26] Security Council Official Records, 1st year, Supplement No. 1, Annex 3, p. 73.

pose insurmountable obstacles.'[27] In effect, Zachariades was saying in 1950 that the 'Third Round', far from being a spontaneous reaction of 'democratic citizens' to the alleged oppression by the British and the Greek authorities, was a deliberate decision made in February 1946 by the High Command of the Greek Communist Party, aiming at expanding Communist control to the shores of the Aegean.

A 'tactical error'

The decision of the 2nd Plenum was soon translated into action. On the night of 30–31 March 1946 a band of Communist-led guerrillas attacked Litokhoron, a village in Thessaly. The attack took place on the eve of the first post-war parliamentary election in Greece. The British, in their effort to restore political stability, had promoted to the premiership Themistokles Sofoulis, the veteran Liberal statesman, who enjoyed the prestige needed to prepare and conduct fair and unimpeachable elections. Furthermore, they had suggested that foreign representatives should come to Greece as observers to attest on the spot how the election was carried out. The Soviet Government was urged to join the group of foreign observers, but they refused on the grounds that this would constitute interference in the domestic affairs of an Allied country. Presumably Moscow did not want to set a precedent which could create problems in Eastern Europe. Finally, the observer force was made up of British, French, and American representatives. Its official title was Allied Mission for Observing the Greek Elections (AMFOGE).

The Communists claimed throughout this period that EAM represented the great majority of the Greek people. An election, especially one conducted by a government headed by Sofoulis, under the watchful eye of more than a thousand foreign observers, was bound to expose this myth. Already, on 16 June 1945, the Politbureau had publicly declared that 'in the event of the conditions for a free expression of public will not being secured, the KKE, in consultation with the rest of the democratic [republican] forces, will consider abstaining from the election'.[28] In February 1946 the pro-republican forces in Greece were not only ready to participate in the election but,

---

[27] N. Zachariades, *Kenourghia Katastasi, Kenourghia Kathikonta* (Nicosia, Cypriot Edition, 1950), p. 38.   [28] *Rizospastis*, 16 June 1945.

with Sofoulis in the premiership, they were in charge of the election itself. Although conditions were not ideal, especially in the remote parts of the country, the opportunity for a return to normal was finally at hand.

The Communists and their fellow-travellers within EAM were not certain what course they should follow. In mid-January EAM publicly instructed all its members to register so as to be able to vote; this action was approved two days later by the Politbureau of the KKE.[29] But as the time drew nearer even the rank and file began to lose confidence in the outcome. The forthcoming election was reportedly the subject of private talks which Partsalides had in Moscow in late January with Molotov, Zhdanov, and others. Their advice was that the KKE should try to form a 'pan-democratic front' around EAM and participate in the election. They allegedly told Partsalides that the Soviet Government was committed to recognizing the results of the elections. This Soviet advice did not reach the Politbureau of the KKE till 21 February, two full weeks after the EAM Central Committee had decided to abstain from the election unless the Greek Government 'restored public order, eliminated Nazi collaborators and former members of the Security Battalions from the police, granted a general political amnesty, cleared the electoral lists of unqualified persons, and assisted in the formation of a representative democratic government with the participation of the parties of EAM'.[30] A few days later the 2nd Plenum of the Central Committee of the KKE had endorsed this statement.

Partsalides' report, which reached the Politbureau on 21 February, created some confusion. For a time the decision to abstain was on the point of being reversed. The Politbureau even issued a mild statement asserting that 'if goodwill exists and British opposition ceases, the requisite conditions for substantially free elections can be established'. The Politbureau went on to say that the KKE was 'ready to assist in every way in making sure that substantially free elections are held'.[31] Partsalides reportedly made it clear that the Soviet advice was in the form of a suggestion, not a directive, and that the final decision rested with the party. In the end the Communist

[29] *Rizospastis*, 16 June 1946.
[30] Ibid., 8 February 1946; see also ibid., 17 February 1946.
[31] Ibid., 22 February 1946.

leadership decided in favour of abstaining. EAM followed suit.

In 1950 Zachariades called the decision to abstain 'a tactical error'.[32] At the same time he revealed that the reasons for their decision were not those proclaimed in 1946. 'Monarcho-Fascist terrorism' had nothing to do with the KKE's decision.

> In deciding to abstain [Zachariades wrote] we believed that we were unmasking the British and depriving them of the opportunity of presenting Greece as an orderly and peaceful western European country, after a popular, parliamentary verdict. We believed that by taking part in the election we would cultivate parliamentary illusions among the masses. We believed that by abstaining we deprived the enemy of such an opportunity and that we prepared the People in the best possible way for the new armed conflict. . . . If we had participated in those elections [he added] and if we had used the opportunities offered by the parliamentary rostrum and by the activities of our deputies of unmasking the British and the Monarcho-Fascists, isolating most effectively the democrats of the Centre, uprooting the parliamentary illusions with the inevitable bankruptcy of the Parliament, we could have a more effective and a broader preparation for the new armed conflict.[33]

These statements need little comment. Participation or abstention were viewed by Zachariades in retrospect as alternative policies for the preparation of the 'new armed conflict'.

As an extra dividend the Communists expected, by abstaining from the election, to claim as their own followers all those who for various reasons normally fail to vote. In the election, as an indirect endorsement of King George, who was still abroad, the voters elected 191 candidates of the Populist (pro-royalist) Party, 56 of the National Political Union, 42 Liberals (pro-republicans), 17 of EDES, and 11 others representing minor groups. According to the AMFOGE observers, politically inspired abstentions amounted to no more than 9·4 per cent.

Following this setback, a serious intra-party quarrel broke out within the KKE. It was easily settled by expelling from the party the principal dissenters, Yiannis Petsopoulos, Andreas

---

[32] Significantly Kostas Koliyiannis, the present leader of the KKE, stated at the Eighth Party Congress (September 1961) that the abstention was one of the party's major tactical errors. 'The Party Central Committee,' he said, 'starting from the assumption that a revolutionary situation existed in the country, decided to abstain from the elections and turned towards an armed struggle' (text from Koliyiannis' report).

[33] Zachariades, *Dheka Khronia Palis*, p. 28.

Mountrihas (*Kapetan* Orestis), and *Kapetan* Zacharias.[34] Zachariades was in fact biding his time before launching his new rebellion. He was facing the difficult tactical problem of how to preserve the freedom of movement enjoyed by the party as a 'legal' political organization while organizing the new guerrilla army. This required a high degree of deception. While constantly hammering at the 'Monarcho-Fascist oppression' and the 'British occupation', the KKE sought to conceal its plans by constant appeals for 'popular unity'. In a speech to the KOA (Communist Organization of Athens) on 12 May 1946, Zachariades even insisted that the KKE ought 'to seek a political solution with the co-operation of all workers, even those who are rabidly nationalistic'. Such co-operation, he added, could be achieved by supporting the elemental political and economic demands of the working people, namely 'economic improvement, freedom, democracy, and independence and integrity for the nation'. It was all very confusing, even for party members. Zachariades had a good reason for trying to build up a seemingly conciliatory front. Although the first Soviet complaint at the UN Security Council in January had ended, after ten days of fruitless recriminations, when Vyshinsky proposed that 'a formal resolution . . . be dispensed with', it was quite evident that British troops could not remain in Greece much longer. When the Greek Parliament fixed 1 September 1946 as the date for the plebiscite on the King's right to return, it was generally accepted that with this final step the mission of the British troops would come to an end. The gradual thinning out of these units was already a telling sign. The vacuum of power on which the KKE counted so heavily seemed to be approaching.

[34] 'Politika kai Esokommatika Zitimata', speech by N. Zachariades, 12 May 1946; also Decision No. 40, Central Control Commission of the KKE; Decision of KOA, 2 June 1946.

16. Guerrilla War

Was the situation 'ripe' for armed revolution?

Intra-party quarrels have a peculiar after-effect: they bring to the surface the secret calculations of Communist leaders and lay bare for the use of the historian or the political scientist what would otherwise have remained for ever concealed. What was the thinking of the Greek Communists in 1946 as they embarked on their fateful drive to win power by force? Zachariades, in his book *Dheka Khronia Palis*, has provided a revealing insight.

What was the situation in 1946? First of all, domestically: on this there was no disagreement. We all agreed that the situation was ripe, that we should take up arms and fight. But we had also to examine the external factors. What backing did we have? The People's Democracies were behind us. But we had to start the struggle under British occupation. Therefore, we had to take into consideration the fact that we should not provoke the British into intervening immediately. Our policy ought to be *ostensibly* [*fenomenika*] defensive in order to unmask the reaction, to unmask British policy. Our effort in this area was directed towards isolating the British, to prevent their immediate armed intervention, while relying on the People's Democracies—in order to begin the attack on domestic reaction.[1]

It is not incidental that Zachariades and other Greek Communists attached so much importance to the attitude of the People's Democracies. There are many indications, from various sources, suggesting that the Third Round was sponsored by Tito, supported at first and then opposed by Stalin.

Even Zachariades' peculiar wording cannot obscure the strategic plan of the KKE in 1946. It was in fact based on two major considerations: first, that the movement would have the support of the Communist states to the north, and secondly, that the British should be successfully prevented from entering the fight, so that the KKE would have to cope only with the domestic 'reaction'.

---

[1] Zachariades, *Dheka Khronia Palis*, p. 40; author's italics.

On the surface, at least, conditions in Greece seemed to justify Zachariades' assertion that 'domestically the situation was ripe' in 1946. The non-Communist political parties were sharply divided on the so-called constitutional issue; the excesses of the extreme Right were forcing many vacillators back into the Communist fold; the economy was disorganized after five years of war, occupation, and revolution; the Civil Service, ill-paid and permeated by Communist sympathizers, was inefficient; the Army was weakened by the infiltration of Communist agents, while it lacked both the organization and the tactical experience to wage anti-guerrilla warfare. On the other hand, the KKE, in spite of its defeat in the streets of Athens in the December Revolution, enjoyed a number of important advantages in 1946. Recognized by the Varkiza Pact as one of the legitimate political parties, the KKE was free to carry on its propaganda and agitation through its own newspapers and numerous publications; it had carefully concealed large quantities of weapons in mountain hide-outs; it had more than 3,000 die-hards still at large, ready to take up the fight; its cadres were schooled in the conduct of guerrilla warfare during the Occupation; in addition, the KKE enjoyed the active support of the neighbouring satellites, Albania, Bulgaria, and Yugoslavia. This last was a decisive factor in the calculations of the Communist leadership. In March 1946 Zachariades, on his way back from a Communist meeting in Prague, stopped in Yugoslavia for talks. He was promised 'all-out help'.[2] While in Yugoslavia, Zachariades visited Boulkes and spoke to a settlement of Greek ELAS guerrillas and refugees who had fled to Yugoslavia after the Varkiza Pact. In a short speech he openly predicted that the 'Third Round' was approaching, and assured his listeners that the Greek people and eighty per cent. of the Army were already on the side of the revolution. One month later, with the approval and support of the Yugoslav Government, Boulkes became a military camp for the training of Greek guerrillas.

A formidable array of domestic problems and the promise of all-out assistance from the north seemed to justify the assertion of the Communist leadership that the situation was 'ripe'. But below the surface there were forces which in time were to frustrate Communist efforts. With the plebiscite of 1 September 1946 the thorny issue which divided the national leadership

[2] *Report* by Vassilis Bartzotas to the 6th Plenum, 9 October 1949.

was at last removed. Seventy per cent. of the voters called for
the return of the King. The republican leadership accepted the
popular verdict, thus leaving the Communists and their fellow-
travellers in a very uncomfortable isolation. True, the political
parties did not immediately close their ranks against the Communist challenge, but at least they were no longer wasting their
energies on an outdated feud. King George returned to Greece
on 27 September, welcomed (as this writer vividly remembers)
by a hysterically enthusiastic multitude. The lessons of the past
were not lost on the controversial monarch. He immediately
made repeated efforts to bring about a coalition government of
Liberals and Populists, in spite of the fact that the Populists and
their allies in Parliament had an overwhelming majority, which
technically made a coalition government unnecessary. These
efforts failed at first because Constantine Tsaldaris, the leader
of the Populists and a nephew of Panagis Tsaldaris, refused to
give up the premiership, while on the other hand even such
right-of-centre Liberals as P. Kanellopoulos, G. Papandreou,
and S. Venizelos made their participation in a coalition government conditional on the transfer to Liberal control of such
Ministries as Foreign Affairs, War, and Economics. Yet whatever the intensity of these disagreements, it was clear that with
the royal issue out of the way, the time would soon come for the
national leadership to close its ranks against the Communists.
In fact, the intensification of Communist provocation could
only bring closer the moment for co-operation among the
national parties.

Another important element in any assessment of the situation
in 1946 was the attitude of the British. Zachariades showed
repeatedly that he was fully aware of this factor. There was
already evidence that with British assistance the Greek Army
could be greatly strengthened. By the end of 1946 the Greek
armed forces had already reached the 90,000 mark. True, some
40,000 of these troops were in auxiliary units and there was
considerable infiltration by Communists and fellow-travellers,
but it was clear that, with sufficient supplies and a proper per-
sonnel policy, great reserves could be tapped, since the Greek
Government effectively controlled the urban centres and most
of the countryside.

All in all, the Communists did have a number of advantages
on their side in 1946, but to conclude from this that the situation

was 'ripe' for armed revolution could hardly have been supported by a sober and realistic analysis.

The KKE launches its 'Third Round'

On the night of 30 March 1946 a band of 'persecuted democratic citizens' (to quote *Rizospastis*, 31 March 1946) attacked the village of Litokhoron, on the eastern slopes of Mount Olympus. This was actually 'the beginning of the revolution', to quote another Communist source, the report of Dimitrios Vlantas to the Third Conference of the KKE (1950).[3] The attack on Litokhoron left corpses and charred ruins in its wake. It was an operation in the classic guerrilla hit-and-run style. In the months that followed, several other exposed villages with only detachments of gendarmes for their protection met with a similar fate. The tactics of the guerrilla bands were simple but effective: selection of target; concentration of forces; surprise attack at night against the gendarmerie station; forcible or voluntary recruitment of young villagers;[4] pillaging of foodstuffs; then retreat to mountain hide-outs. Throughout the summer of 1946 the guerrilla bands, portrayed by their colleagues in Athens as 'persecuted democratic citizens', continued their sudden, hit-and-run attacks, while the Communist Party, safe under the protection of the Greek laws, with its headquarters housed in a lofty building in the centre of Athens, carried on its open propaganda and subversive activities. *Rizospastis* and *Eleutheri Ellada* were calling daily for insurrection under the guise of 'mass self-defence'. The Greek Government, trying to disprove Communist allegations that an oppressive, Fascist régime was driving 'a desperate citizenry to armed resistance against Fascism', extended complete protection to the Communist leaders, thus leaving the field for a more violent reaction to the Rightist extremists. This policy was interrupted once in the summer of 1946, when intelligence reports indicated that Saraphis, Bakirtzis, and several other former high-ranking officers of ELAS were preparing to join the guerrillas in the mountains. The Greek Government ignored Communist protestations and exiled more than a hundred such officers to the Aegean Islands. The reports were probably exaggerated, but at

[3] *Pros tin III Synthiaskepsi tou KKE* (edition of the Central Committee of the KKE, 1950), p. 65.

[4] Markos, in his 'platform' of 1948, revealed that 'from the middle of 1947 practically all recruitment was effected by force'.

least the potential danger that the guerrillas might be given a respectable cover was eliminated.

In August the Politbureau, on the insistence of Zachariades, instructed Markos Vafiades,[5] one of the leaders of ELAS, to leave for the 'mountains' to co-ordinate the activities of the bands.[6] At about the same time the Greek Government resolved that the gendarmerie units were totally inadequate to cope with guerrilla warfare. A guerrilla movement is weak at the initial stages and can be checked, provided that it is met with an all-out campaign by strong military forces especially equipped for maximum mobility, which do not rest till the last of the guerrillas is captured or physically exterminated. But in most cases democratic governments are not prepared or equipped to launch such an attack against the guerrillas. The Communists often successfully create the impression that it is a non-political movement of disgruntled citizens, while they seemingly leave the door open for a peaceful resolution of the conflict. The Greek Government lacked the necessary experience in 1946, while even non-Communist circles in Greece and abroad supported Communist allegations for a while. It took the destruction of several villages before, in August 1946, the Greek Army was finally called in to take over from the hard-pressed gendarmes. It was only a beginning.

The leadership of the Army and their British advisers, partly

[5] See biographical note No. 5.

[6] The organization of the guerrilla forces in Greece followed this pattern. During the first stage (March–September 1946) there were small groups (*omathes*) of 7–10 men armed with old-fashioned firearms and a small supply of ammunition. They moved swiftly and joined forces only before an offensive operation. During the second stage (October 1946–March 1947) the guerrillas were organized into detachments (*syngrotimata*) of 70–100 men, each under a commander and a *kapetanios* (political officer). They were armed with rifles, some automatic weapons, and a small supply of ammunition. The detachments in each area were under the supervision of the regional 'self-defence' party organization, which was responsible for intelligence, supplies, and information. By the end of this second period, regional commands (*archighia*) were organized in the various mountainous complexes. These *archighia* had a military commander, a *kapetanios*, and a logistics officer. On 26 October 1946 the General Command (*Gheniko Archighio*) of the Democratic Army of Greece (*Dimokratikos Stratos Ellados*, DSE) was organized, with Markos Vafiades as the commanding officer. Under the General Command there were the following regional commands: Peloponnesos, Roumeli, Epirus, Thessaly, Central and Western Macedonia, Eastern Macedonia, and Western Thrace. During the third period, beginning in the spring of 1947, the forces of the DSE were organized into brigades (700–1,300 men), battalions (200–400), companies (50–100), platoons (20–60), and battle groups (10–30). The organization of the brigades into divisions began in September 1948.

from lack of experience and partly from a shortage of adequate forces, adopted two erroneous tactics, 'static defence' and 'time-limited cleaning-up operations'. The static defence proved particularly costly. It meant that whenever the garrison of a village or a small town was attacked by superior guerrilla forces, nearby garrisons were not allowed to leave their assigned posts and rush to the rescue. There was always the danger of falling into a guerrilla ambush or of another guerrilla force attacking and destroying the defenceless village. Static defence would have made sense if mobile forces had been available to come to the assistance of the besieged garrison and attack the concentrated guerrilla force from behind. As there were no such forces available, many villages paid a heavy toll. It was a hapless tactic, but one dictated by the existing circumstances. The tactic of 'time-limited' cleaning-up operations was not as costly in human life, but was almost totally ineffective. The failure of 'Operation Terminus' in the spring of 1947 was largely due to this tactic, which prescribed a specific timetable for each target area (e.g., five days for Parnassos, seven days for Elikon, etc.).[7] When the time prescribed for each cleaning-up campaign was over the troops were pulled back regardless of any actual results. The guerrillas, on the other hand, following in this Mao's familiar dictum, as a rule avoided any direct clashes with the regular troops and sought refuge either in remote hideouts or among villagers, posing as villagers themselves. After the departure of the Greek Army the guerrillas would reappear, ready to mete out severe punishment to anyone who might have been indiscreet or too friendly with the 'Monarcho-Fascist Army'. No wonder the intelligence information indispensable for flushing out guerrillas from their hiding-places was not forthcoming. The villagers, regardless of their personal feelings or political views, had no incentive to cooperate with a *visiting* army if they were to bring on themselves the iron fist of the ruthless guerrillas. On the other hand, a well-structured underground apparatus, manned by former Eamites or Elasites, provided the guerrillas with timely intelligence on the movements of the Army. The cleaning-up operations produced only frustration and outcries against the 'inefficiency' of the military leadership.

---

[7] Tsakalotos, op. cit., Vol. II, p. 59.

The basic rules of guerrilla warfare

Several foreign and domestic critics at that time argued that it was incomprehensible that an army of more than 100,000 troops was unable to liquidate 10,000 or even 15,000 guerrillas. The truth of the matter is that guerrilla warfare gives the guerrilla bands a power-ratio advantage over their opponents of almost ten to one. This is because the number of regular and special troops required for a successful anti-guerrilla fight is not determined by the numerical strength of the guerrillas, but by the area which must be protected against guerrilla attacks (defence) or saturated to cut off all possible avenues of escape for the guerrillas (offence). The Greek Communists were fully aware of the peculiar advantages enjoyed by a guerrilla force. In an article which appeared in the *Komep* issue of May 1947 it was succinctly stated that:

Greece has approximately 25 mountain ranges on the mainland, exclusive of the islands. If we visualize a radius of 20 kilometres from the centre of each mountain complex, we have a periphery of approximately 120 kilometres. Thus we have a total front-line of 3,000 kilometres. This will require huge forces on the part of the enemy.

From a strictly military standpoint this assessment was correct. Moreover, the guerrilla bands were able to move swiftly, select their targets, attack–destroy–depart, and immobilize large opposing forces by simply threatening to attack. Yet, in spite of these impressive tactical advantages, Communist guerrilla warfare is one of the least promising forms of aggressive military action, particularly now, in this period of 'peaceful coexistence' or rather 'mutual nuclear deterrence'. A guerrilla force can hardly expect to achieve a decisive and lasting change of the *status quo* as long as it remains a host of loosely organized bands, roaming the countryside without permanent bases, unable to establish continuous control over populated areas in the target country. If carried to extremes, the *tactical* advantages of the guerrilla forces may turn into a fatal *strategic* liability.

Guerrilla warfare is one form of sub-conventional warfare which may be used in this period of mutual nuclear deterrence or stalemate by the Communists in an effort to alter the political and social set-up in countries with residual economic and social problems due to inadequate economic development. The ultimate objectives of Communist-directed guerrilla operations are political in nature, and the tactics reflect a strange mixture of military and political considerations and techniques. In the last twenty-five years accumulated experience has shown that a guerrilla type of operation[8] may serve a practical purpose if it is used to prepare the ground for the time when: (*a*) foreign or outside intervention by regular military forces may become feasible; or (*b*) the morale of the loyal military forces in the target country is sufficiently undermined for the troops to become apathetic or even shift their allegiance in large numbers to the guerrillas; or (*c*) the leadership of the target country is discredited so that a substantial majority of the people accepts the guerrillas as liberators; or (*d*) after a protracted and inconclusive anti-guerrilla war Communists and sympathizers are admitted to a coalition government as a compromise solution.

It is quite evident that all these conditions are primarily political in character; even a foreign military intervention will depend on an assessment of the international political climate. During the Second World War the guerrilla forces in Europe and Russia were used to prepare the ground for the time when Allied troops would reach their area. As an auxiliary force, disrupting enemy communications and pinning down some sorely-needed forces, they played a useful role, though at a high cost in human life and resources. Under conditions of 'peaceful coexistence', however, outright military intervention in support of the guerrillas may not be forthcoming, for political reasons. Barring military intervention from the outside, a Communist guerrilla force must make full use of a host of political devices to attract popular support, discredit the national leadership, demoralize the opposing army, and sow the seeds of frustration among the people. To broaden its popular basis, a Communist guerrilla force will in most cases conceal its true identity behind a smokescreen of attractive demands for national integrity and social justice. At the same time such a force will, of necessity, rely on the use of selective terror to intimidate and neutralize those unwilling to support the movement. In the end, to consummate its plans, a guerrilla force must pass from the

---

[8] A guerrilla type of operation directed against a foreign army occupying a country against the will of the inhabitants presents somewhat different problems. Yet it, too, follows the general rules of guerrilla warfare as expounded here.

R

subconventional to the conventional stage, replacing hit-and-run tactics with conventional military operations aiming at lasting territorial gains. This is the crucial point in a guerrilla campaign. Once this transition takes place, the guerrillas lose the tactical advantage of their ten-to-one ratio and are forced to face their opponent on equal terms. In fact, the guerrilla army is placed at a serious disadvantage because, as a rule, it is inferior in numerical strength, supplies, and ammunition. This is the Achilles heel of a guerrilla operation, *provided that* at the crucial moment of transition the people and the armed forces of the target country are at a high level of morale and preparation.[9]

The passing from the sub-conventional to the conventional level poses a harsh dilemma to the leadership of a guerrilla movement. Without it, no lasting results can be expected; yet, if the transition is effected while the opponent is strong, the guerrilla army will be exposed to mortal danger. For this reason, a guerrilla force will first conduct a prolonged, demoralizing, destructive campaign to break the morale of the opponent. Needless to say, tactics such as the 'static defence' or the 'time-limited' sweeps through the countryside mentioned above can play directly into the hands of the guerrilla leadership by causing frustration, fatigue, and disillusionment.

Full-scale rebellion

Soon after the arrival of Markos Vafiades in the mountains, the guerrillas stepped up their activities. In the last week of September 1946 the village of Dheskati on the borders of Thessaly and Macedonia was briefly occupied by the guerrillas, who withdrew to the mountains after recruiting a number of young villagers and carrying away foodstuffs and other supplies. In November the guerrillas attacked the small frontier town of Skra, near the border with Yugoslavia. To discredit government charges that the guerrilla movement was assisted by the Balkan People's Democracies, Communist bands carried out some spectacular raids in the south, in Peloponnesus. Nevertheless, the Greek Government amassed a great deal of evidence proving the complicity of Greece's northern neighbours, and on 30

[9] D. G. Kousoulas, 'The Crucial Point of a Counter-guerrilla Campaign', *Infantry*, January–February 1963; also Kousoulas, 'The Guerrilla War the Communists Lost', *Proceedings*, U.S. Naval Institute, May 1963.

November instructed the Greek representative to the United Nations to request the Security Council to consider, under Articles 34 and 35 (1) of the Charter, the situation which was leading to friction between Greece, on the one hand, and Albania, Bulgaria, and Yugoslavia, on the other.[10] The Greek Government alleged that the guerrilla movement in Greece was receiving support from these three Balkan countries, and asked that the world organization should verify these charges by conducting an on-the-spot investigation. This was the third time within a year that the 'Greek case' had come before the United Nations. It had been discussed previously in January, following the Soviet charges, and again in August after a cable from the Ukrainian Foreign Minister, who accused the Greek Government of creating in the Balkans a situation endangering international peace and security. On both previous occasions the majority of the Security Council had refused to accept the Soviet allegations. In December, with Greece now the complaining party, the Security Council unanimously agreed to establish a UN Special Committee on the Balkans (UNSCOB), on which all eleven members of the Security Council were represented. The Soviet Union reluctantly agreed, for the simple reason that to refuse outright would have amounted to a tacit admission of the Greek charges. When, on 23 May 1947, the majority of the Commission members stated in their report that Albania, Bulgaria, and Yugoslavia had, indeed, been assisting the Greek guerrillas, the representatives of the USSR and Poland, in a dissenting report, held the Greek Government solely responsible for the troubled situation along Greece's northern frontiers.[11]

The deliberations of UNSCOB, the discussions at the Security Council in June, the transfer of the Greek question to the General Assembly, and the heated arguments which followed there proved, if nothing else, that the trouble in Greece, far from being an isolated case of popular discontent against an allegedly oppressive régime, was a reflection of the progressive disintegration of the wartime alliance. More important, the early discussions in the United Nations showed that the Americans were slowly but inexorably shifting to new vistas of foreign policy. The task of American diplomacy in 1947 was to avert the possibility of a new war by stating clearly the limits

[10] U.N. doc. S/203.   [11] Ibid., S/360.

of Soviet expansion, while at the same time offering the cool-headed realist in the Kremlin every incentive for renewed co-operation. The Truman Doctrine enunciated on 12 March 1947 was deliberately designed to serve the first objective; the Marshall Plan for aid to Europe, including the Soviet Union, the second. When the Soviet Union rejected the Marshall Plan and forced the East European governments to do the same, the cold war had clearly begun.

The Truman Doctrine, promising help to Greece at the time when Britain had openly stated her inability to carry the burden further, should have caused the leaders of the Greek Communist movement to have second thoughts. There was still time to pull back. The Communist Party remained 'legal', its leaders freely operating in Athens. Siantos was one of the Communist leaders who dared to voice serious misgivings and argue against the continuation of the armed struggle. Zachariades, supported in this by most of the members of the Politbureau, rejected Siantos' suggestion. The conflict was finally resolved by the sudden death of G. Siantos on 20 May 1947. He died reportedly of a heart attack in the clinic of a Communist physician named Petros Kokkalis. Zachariades later, in 1950, denounced Siantos as a life-long agent of the British, and advanced the bizarre theory that the British murdered Siantos to prevent him from being forced by Zachariades to go to the mountains and there made to reveal all his past dealings with them. Significantly, Kokkalis reappeared in December 1947 as 'Minister' of Health, Education, and Welfare in the first Cabinet of the 'Temporary Democratic Government' (PDK), established by the Communist guerrillas in the mountains on 24 December 1947. Zachariades, in his own brochure *Provlimata Kathothigisis* (1950), stated that 'Siantos' presence was a serious obstacle then to the entire work of the Politbureau . . . in the field of military preparation and the armed struggle'. With Siantos conveniently out of the way, Zachariades was free to proceed with his plan for an armed drive to seize power.

In July 1947 a strong guerrilla force from the mountain regions of Grammos, on the Albanian frontier, thrust out in the direction of Ioannina in Epirus. They did not attack the town but established centres of control in a wide area, in Zagorokhoria. Throughout the summer strong guerrilla units attacked several villages and small provincial towns. They did not succeed in holding any worth-while urban centre, but their objective was mainly to cause fear and frustration, and this they largely achieved.[12]

On the political scene the process of conciliation within the non-Communist camp moved forward. In January 1947 Tsaldaris' Government had been replaced by a coalition which included P. Kanellopoulos, G. Papandreou, and S. Venizelos from the Centre, and had as its Premier the elder statesman Dimitrios Maximos, a respected Populist. Constantine Tsaldaris kept the Ministry of Foreign Affairs, while Napoleon Zervas, the former guerrilla leader, headed the Ministry of Security. The death of King George on 1 April 1947 brought to the throne his brother Paul and his intelligent wife, Frederika. King Paul and Queen Frederika had not been directly involved in the old dynastic quarrels; under them, co-operation among the political leaders was made much easier. By the end of the summer a new coalition Government was formed under the leadership of eighty-seven-year-old Themistokles Sofoulis (Liberal), with Constantine Tsaldaris (Populist) as Minister of Foreign Affairs, and an array of top political personalities from all major parties.

The Communists were totally isolated. It was high time for them to pull back from the brink and call off the fight. This could have been done without even a formal declaration. The guerrillas could have taken advantage of the standing amnesty offer and returned to their villages. Instead, the 3rd Plenum of the KKE Central Committee, which met on 12–15 September 1947 with only six out of its twenty-five regular members,[13] decided 'to transfer the centre of gravity of the party's activities to the military–political sector in order to make the Democratic Army the force which will bring about in the shortest possible time the establishment of a free Greece, basically in all the areas of Northern Greece'. In other words, the 3rd Plenum decided to prepare for the passing into the conventional stage. Markos was already opposed to the decision, but he was forced to accept Zachariades' lead. The Plenum further decided 'to mobilize all the party's forces for the unqualified support, expansion, and leadership of the Democratic Army's war effort'. Up to this

---

[12] By now the guerrilla bands had assumed the lofty title of 'Democratic Army of Greece' (DSE).

[13] *Neos Kosmos*, Vol. 8, August 1950, p. 478.

time the KKE had not formally associated itself with the Democratic Army. But on 8 October 1947 *Rizospastis* published a summary of the decisions taken by the 3rd Plenum, together with an interpretative article by Zachariades himself, openly calling for all-out war. Ten days later, *Rizospastis* and *Eleutheri Ellada* were closed down by a court order. Zachariades and most of the other Communist leaders went underground and soon joined their colleagues in the mountains. In November a joint Greek–American staff was established for the more effective direction of the fight against the guerrillas. The right to strike was temporarily suspended in December. When Markos Vafiades, against his better judgement, announced in the mountains on Christmas Eve the establishment of a 'Temporary Democratic Government' (PDK),[14] the Greek Government took a long overdue step and outlawed the Communist Party. These decisive measures on the part of the Greek Government could only have been taken by a leadership with a sufficiently wide popular base to offset all the outcry about 'Fascist oppression'. With the lines now definitely drawn, the conflict entered its next critical phase.

[14] The first 'Cabinet' of the Temporary Democratic Government (PDK) was composed of Markos Vafiades as Premier and Minister of War; Y. Ioannides, Vice-Premier and Minister of Foreign Affairs; Miltiades Porphyrogennis, Minister of Justice; Petros Kokkalis, Minister of Health, Education, and Welfare; Vassilis Bartzotas, Minister of Finance; Dimitrios Vlantas, Minister of Agriculture; Leonidas Stringos, Minister of National Economy. Markos later said that the establishment of this 'government' was premature.

17. The Tide Turns

Disunity sets in

Immediately after the establishment of the PDK, UNSCOB called on all governments to refrain from recognizing the rebel 'government' lest they aggravate the situation. To the discomfiture of the Greek Communists their 'government' was not recognized by anyone, not even the Government of the USSR or the People's Democracies. This caused confusion and disillusionment in the ranks of the DSE, but they were assured by their leaders that recognition would be forthcoming as soon as they had permanently established themselves in control of a substantial town. In fact, the first attempt to provide the PDK with a capital had failed miserably. On Christmas Day a strong guerrilla force had attacked the small town of Konitsa, near the Albanian border. This was the first time the DSE had acted as a well-organized, conventional military force. It has already been stated that passing from the sub-conventional to the conventional stage is the most crucial step in a guerrilla operation and can only succeed if it is taken at the moment when the opponent is demoralized and in the process of disintegration. The Greek Communists made the fatal strategic error of passing from the sub-conventional to the conventional stage at a time when their opponent was entering a new period of strength and cohesion, mirrored in the American presence and the co-operation of the national leadership under King Paul and Themistokles Sofoulis. The Greek Army, far from being on the verge of disintegration, was growing steadily and rapidly in both strength and experience. The Battle of Konitsa showed that a guerrilla army, acting prematurely as a conventional force, loses most of its tactical advantages when it exposes itself to the superior power of its opponents. The leadership of the Greek Army, under the stern and energetic General Constantine Ventiris, reacted swiftly. Strong forces converged on the scene, and the guerrillas who had laid siege to Konitsa found themselves surrounded by national forces.[1] During the night of 31 December 1947 to 1 January 1948 the DSE command gave the signal for a hasty retreat. By its own reckoning the DSE lost

[1] Tsakalotos, op. cit., Vol. II, p. 69.

650 dead and wounded. This, together with the disclosure that Queen Frederika had been inside Konitsa visiting the besieged town during the fighting, gave a great boost to the morale of both the Army and the people.

The Communists' failure to capture Konitsa for their 'capital' was only one, rather marginal, reason for the refusal of the USSR and the People's Democracies to recognize the PDK. Behind the façade of Communist solidarity, reflected in the establishment of the Cominform, divisive forces were already stirring ominously. Stalin disliked the air of independence displayed by Tito, while the idea of Albania's union with Yugoslavia had not received unanimous support in Tirana. The agreement reached in August 1947 between Georgi Dimitrov, the Bulgarian Premier, and Tito to take gradual steps towards a Balkan federation was foundering on the rocks of Soviet opposition, and the traditional Bulgaro-Yugoslav disagreements focused as usual on the Macedonian issue. Tito's idea was that Macedonia as a whole should form an autonomous state to be incorporated in the proposed federation. To the Bulgarians this meant that Bulgaria, instead of gaining the whole of Macedonia, would lose her part of Macedonian territory (Pirin) to the new Macedonian state, and her position within the federation would be reduced to that of Serbia or Montenegro. Stalin had been infuriated by Tito's triumphant trip through Bulgaria and Rumania in September 1947 and his 'presumption' in thinking that he had an international role to play. *Pravda*, on 28 January 1948, issued a stern warning against any plans 'for a Balkan or Danubian federation including Poland, Czechoslovakia and Greece'. Shortly afterwards, on 10 February, according to Milovan Djilas, Bulgarian and Yugoslav representatives received a severe dressing-down from Stalin himself, while the Yugoslavs were unequivocally told that the revolt in Greece 'should fold up immediately'.[2]

All the evidence that this writer has been able to obtain from persons who were close to the top Communist leadership at that time indicates that in all probability neither Markos nor Zachariades knew of Stalin's 'advice' to the Yugoslavs to end the rebellion in Greece.[3] However, the fermentations behind the

[2] Djilas, op. cit., p. 181.
[3] Rear-Admiral Ellis M. Zacharias, in his book *Behind Closed Doors* (p. 157), relates that there was an intelligence report which indicated that '. . . in a special

Iron Curtain, revealed as they were in sporadic, cryptic statements or moves, together with the growing strength of the
Greek Government, could not but have a serious impact on the
cohesion and effectiveness of the Communist Party and its
'Democratic Army'. Greek, Bulgarian, Titoist, Bulgaro-
Macedonian, Soviet, and Albanian influences were often working at cross-purposes behind the scenes. As was the case with
ELAS, the ordinary guerrilla of the DSE was separated from
the leaders by a wall of differing motives. In the course of his
service in the Greek armed forces, this writer met and spoke at
the time with a great number of guerrillas after their capture or
surrender. For the rank and file, the influence of their Greek
background seemed to predominate. The great majority of
the ordinary guerrillas wanted a free and prosperous Greece
with social and economic justice. This was all simply translated
into a better deal for the downtrodden. As most of them came
from the poor villages of the mountainous areas, they lacked
sophistication and could easily be swayed and duped by appeal-
ing slogans. At the same time most of them had a fairly low
margin of perseverance, and of awareness of, or fanatical attachment to, the ultimate goals of the movement.

Somewhat different influences moved those guerrillas who
came from the so-called Slavo-Macedonian minority. Some
considered themselves to be Bulgarians and looked to Bulgaria
as their mother-country. Others believed in the existence of a
separate Macedonian nationality and tended to accept more
readily the Yugoslav point of view.

Above this line of limited awareness were the leaders, the
few who knew what was really happening. Among them, all the
foreign Communist centres of power could find amenable
clients. As long as Stalin and Tito appeared as the senior and
the junior partner in a well co-ordinated enterprise, all the conflicting influences could be reconciled and channelled into the
mainstream of Communist expansion into the southernmost tip
of the Balkans. The trouble started when these two luminaries
collided, with a bitter exchange of recriminations, in June 1948.
It has been suggested that Markos sided with Tito, and Zachariades with Stalin. This is only a surface judgement. For one

---

Politburo session held on Aug. 21–23, 1949 . . . the Kremlin decided to liquidate
the Greek guerrilla movement . . .'. By that date, of course, the DSE was rapidly
disintegrating under the blows of the Greek Army.

thing, Stalin is said to have suggested an end to the Third Round as early as February 1948. Yet it was Zachariades who became the champion of 'war to the bitter end', while Markos advocated a return to a more limited, sub-conventional type of operation. This seeming contradiction calls for a more thorough analysis.

Zachariades versus Markos

The DSE had passed into the conventional stage at a time when there were no signs of impending disintegration in the Greek Government or Army. On the other hand, Tito's break with the Cominform, and his reluctant, at first, but inevitable change to a less militant policy towards the West ruled out any prospect of a direct military intervention by Tito on the side of the DSE. This turn of events posed a crucial strategic problem to the leadership of the DSE. Markos tackled the thorny issue realistically, at least up to a point. In a revealing analysis written in the autumn of 1948, he laid bare the serious weaknesses of the movement. He pointed out that the recruitment of new guerrillas 'did not even reach 10 per cent. of young Greeks', while 'since the middle of 1947, recruitment to the DSE was achieved almost entirely by force'. He acknowledged that 'the Monarcho-Fascist régime' had achieved a 'relative stabilization', while 'the people's democratic forces' could not expect any serious support in the urban areas, nor did they have the necessary strength to attack the cities. He concluded by saying:

The DSE cannot overthrow Monarcho-Fascism in the near future by its own armed strength, but only with direct military aid from outside, following the recognition of the PDK by those countries that are friendly to us. However, there is no such possibility because the DSE has been unable to create the proper conditions, and because the international situation does not at the moment seem to allow such a step.[4]

Markos did not suggest an end to the struggle. The amnesty provisions offered by the Greek Government did not include the Communist leadership or those directly accused of common crimes. No Communist leader dared even to hint at what would amount to an unconditional surrender. Instead, Markos advised a return to the sub-conventional stage,

[4] *Neos Kosmos*, Vol. 8, August 1950, pp. 476–83.

intensive, guerrilla-type activity, by small, mobile, lightly armed contingents, saboteurs, and snipers, able to choose where and when to fight . . . to cause the Americans and the Monarcho-Fascists a continuous military and economic haemorrhage, a deepening political instability—and finally, taking advantage of the deteriorating conditions of the Greek workers, to intensify the movement in the urban areas, strengthen the DSE, and deliver strong and co-ordinated blows.'[5]

Markos had rightly concluded that the DSE had entered the conventional stage prematurely, but to return to the sub-conventional stage was easier said than done. It is not difficult to visualize the effect of such a decision on the morale of the rank and file. Guerrilla warfare had its own process of development, and if that process is abruptly reversed the entire movement is threatened with disintegration. Besides, with the Greek Army now strong and experienced, the villagers armed and placed under the command of regular officers, the nation united and confident, sub-conventional guerrilla bands would fall an easy prey to a concerted counter-guerrilla campaign.

Zachariades fought bitterly against Markos' ideas and decreed that 'what happens to Monarcho-Fascism and the American occupation depends entirely on the military activities of the DSE, the popular uprising in the towns . . ., the decisive solution of our problems of reserves . . ., the decisive and consistent application of our policy for brotherhood, understanding and peace'.[6] The last phrase was obviously designed for popular consumption.

This fundamental conflict about the strategic development of the struggle which started in the spring of 1948 was at first suppressed by Zachariades. During the 4th Plenum, which met in Petra Bouka on the Grammos on 28–29 June 1948, the 'Leader' of the KKE forced Markos, the Premier, Minister of War, and Commander-in-Chief of the 'Democratic Army', to forget his differences of opinion and present a resolution written by Zachariades. In it the Central Committee, or rather ten of its twenty-five members, resolved that the end of 'Monarcho-Fascism' was 'closer than ever, provided every Greek fully performs his duty to the country'. Shortly afterwards, Zachariades was able to point with some justification to the outcome of the large-scale offensive carried out by the Greek Army

[5] Ibid., p. 478.   [6] *Pros tin III Synthiaskepsi tou KKE*, p. 117.

against the Communist stronghold of Grammos in the summer of 1948. As we shall see later, Grammos fell after seventy days of bitter fighting, but the Communist forces, taking advantage of their freedom to pass through Albania, successfully disengaged and transferred their forces to the area of Vitsi in North-Western Macedonia. This seeming success could only postpone the inescapable end. That Markos wrote his 'opportunistic platform' three months after this 'strategic manoeuvre' shows that he had not been fooled by the apparent achievement.

Successful anti-guerrilla tactics

Caught in a web of their own making, both Markos and Zachariades had proposed the wrong solutions. Neither had the courage or the integrity to call off the entire operation and face the political consequences. While Markos' strategy of returning to the sub-conventional stage would have led to the gradual decomposition of the movement, Zachariades' desperate decision to continue the fighting on a conventional plane amounted to virtual suicide.

Markos had correctly assessed the 'relative stabilization of Monarcho-Fascism'. This stabilization, already quite evident in the summer and autumn of 1948, was the end-product of a successful anti-guerrilla strategy. The strategy was based on two foundations, political and military, in full recognition of the dual character of a Communist guerrilla operation. Politically, the Communists had been isolated as the national parties had closed ranks around King Paul and his democratic Prime Minister, the venerable Sofoulis. The significance of this cannot be over-emphasized. A Communist guerrilla operation is, at least partly, political in character, and no traditional military techniques can suffice to overcome the challenge. In fact, successful anti-guerrilla tactics require a direct reversal of the concepts which form the basis of a guerrilla offensive. The ultimate success of the guerrillas—barring military support from the outside—depends on the gradual subversion of their opponent's morale. Thus, to strengthen the morale of the nation and of its armed forces becomes the first essential in a successful anti-guerrilla operation. A parochial, narrow-minded leadership, with anti-Communism as its only credential, cannot possibly provide the required foundation for a successful war against a Communist guerrilla offensive. The Communist

leadership of a guerrilla force relies, as a rule, on an assortment
of attractive slogans for political and social reforms, designed
to gain the support of wide segments of both the peasantry and
the urban lower-income groups. As long as the war continues,
no such reforms can be implemented. But it is the *promise* that
counts, not the implementation. Similarly, the national leadership of the target country must present a programme for the
solution of the major social and economic problems, together
with the hope of an all-round attack on poverty, disease, illiter-
acy, economic stagnation, and exploitation. As in the case of the
guerrillas, the national leadership cannot carry out its programme while the war is on. Again it is the promise that really
counts. The value of a promise depends on the reliability of
those who make it. For this reason, it becomes imperative to
form a leadership which, by its composition alone, can justify
the expectation and the faith that the promise is genuine, not
merely a propaganda sham. The Sofoulis Government, with its
broad, representative basis, had provided exactly this all-
important requirement for a successful anti-guerrilla strategy.

In the military sector the errors and the inadequacies of the
recent past could not be eradicated overnight with one swift
stroke. The Greek Army had to be reorganized, its strategy and
tactics reshaped. By trial and error, a strategy which could be
called the strategy of staggered expansion of control gradually
evolved. The 'time-limited' sweeps through the countryside and
the spasmodic cou   measures against Communist initiatives
were abandoned. Instead, the Army began systematically to
expand its control over well-defined areas. This meant, up to a
point, a reversal of the guerrilla tactics; it involved the selection
of a target area, the concentration of regular and special anti-
guerrilla forces, continuous offensive operations, the extermination or capture of the guerrilla force in the area, mopping-up
operations by auxiliary units, the establishment of local units
for static self-defence, the extension of permanent government
control over the cleared area, measures to prevent re-infiltration
of the area by guerrilla units, then the selection of another
suitable area and a repetition of the process. A good example of
this strategy was 'Operation Dawn' in Roumeli. It started on
15 April 1948. The army high command, disregarding the
protests of some military leaders on the field, transferred several
units to Central Greece and placed them under the command

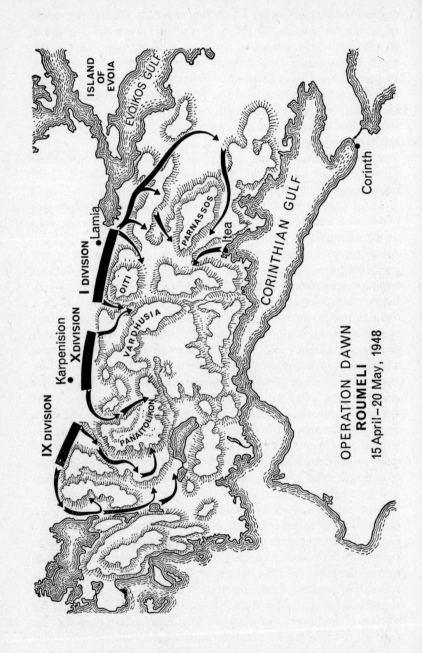

OPERATION DAWN
ROUMELI
15 April – 20 May, 1948

of the First Army Corps. The other two Army Corps were left with only the necessary force for defensive action. The First Army Corps, augmented to the level of 27 infantry battalions, 16 National Guard battalions, 6 gendarmerie battalions, 2 battalions of LOK (Mountain Commandos), 48 pieces of artillery, and a regiment of armoured cars, completely surrounded the area of Roumeli, establishing three or four successive and overlapping lines of interception, while the main infantry and LOK forces carried the thrust from north, west, and east against a force of approximately 2,500 guerrillas. Escape to the south was blocked by the Corinthian Gulf, heavily patrolled by the Greek Navy.[7]

The tactic of establishing several lines of interception deprived the guerrillas of their familiar advantage of being able to slip through the army lines into other safe areas. The First Army Corps did not end the operation till almost the entire guerrilla force was for all practical purposes destroyed. The weather also played into the hands of the national forces. A heavy snowfall in the mountains, followed by storms and a drop in temperature, exposed the pursued guerrillas to added hardships. The national troops, better clothed and equipped, could more easily withstand the rigours of bad weather. Moreover, the tracks of the guerrillas could be easily traced on the snow. The national troops, in this reversing their previous tactics, moved, as a rule, during the night, taking up positions under cover for surprise offensive operations during the day. Speedy movements were carried out only when detachments were in actual contact with retreating guerrillas. Otherwise, the national forces proceeded to new positions only after they had completely exterminated or captured the bulk of the guerrillas in a given sector.

After one month of continuous pursuit 2,000 guerrillas were either dead or taken prisoner. At the same time the First Army Corps broke up the underground organization in the villages, removing both agents of intimidation and sources of information and supply for the guerrillas from among the villagers. After that, intelligence started to flow in freely. The remnants of the Roumeli guerrilla force, hunted constantly, with their sources of food and supply cut off, were gradually eliminated by the battalions of the National Guard, the gendarmerie, and the

[7] Tsakalotos, op. cit., Vol. II, pp. 115–22.

militia which was formed in every village under the command of regular or reserve army officers. The entire operation, which at its critical moments was observed by General James Van Fleet, the chief of the US Military Mission, and Marshal Alexander Papagos, lasted approximately three months.

During 1948 the army leadership took a series of measures designed to eliminate past shortcomings. First, the 'selective recruitment' of ideologically reliable young men, which was being used as a protection against the infiltration of the armed forces by Communist agents, was abandoned. Under this mistaken method pro-Communist draftees were deferred 'for health reasons', thus leaving them free to go on with their subversive activities or even join the guerrillas in the mountains. Under the new system all those eligible for military service were inducted without exception. Those of questionable loyalty were placed in unimportant posts. The most dangerous among them were held in a concentration camp on the island of Makronisos off the coast of Attica, where they received intensive indoctrination. Some of the most celebrated anti-Communist military battalions came out of this camp.

Secondly, with American economic assistance the Army doubled its forces. Its units were trained to meet the challenge of this type of warfare. With American supplies, their mobility and fighting strength increased. Special commando units were organized, known by their Greek initials as the LOK.[8] The Air Force was supplied with American dive bombers and other equipment.

Thirdly, with the experience gained after almost two years of anti-guerrilla fighting, with the co-operation of the American military mission (under the command of General Van Fleet since February 1948), and in close contact with Marshal Papagos, who held the honorary position of Chief of the King's Military House, the military leaders devised the plan of staggered or progressive expansion of control over specified areas of the country, moving in the general direction of the Communist strongholds in the north. The plan included: (*a*) the relentless

---

[8] These units proved extremely useful in carrying out probing operations, obtaining intelligence, delivering surprise blows often behind the lines of guerrilla control or deep in their hide-outs. Nevertheless, such units cannot by themselves establish and maintain permanent control; a combination of such special anti-guerrilla units with regular army forces is an indispensable foundation for a victorious anti-guerrilla strategy.

eradication of the underground organizations used by the KKE
for information, recruitment, and supplies; (*b*) the continuous
pursuit, day and night, of the guerrilla bands, the discovery and
destruction of their camps and supply depots, and the engage-
ment and liquidation of all remaining guerrilla units in a given
area; (*c*) a systematic effort to prevent the re-entry of guerrilla
bands into areas already cleared, by organizing village militia
units; (*d*) the establishment of a 'no-man's-land' by removing
the population of entire villages located near Communist
strongholds, to deprive the guerrillas of indispensable sources of
information and food at critical moments.[9] This tactic of removing people from exposed areas has some disadvantages and
must be used with caution. It resulted in the concentration of
thousands of villagers, under difficult conditions, in the major
provincial towns, and imposed a heavy burden on the country's
already overtaxed budget. Furthermore, a prolonged concentration of people in the 'evacuee camps' could have produced an
explosive situation which might have played right into the
hands of Communist agitators. In Greece it proved successful
because it was applied at decisive moments and for a relatively
short time.

There is one more point of general interest. The young draftees were not merely trained militarily. At the same time they
were given a political indoctrination at the training centres that
was designed to evoke in them strong patriotic feelings, contempt for the enemy, and an abiding determination to fight.
The leaders of the Greek armed forces had correctly understood
that in this type of warfare military training alone cannot
suffice. After all, a well-trained soldier may become a very
dangerous guerrilla if he ever decides to cross the line to join the
other side, while the best-trained and equipped soldier will be of
limited value if he is unwilling to stand up and fight.

The final act

The success attained in the early part of 1948 by the strategy
of staggered expansion of control convinced the military leadership that the time had come for a final offensive against the

---

[9] 'The greatest difficulty which our troops faced during enemy operations was
hunger, as a result of the evacuation of the peasants and their concentration in
the towns.' D. Vlantas, 'Triamisi Khronia Palis', in *Pros tin III Synthiaskepsi*,
p. 109.

S

Communist stronghold of Grammos, along the border with Albania. The operation which started in early June 1948 was bogged down for almost forty days; tactical errors were committed by the leadership of the Greek Army and by some military commanders in the field, while the guerrillas, supplied freely from Albania, fought from strongly-fortified positions. Finally, the First Army Corps, which had remained in Roumeli to complete its task, entered the fighting. The offensive was stepped up, and by 20 August 1948 the last positions of the guerrillas in Grammos were captured.[10] At this point the DSE retreated into Albania and re-entered Greece in the area of Vitsi in North-West Macedonia. Finding the area weakly defended, they penetrated southwards as far as the outskirts of Kastoria and Florina. The DSE 'manoeuvre' was completed by 25 August. Four days later the Politbureau of the KKE discussed the entire operation and passed this resolution:

With unshakable determination and confidence in our final victory, we declare once again: We want independence and democracy; we want peace and tranquillity; we shall accept any honest, democratic understanding. We proffer our hand to all who believe in the People, in Democracy, in Independence and Peace. Our strength is the confidence of the People, our slogan, till the rights of the People win, remains ALL IN ARMS, ALL FOR VICTORY.

What was the meaning of this statement? During the deliberations of the Politbureau, Markos, not deceived by the DSE's 'successful manoeuvre', suggested that now was the time to seek some negotiated settlement, using as a lever the inevitable disillusionment of the 'Monarcho-Fascists' after the successful re-entry of the DSE into the Vitsi area. Zachariades and most of the other participants felt that there was little chance of coming to an understanding with the 'Monarcho-Fascists and their American masters'. So the argument came back to the fundamental dispute between Markos and his suggestion for a return to the sub-conventional stage, and Zachariades and his insistence that the DSE should continue operating as a conventional army even though no foreign intervention was forthcoming, nor was a collapse of the opponent in sight. The decision of the Politbureau mentioned above reflected, under a deceptive screen of reasonableness for the sake of the rank-and-file, the

[10] Tsakalotos, op. cit., pp. 145–60. See also Lt.-Gen. E. Vasilas, 'I X Merarkhia', *Eleutheria*, 16–29 July 1961.

conflicting viewpoints at the summit of the Communist hierarchy—and also Zachariades' pre-eminence.

Behind the scenes the dispute went on. At another meeting of
the Politbureau on 15 November 1948 Markos submitted in
writing his views on a return to the sub-conventional stage. It
was this memorandum that was later labelled 'the opportunistic
platform' by Zachariades.[11] At the meeting Markos was supported only by Khryssa Khatzivassiliou. From that moment,
Markos was removed from any position of real power. Zachariades now moved to put into effect his strategy of conventional
warfare. In early November the 18th DSE Brigade attacked
Siatista, and held the town for a day. On 13 November two
guerrilla brigades attacked Voulgareli and overpowered the
garrison. During the same period the DSE made a determined
effort to strengthen the guerrilla forces operating in Peloponnesus by dispatching a caïque carrying more than 1,500 rifles,
100 machine-guns, more than 1,000 land mines, and other
weapons and explosives. The attempt failed as the caïque was
intercepted and sunk by a Greek naval unit.

On 11 December 1948, just before midnight, a strong
guerrilla force attacked Karthitsa and quickly overpowered the
outnumbered garrison. The guerrillas remained in the town for
two days, looting and burning. Attacked by the 77th Brigade,
they withdrew towards the Agrafa range, taking with them
more than 500 'recruits', many of them young women.

During the night of 22 December, three guerrilla brigades
which had moved south from the area of Kaimaktsalan attacked Edessa and Naoussa, two important towns on the road
from Salonika to Florina. At Edessa the attack failed, but at
Naoussa the guerrillas succeeded in entering the town. They
were forced to withdraw three days later, but before leaving
they managed to abduct more than sixty 'recruits' and quantities of foodstuffs and pharmaceutical supplies.

Emboldened by these successes, the same three guerrilla
brigades prepared another attack on Naoussa. They struck on
the night of 11–12 January 1949, and a few hours later they
penetrated the town's defences. Efforts to recapture the town
started the next day, but had little success. The guerrillas held
their ground for three days. They left in good order on the
night of 14–15 January, taking with them great quantities of

[11] See page 252.

supplies and more than 600 'recruits', most of them teenage boys and girls.

The guerrilla forces which had attacked Karthitsa in December moved slowly southward through the Pindus range and by 5 January they reached the area of Karpenision, a key town on the road between Larissa and Agrinion. On the night of 19–20 January the guerrilla force, numbering more than 3,000, attacked the town. The garrison was outnumbered by five to one and was finally beaten on the following day, 21 January. The guerrillas remained in control of the city until 8 February, when, attacked by strong national forces, they withdrew into the mountains.

Apparently encouraged by these successes, Zachariades, since November the real leader of the DSE, decided to move into the forefront and put an end to the fiction of Markos' leadership. On 8 February 1949 the *Dheltion* (Bulletin) of the DSE announced that Markos had resigned from all his positions 'for reasons of health'. This was too transparent an explanation even for the most gullible among the Communists. At the time, of course, few knew that at the 5th Plenum, which met on 29–30 January 1949, Markos had been charged with defeatism, if not outright treason, and placed under what amounted to house arrest. He was angrily denounced by Zachariades for holding that 'our struggle for the liberation of our country is doomed, that the liberation of our country can only be achieved with foreign armed assistance'.[12]

The 5th Plenum, completely dominated by Zachariades, tackled the thorny 'question of reserves'. This was a euphemism, a play on words, to cover up the inability of the DSE to replace its losses and increase its strength by new volunteers. The 'question of reserves' was indeed at the basis of its predicament. However premature the passing into the conventional stage, the DSE might have survived and even successfully surmounted its difficulties if it had had wide popular support translated into new forces for the dwindling guerrilla army, culminating possibly in wholesale desertions among the national troops. This did not happen. The Communist attempt to seize power by force remained a terroristic enterprise with a narrow popular base, devoid of any real social content. To most Greeks the DSE, contemptuously referred to as the '*katsapliades*' (goat-

[12] *Pros tin III Synthiaskepsi tou KKE*, p. 115.

thieves), represented a foreign-directed spearhead against the freedom of Greece. Its narrow base was mainly made up of poor peasants who had usually been forced into the ranks. The leaders in the mountains, as well as the Communists and the Communist-sympathizers in the urban centres, were mostly of petty-bourgeois origin, often seeking in a Communist victory the satisfaction of petty personal ambitions.[13] They were not too eager to risk their lives in a futile and unpromising campaign. For these reasons the problem of 'reserves' remained acute throughout the war. While there were no defections of any consequence from the National Army, there was a constant trickle of deserters from the 'Democratic Army'.

At the 5th Plenum, in a last-ditch effort to tap the few remaining sources of manpower, Zachariades reversed his position on the Macedonian question and returned to the old, discredited policy of supporting an 'independent Macedonian state'. In 1949, with Yugoslavia already out of the Communist fold, the establishment of an independent Macedonian state of Communist making could only have served the designs of the Bulgarians. Significantly, a little over a month before the 5th Plenum, Zachariades, accompanied by Ioannides and Vlantas, took time off from the direction of the fighting and the intra-party squabbles to attend the Fifth Congress of the Bulgarian Communist Party in Sofia. There, by all indications, he was promised sorely-needed aid in exchange for a return to the old policy of an 'independent' Macedonia. The KKE, in a desperate effort to gain the support of the 'Bulgaro-Macedonians' or 'Slavo-Macedonians' located in villages controlled by or accessible to the DSE, passed a resolution openly advocating an 'independent' Macedonian state including the portion of Macedonia inhabited by more than 1,500,000 Greeks. At the same time it formally admitted the NOF, the Slavo-Macedonian 'National Liberation Front', into the leadership of the movement. An ill-considered move, made in desperation, the resolution on the Macedonian question furnished one more argument for branding the party with the stamp of treason.[14]

---

[13] *Pros tin III Synthiaskepsi tou KKE*, pp. 22–24.

[14] Zachariades later explained the reasons behind this policy decision. 'With this change we were striving to mobilize the Slavo-Macedonian forces and frustrate Tito's divisive and subversive efforts.' *Dheka Khronia Palis*, pp. 122–3.

The 5th Plenum, in complete disregard of what actually lay within the power of the DSE, decided to,

first, continue without respite a war of attrition . . . , transfer the war into the towns and cities with large offensive operations and partisan attacks by sniper forces . . . , solve the problem of reserves through mass recruitment and a reduction of [DSE] losses . . . , improve the quality of [DSE] cadres and fighters through intensive training and political education. Second, break up the offensive thrust of the enemy in Peloponnesus, Roumeli, and Thessaly, give a bloody answer to the approaching enemy offensive against Grammos and Vitsi, follow this up with a strategic counter-offensive to throw the enemy back, and with a broad manoeuvre re-enter and liberate Epirus.[15]

But by January 1949 the DSE no longer possessed the strength to carry out such an ambitious plan.

While the Communist camp was going through the convulsions of a major crisis—as intimated by the removal of Markos—the Greek national forces had gained an added element of strength: Marshal Alexander Papagos was entrusted on 20 January 1949 with the supreme command of the Greek armed forces. The operation against Grammos in the summer of 1948 and the guerrilla attacks on Karthitsa, Naoussa, and Karpenision had revealed, at least to those in high positions, one of the major weaknesses of the national armed forces. There was no truly unified command. Ostensibly the supreme command was in the hands of the Chief of the General Staff. But his authority was curtailed by the interference of political groups, foreign advisers, and the inability of successive Chiefs to impose strict discipline over the major military commanders in the field. Most of the field commanders had been fellow-students with one another and with the successive Chiefs of Staff, with personal friendships and animosities. There were frequent and occasionally ill-considered replacements of general officers.[16]

Marshal Papagos, as the Commander-in-Chief in the Albanian campaign in 1940–1 and the only Marshal of the Greek Armed Forces, had attained a stature seldom achieved by any military leader in the history of modern Greece. A suggestion to place him in the supreme command of the armed forces was first discussed in government circles in the spring of 1948. Papa-

[15] *Pros tin III Synthiaskepsi tou KKE*, p. 117.
[16] Tsakalotos, op. cit., Vol. II, pp. 161, 177; also Vasilas, op. cit.

gos, thinking of his reputation, was unwilling to accept unless a number of steps were taken to prepare the ground for an all-out offensive. He participated as an observer in the operation in the summer of 1948 and kept in close touch with the military leadership and with General Van Fleet, the chief of the American mission. Many of his ideas were put into effect, both in the organization and training of the armed forces and in formulating the strategy for a staggered expansion of control.

The Greek Army, employing this strategy experimentally during 1948, had scored some victories, as in Roumeli, but had not succeeded in stamping out the Communist rebellion. At times the indecision of field commanders or even their unwillingness to carry out the orders of their superiors allowed the guerrillas to slip through the army lines and regroup in other mountain ranges. The DSE 'manoeuvre' from Grammos to Vitsi in the summer of 1948 had inevitably caused frustration. Its 'conventional' operations in Karthitsa, Naoussa, and Karpenision had showed that lack of effective co-ordination had robbed the Greek Army of precious opportunities to corner and destroy large guerrilla forces. It was clearly a question of leadership at the highest level. Papagos filled the bill. On taking over the reins he was given full authority, and he had the will and the ability to use it. Ineffective commanders were summarily removed, and those guilty of serious violations of military discipline were court-martialled. Within a few weeks a new spirit of aggressiveness and determination was instilled in the armed forces. It was clear to all that 'Papagos meant business'.

The first major success came with the guerrilla attack on Florina. Alerted by information obtained from a captured guerrilla, the new military leadership prepared not only for the defence of the town but also for a counter-attack. A guerrilla force of over 3,000 attacked in the early hours of 11 February. After some minor successes the guerrillas were pushed back. Then national forces, including tanks and armoured cars, brought in from adjacent areas struck against the guerrillas in a pincer movement. In the fierce fighting which followed more than 500 guerrillas were killed and over 350 were taken prisoner. With one-third of the force destroyed, the DSE command signalled a hasty retreat into the mountains towards the area of Vitsi.

Following this major success, the Greek Army pressed hard

on one area after another. 'Operation Pigeon' in Peloponnesus, which had started with mixed results in December, was pressed decisively, and, by 25 March 1949, of the 2,000 DSE troops there only a few scattered bands remained, hunted without respite by light infantry and gendarmerie units. This was another successful application of the strategy of staggered expansion of control.

The 2nd guerrilla division, which had withdrawn from Karpenision on 8 February, came under the relentless pursuit of strong Greek forces as it tried to move south into Roumeli. Other forces attacked the 1st guerrilla division, which had also taken part in the operation against Karpenision. Constantly hunted, the guerrillas had no chance to prepare and carry out any new looting and recruiting raids. Diamantis (Yiannis Alexandrou), the commander of the 2nd guerrilla division, was cornered in Roumeli in late June and killed. Finally, the remnants of the two divisions, broken into scattered bands, hungry and demoralized, reached the Grammos and Vitsi strongholds.

Similar operations were carried out with renewed vigour in other parts of Greece. The essential ingredients of success were the concentration of forces against selected areas, attack from many directions by day and night, relentless pursuit and extermination.

With most of Greece freed of Communist bands through methodical mopping-up operations, the Greek Army prepared for 'Operation Torch', the final assault against the two major Communist strongholds of Grammos and Vitsi.

In a last effort to rally popular support the KKE reshuffled the 'Temporary Democratic Government' on 5 April, and Dimitrios Partsalides became the new 'Premier'. Yiannis Ioannides, the Vice-Premier, who since Markos' resignation had served as 'Acting Premier', returned to his previous post. Petros Roussos became 'Minister of Foreign Affairs'; D. Vlantas, 'Minister of War'; V. Bartzotas, 'Minister of the Interior'; Leonidas Stringos, 'Minister of Economics'; K. Karayiorgis, 'Minister of War Supplies'; Dimitris Papadimitris (Agrotikon Komma Ellados), 'Minister of Agriculture'; S. Savidis (AKE), 'Minister of Co-operatives'; Miltiades Porphyrogennis, 'Minister of Justice'; P. Avelides (AKE), 'Minister of National Economy'; Dr. Petros Kokkalis, 'Minister of Health and Education'; G. Tsapakidis (AKE), 'Minister of Welfare'; Paskal Mitrofski (NOF), 'Minister of Food'; I. Vournas (AKE),

'Minister of Transport'; Apostolos Grozos (ERGAS), 'Minister of Labour'; Kraste Kotseff (NOF), 'Under-Secretary for National Minorities'.[17] The War Council—originally established in the spring of 1948—was reconstituted with N. Zachariades, Y. Ioannides, V. Bartzotas, D. Vlantas, G. Gousias or Georgios Vontissios, K. Karayiorgis, Kostas Koliyiannis, S. Ekiouzelis, G. Erithriades, Constantine Loulis, and Vangel Kotseff (NOF).[18] Neither the names of the 'ministers' nor the fact that an organization such as NOF was represented in the new 'government' could inspire much confidence to the average Greek. In fact, the pretentious titles of the 'ministers' sounded ludicrous, considering how little they had to administer. The reshuffle, instead of solving the problem of 'reserves' or undermining the morale of the national forces, merely strengthened their determination to stamp out the rebellion.

Tito's decision in July 1949 to close the Yugoslav–Greek frontier and discontinue all aid to the Communist guerrillas removed the possibility of their using Yugoslavia as a sanctuary to enable them to recoup and re-enter Greece with renewed vigour. Although they still had Albania as a convenient refuge and presumably could count on Bulgarian assistance, the stage was now set for the final act. The Communist leadership had manoeuvred itself into the unenviable position of having to face vastly superior conventional forces in conventional warfare.

Prior to commencing Operation Torch, the Greek Army conducted a preparatory operation against a guerrilla force in the Kaimaktsalan area to the north-east of Vitsi, on the Yugoslav border. By moving along the Yugoslav frontier on the Greek side, the Army outflanked the guerrilla contingent and captured substantial quantities of supplies and ammunition. Some guerrillas escaped into Yugoslavia, where they were disarmed by the Yugoslav authorities. The operation was successfully completed by 28 July. The ground was now fully prepared for Operation Torch.

The Greek Army's plan for the operation against Grammos

[17] The AKE (Agrarian Party of Greece) was a creation of the KKE without any independent standing. NOF was the new version of the wartime organization SNOF. ERGAS was the Communist-led labour organization.

[18] Of the various 'ministers', A. Grozos, Dimitrios Partsalides, and K. Koliyiannis are of special interest because they are the ones who pushed out Zachariades in 1957 and are now holding the reins of the KKE in exile.

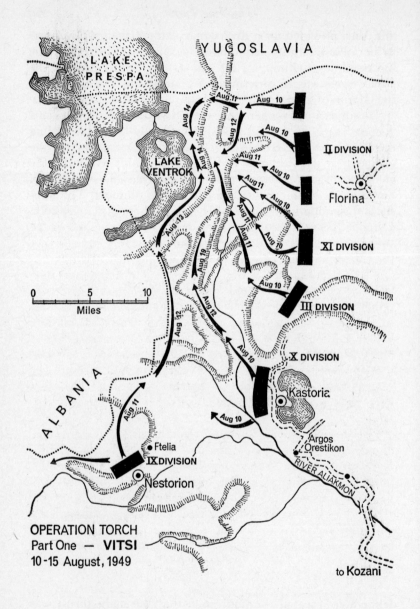

OPERATION TORCH
Part One — **VITSI**
10-15 August, 1949

and Vitsi provided for a diversionary attack against Grammos
to be followed by a major offensive against Vitsi. With the
successful termination of this phase, the largest part of the
Greek forces was to concentrate on an all-out assault against
the Grammos stronghold.[19]

The diversionary operation against Grammos started on 1
August 1949. In a swift operation, shortly before launching
the offensive, the Greek Army removed all villagers from the
villages near the Grammos and Vitsi strongholds, to deprive the
guerrillas of any potential source of information and supply.
For nine days the offensive proceeded as planned. The Supreme Command, using dive bombers and field artillery,

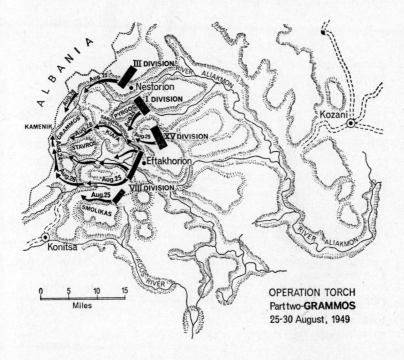

OPERATION TORCH
Part two-**GRAMMOS**
25-30 August, 1949

deliberately created the impression that the main thrust was
directed against Grammos—seemingly a repetition of the 1948

[19] Of the 17,000 guerrillas remaining in Greece by the end of July 1949, more
than 12,000 were concentrated in the Grammos–Vitsi area. The rest were scattered
in small groups, isolated and facing constant pursuit.

operation. The DSE strategists fell for the trick and concentrated their reserves on Grammos, leaving Vitsi relatively weak. Suddenly, on the night of 10 August, after heavy shelling, the Second Army Corps with five Divisions (II, XI, X, IX, and the III Division of Mountain Commandos) moved against the fortified Communist positions in the Vitsi mountain complex. With swift and deep penetrations, pincer movements, and frontal attacks, the Communist positions were blasted open and hundreds of *katsapliades* were killed, wounded, or captured.[20] The offensive on Vitsi had progressed with such speed that of the six guerrilla brigades only one managed to withdraw intact towards Grammos. In their flight the guerrillas left behind 39 artillery pieces, 33 anti-tank guns, 16 anti-aircraft guns, more than 100 mortars, more than 400 machine-guns, and great quantities of ammunition and food.

Ten days later, in the presence of King Paul, the First Army Corps, augmented by some of the units which had been brought in from the area of Vitsi, opened a broad attack from east and west on the guerrilla forces in Grammos. After fierce battles the Greek forces broke through the fortified positions of the DSE, and on 30 August, at five o'clock in the morning, the VIII Division reached the summit of Kamenik. The remnants of the guerrilla army beat a hasty retreat into Albania. By ten o'clock that morning all organized resistance in Grammos had ceased.[21] For all practical purposes the Third Round was over.

[20] According to Greek General Staff reports, guerrilla losses during the operation in Vitsi were 997 killed, 642 captured.

[21] The retreating guerrillas were reported to have left behind in both Vitsi and Grammos a total of 1,919 dead, 1,586 prisoners, 57 artillery pieces, 21 anti-tank guns, 19 anti-aircraft guns, 227 heavy machine-guns, 216 heavy mortars, 416 light machine-guns, 102 light mortars, 142 rocket launchers, more than 6,000 rifles, and large quantities of ammunition, supplies, and food-stuffs. Greek National Army casualties during Operation Torch were 472 dead, 2,568 wounded, and 14 missing. During the Third Round, 1946–9, the Greek armed forces, including the gendarmerie, suffered 16,753 dead, 40,398 wounded, 4,788 missing. In the same period the guerrillas burned 11,788 houses, destroyed 98 railroad stations, derailed 96 trains, executed 4,123 civilians, and carried out 1,611 major sabotage operations against bridges, tunnels, and railroad lines.

18. After the Defeat

Behind the Iron Curtain

The period since the end of the Third Round is much too near for any fully-fledged historical appraisal. One can only sketch the highlights. With the collapse of the front, the leaders of the KKE, followed by the pitiful remnants of the DSE, sought refuge inside neighbouring Albania; there, on 9 October, the 6th Plenum of the Central Committee went over the causes for the débâcle. They found in Tito a convenient scapegoat. Vassilis Bartzotas, in his report to the Plenum, asserted that the party,

primarily because of Tito's treachery, found it impossible to solve the DSE's basic problem of reserves, and the problem of supplying its forces in Central and Southern Greece; the DSE further proved unable to change the situation which Monarcho-Fascism had created in the towns, thus failing to co-ordinate a strong mass movement in the towns with the operation of the DSE in the mountains.[1]

Zachariades, too, in his book *Dheka Khronia Palis*, repeated the charges against Tito, but at the same time acknowledged that the real reasons for the defeat were the familiar problem of reserves (more accurately the unwillingness of the Greek people to rally around the KKE and DSE) and the inability of the KGANE—DSE forces in Central Greece—to engage the National Army and allow the DSE forces in Grammos and Vitsi to hold their positions 'and pass over to the counter-offensive'.[2]

The reasons given by Zachariades and Bartzotas were valid only in part. Their most basic error was the decision to start a guerrilla operation and then pass into the conventional stage at a time when the Greek Government, supported by American aid and with the great majority of the people united around the national leadership, was getting stronger and more stable every day. For obvious reasons, Zachariades and Bartzotas passed

[1] *Nea Katastasi kai ta Kathikonta mas* (Central Committee of the KKE, 1950), p. 9.
[2] Zachariades, *Dheka Khronia Palis*, p. 61.

silently over their own responsibility for the disastrous policies which had led to the routing of the Communists.

Now that the reasons for supporting Macedonian independence were no longer relevant, the 6th Plenum, with a mere stroke of the pen, gave up that slogan and returned to the less ambitious policy of support for 'the equal rights of the minorities'. Zachariades, in 1950, offered a disarming explanation for the repeated changes in party policy on this tricky subject.

The KKE [he wrote] recognizes the right of the Slavo-Macedonians, the right of the people of [Greek] Macedonia, to self-determination including separation. . . . The right of self-determination means that the nation has a right not only to autonomy but also to separation. . . . Now, depending on the situation and the interests of the proletarian struggle, of the Revolution, each time the Party promotes the one [autonomy] or the other [separation] side of the national question, because the national question is subordinate to that of proletarian revolution. The change of the slogan each time from separation to autonomy is dictated by the concrete interest of the Revolution. . . . When we say 'equal rights', we mean nothing else but autonomy in its true Leninist–Stalinist sense, that is political self-government.[3]

The statement speaks for itself.

The 6th Plenum outlined the 'duties' of the party in the wake of defeat. In a somewhat tragi-comic statement, considering that the fight was all over, it declared that 'the Party has decided to discontinue the armed struggle for the time being, leaving only small guerrilla detachments as a means of exerting pressure'. This was, in effect, a return to the strategy of sub-conventional warfare which Zachariades had bitterly fought against when it was advocated by Markos in 1948. This time such a strategy was even less realistic. Guerrilla bands have little chance of survival, much less of success, if they meet decisive, concerted, and well-organized resistance. In the autumn of 1949 the Greek Government was fully equipped to deal with any attempt to renew 'the guerrilla struggle'. Nevertheless the Politbureau, in a detailed decision on 14 November 1949, outlined the familiar guerrilla tactics and ordered the scattered small bands that remained in remote areas, hunted, hungry, and demoralized, to begin 'the struggle' anew. It never materialized. In the following months the few remaining bands were

---

[3] Zachariades, *Dheka Khronia Palis*, pp. 122–3.

liquidated one after the other. In the end the Communist leadership grudgingly recognized that the armed fight was definitely over and directed their followers in Greece to concentrate on political and subversive activities. It was clear that the novel situation in which the party found itself required new operational tactics. The KKE's new strategy evolved around two major objectives: the staging of a political come-back, under some convenient disguise, since the party remained outlawed; and the establishment of a network of clandestine communications with the scattered party forces within Greece to reorganize the illegal apparatus. Several small groups of agents, trying to slip into Greece across the frontiers with Albania or Bulgaria, were intercepted. Some of them carried expensive radio equipment. How many agents were able to elude capture is not known.

With the return to normal, Greece went to its first post.war election to be held in conditions of genuine peace. With the KKE label politically taboo, several Communists and sympathizers formed an electoral coalition called the 'Democratic Group'; in the elections of March 1950 the group succeeded in winning eighteen out of 250 parliamentary seats. Soon after the opening of the Parliament this electoral coalition broke up into factions, most of them unwilling to follow the KKE's directives.

On 14 May, when the 7th Plenum of the Central Committee of the KKE met behind the Iron Curtain, Zachariades, seconded by Vlantas and Bartzotas, presented a set of operational directives which were incorporated in the decisions of the Plenum. The emphasis was placed on 'illegal work'. At the same time the Plenum singled out the areas of legal activity still open to the party:

1. We must enter the existing [non-Communist] mass organizations and recruit party members from among their membership; we must use those organizations very cleverly.
2. We must create new mass organizations. To do so we must know what issues interest the masses at any time, and then we must find suitable persons who can take the initiative in forming such mass organizations; these organizations must avoid open Communist agitation so as not to expose themselves, thus allowing the enemy to take measures against them, including their dissolution.
3. Since the Party remains outlawed, we must not hang on the chest of each party member a sign saying that he is a party member;

whenever party members speak they should not say that they express the opinion of the Party, but they should present the party directives as their own personal views.

4. Whatever we cannot say openly to the masses we should say in illegal [clandestine] meetings, as well as through secret circulars.

5. We must never use in our illegal apparatus party members who are currently engaged in legal activities within the [non-Communist] mass organizations; we must preserve the illegal apparatus like the apple of one's eye. . . .[4]

The lasting significance of these operational tactics cannot be over-emphasized.

Defeat breeds dissension

The unity of purpose seemingly reflected in the clear-cut resolutions of the 7th Plenum was largely deceptive. The disaster could not but bring the inevitable party crisis as defeat had so often done in the past. Once the leaders of the party regained their composure in the safety of the People's Democracies, they began to search for the real causes of the débâcle. Timidly at first, with increasing boldness and intensity as the months went by, some members of the Central Committee, with Partsalides as their spokesman, began a campaign of criticism against Zachariades and his intransigent policies. It was mostly a whispering campaign behind closed doors. On the surface, at least, the criticism centred on the policy of 'United Front from below only' which Zachariades advocated and which, they felt, would prevent the remaining party forces in Greece from breaking through the smothering ring of political isolation. Zachariades quickly realized that the dispute over the united front tactics would not stop there; once his leadership was successfully challenged on one point, his past policies, which had led to the routing of the DSE, could not escape a searing review. At the 7th Plenum Zachariades, preparing the ground for the approaching purge, attacked his critics, and primarily Dimitrios Partsalides, and insisted that 'there can be no right of criticism, no democracy, no free expression for the enemies of the party, for the anti-party elements who seek to use criticism and democracy to damage, bankrupt, and liquidate the Party'.[5] He went on to say that:

[4] *Report* by D. Vlantas to the 7th Plenum of the Central Committee of the KKE, 4–18 May 1950.
[5] Zachariades, *Dheka Khronia Palis*, p. 171.

The KKE has remained ever faithful to the October Revolution which nursed it, to the Bolshevik party and to Marxism–Leninism, to Lenin and Stalin, who nurtured us and helped us to grow. . . . The [Russian] Bolshevik party always helped and supported us. This is why our devotion to it is boundless; this is why anyone who tries to strike at the KKE in effect undermines its ties with Bolshevism.[6]

By identifying himself with the KKE, and the KKE with the Communist Party of the Soviet Union and Stalin, Zachariades was cleverly exposing his personal critics to the charge of treason, or at least disloyalty to Stalin. At a time when those suspected of Titoist sympathies faced physical liquidation, his arguments had an ominous ring.

Zachariades proceeded with a purge on a grand scale. The crisis came to a climax during the Third Party Conference which convened in October 1950. It was preceded by a vicious attack on most of the party leaders who had carried the burdens of leadership during the historic decade of the forties. Zachariades, supported by Bartzotas and Vlantas, denounced such party stalwarts as Karayiorgis, Partsalides, Siantos, and Markos. In a torrent of invective published before and after the conference, Zachariades and his supporters provided the future historian with a mass of revealing details which shed new light on the tragic events of the preceding decade. The attacks were most savage against Siantos, long dead, and Markos Vafiades, absent from the Conference and unable to answer the charges. Siantos, the leader of the vaunted 'Resistance' movement of EAM/ELAS, was pronounced by Zachariades to have been a lifelong agent of the 'class enemy'. In a massive presentation of 'evidence' going back to the late twenties, Zachariades charged Siantos with outright treason against the party and the movement. Markos, whose removal from the leadership had up to that time been attributed to 'reasons of health', was ridiculed as 'an incompetent *arriviste* who had never been a true Communist in his life'.[7] These same leaders had received extravagant praise in the past—from Zachariades himself. They had played a leading role in the party's three major attempts to seize power by force. Their policies had caused untold suffering to the

[6] Zachariades, *Dheka Khronia Palis*, p. 197.
[7] *Pros tin III Synthiaskepsi tou KKE*, p. 137; see also *Neos Kosmos*, No. 11–12, November–December 1950, pp. 828–31.

country—and to the party following. Thousands had gone to their death with a blind faith in their leadership. Now, the families of those who had fallen under the party's banner were told that they had been deceived by false prophets. One was entitled to ask what proof there was that the accusers were not equally false and unreliable leaders. It would have been a legitimate question. Within the short span of five years a new group of 'leaders' would denounce Zachariades and his colleagues with equally devastating vehemence.

In 1950 Zachariades was aware of the risks involved in his massive attacks against those who had carried the burden of party leadership in the most critical period of its history. Yet he resolved that he could profitably use the familiar 'stab in the back' theory that Hitler had also used before him in a different context. The movement, he asserted, had been defeated because of treason from within, not because of the inadequacies of its ideology or the competence of its opponents. He was gambling, relying on the gullibility of the party following.

The crisis did not help the party in Greece. Yet it helped Zachariades and his group to remain the undisputed masters of the exiled members, after the Third Conference. In a period when dissident Communists in Eastern Europe were liquidated on the convenient charge of Titoism, Zachariades and his colleagues lived in the luxury of private villas, claiming to be avowed Stalinists 'with boundless loyalty to the Bolshevik party'. They were to feel the first shivers of uncertainty with the death of Stalin in March 1953.

One month after the famous anti-Stalin speech of N. Krushchev to the XX Congress of the CPSU, in February 1956, the Central Committee of the KKE met in what was billed as its 6th Plenum. It had been directed by the CPSU to purge the KKE of its own cult of personality. In the heap of fallen Communist idols Zachariades, Bartzotas, and Vlantas joined Siantos, Markos, Karayiorgis, and Ioannides who had been purged by Zachariades in 1953. A new Politbureau was elected with Apostolos Grozos, Dimitrios Partsalides, Kostas Koliyiannis, and Leonidas Stringos among its members. The new party leadership put an end to the 'sectarian' policy of a 'United Front from below only', and denounced the policies which had led to the defeat of the revolution in Greece. It was not a condemnation of the revolution itself, only a devastating criticism of the policies which had robbed the party of victory. The agreements of the Lebanon and Caserta were denounced as unnecessary capitulations at a time when the movement, they argued, had the means to seize power with the departure of the German army. The abstention from the elections of March 1946 and the subsequent decision to resume the armed struggle were attacked on the grounds that the party had embarked unwisely on that fateful move before trying to convince 'the masses' that there was no other way but the call to arms. More important for the future, the Plenum decided on a policy of 'United Front from below and from above', while it re-emphasized that the future revolutionary changes in Greece 'will have, at the outset, not a socialist but an anti-imperialist democratic character'. The significance of this last point lies in the fact that under this strategy the party espouses policies designed to attract wide social groups which have no interest in a 'socialist revolution'.

Zachariades, Bartzotas, and Vlantas were finally expelled altogether from the party in October 1957. These decisions, adopted by the 7th Plenum in the case of Zachariades and by the Politbureau in the case of Bartzotas and Vlantas, were approved formally only in October 1961 by the Eighth Party Congress.[8] This Congress approved also a decision of the 15th Plenum (1961) on the expulsion of Markos Vafiades, who for a short period had been reinstated as a member of the Central Committee after the downfall of Zachariades. With this, all the leaders in the momentous party drive for the seizure of power passed into oblivion by decision of their former colleagues and aides.

The change in leadership had no significant effect on the ultimate objectives or on the methods of the party. Its new programme, approved by the Eighth Congress, reiterated:

The Greek people will free themselves from every form of exploitation . . . through the socialist revolution, including socialization of the means of production. But in order to reach socialism, Greece must first be free from imperialist dependence and must carry out an anti-imperialist, democratic revolution. This is the true essence

[8] The present Politbureau includes Apostolos Grozos, Chairman of the Central Committee of the KKE; Kostas Koliyiannis, First Secretary of the Central Committee; Dimitrios Partsalides; Leonidas Stringos; Panayiotis Mavromatis; Z. Zographos; and Dimitriou.

of national democratic change, which is an imperative need for the country and which is becoming a nation-wide demand. National democratic changes can be achieved only through the struggle of the people under the leadership of the working class and its party, the Greek Communist Party.

The Communist Party, realizing that the overwhelming majority of the Greek people have no interest in Marxist–Leninist ideology and in a 'socialist revolution', lowered the ideological flag, and now advocates a less offensive intermediate stage. In a further effort to ease the fears of potential adherents, the party programme asserts—following in this the pronouncements of the CPSU—that its 'anti-imperialist, democratic revolution' will come about peacefully. But it hastens to add:

However, having in mind the desire of the plutocracy to remain in power at all costs by resorting to armed force and anti-parliamentary methods, the Greek Communist Party stresses the necessity for the people to be ready for the utilization of non-peaceful tactics to neutralize efforts by the plutocracy to use force to prevent the success of the popular will. In that case, responsibility for a non-peaceful development of events will exclusively fall on the plutocratic reaction.[9]

This statement has a familiar ring.

The new party programme does not conceal the real function of the 'anti-imperialist, democratic revolution'. This revolution, it declares, 'will deprive the foreign-dominated oligarchy of power, freeing the country from foreign rule, and, by achieving a democratic resurgence, will pave the way for the socialist reconstruction of Greek society'. Thus, after a full and disastrous cycle, the KKE has returned to the thesis enunciated by Zachariades in the famous resolution of the 6th Plenum in 1934.

The EDA story

The peace offensive which in the spring of 1950 preceded the Communist invasion in South Korea gave the KKE a seemingly innocuous subject for party activity in Greece. The

[9] The new programme of the CPSU similarly states: 'Lenin teaches, and historical experience confirms, that the ruling classes do not voluntarily give up power. The degree of bitterness in a class struggle under these conditions will not depend so much on the proletariat as on the strength of the resistance of the reactionary circles to the will of the overwhelming majority of the people, and on the use of violence by these circles at various stages of the struggle for socialism.'

party broadcasts from behind the Iron Curtain and the bold efforts of some fellow-travellers to generate public support for the peace movement hardly made a ripple. The peace offensive was part of the policy of 'active defence', meaning a policy of exploiting the numerous social and economic problems left by nearly ten years of war, occupation, and revolution. This policy was cleverly carried out by 'crypto-Communists' using the existing legal 'mass organizations'. There was a wave of labour strikes, yet the political gains of the party remained insignificant. The Communists, shunned by the other political forces in the country, found a convenient refuge in the policy of 'United Front from below only'. In their radio broadcasts from abroad they vehemently attacked 'the traitors of ELD/SKE, and the so-called democratic camp',[10] the 'Fascist' Sophocles Venizelos, the 'traitor' Papandreou, the 'dangerous demagogue' Nikolaos Plastiras.[11] In a way this policy advocated by Zachariades was not without justification. The party forces in Greece, dangerously weakened after the disaster, could not possibly expect to infiltrate and gain influence over the strong democratic parties. Many party members would probably leave the party and seek the satisfaction of their aspirations in the political activity of the non-Communist parties of the democratic Centre, or the mildly Socialist haven of ELD/SKE. Isolation appeared to be the best possible method for regrouping and reorganization. On the other hand, it is doubtful that a policy of 'United Front from below and from above', like the one supported then by Partsalides, would have borne any fruit. In the early years after the end of the Communist rebellion, association with Communism was politically quite unprofitable in Greece.

In 1951 this policy of 'United Front from below only' led to the establishment of a new 'mass organization' which was designed to provide the KKE with a vehicle for 'legal' political activity. This organization, known as the United Democratic Left (EDA), has ever since drawn the support of all those who for social and economic reasons tend to embrace the positions of the pro-Soviet, anti-Western Left.

After 1951 the history of the KKE moves on two separate, yet superimposed, planes. Abroad, it is a sorry tale of intrigues and

[10] Joint Decision of the Politbureaux of the CC of the KKE and the CC of the AKE, 9 March 1951.
[11] Vlantas, *Report*.

frustrated ambitions by revolutionary exiles—a story high-
lighted by Zachariades' resounding downfall in the spring of
1956. In Greece proper it is primarily the story of EDA.

For the first four years of its existence EDA, following faithfully in this the directives of the KKE, practised a policy of
'United Front from below only', later to be denounced by Constantine (Kostas) Koliyiannis, the present Secretary of the
KKE, as 'an inconsistent, leftist, contradictory, sectarian policy
which created difficulties in the practical work of the Party
and slowed down the development of the workers' democratic
movement'.[12] The EDA daily *Avgi*, protected by the laws which
permitted the activity of all other political parties except
the KKE, openly advocated the Communist line. For four
years EDA's political influence remained very limited. In the
elections of 1951, under a system of modified proportional
representation, it gained only ten seats in the 250-seat Parliament. In the following year, when a majority electoral system
was applied, EDA did not elect a single deputy to the 300-seat
Parliament.

EDA's political fortunes took a different course in 1956. The
turning-point came at the parliamentary elections of February
1956. By then, Zachariades was on the way out. His 'leftist,
sectarian' policy had failed to produce any tangible gains. The
group of Partsalides, Grozos, and Koliyiannis pressed successfully for a policy of 'United Front from below and from above'.
The KKE's directives to EDA for non-co-operation with other
political leaders were superseded by new instructions urging a
strong effort to establish an electoral coalition with the parties
of the Centre. EDA's leaders were only too happy to comply.
The previous policy had proved self-defeating. By limiting the
area of mutual concessions, EDA finally persuaded many important leaders of the Centre and even of the moderate Right to
join EDA, with their parties, in a 'popular' or 'patriotic' front
directed against Constantine Karamanlis, the energetic successor to Marshal Alexander Papagos—the Greek Premier since
1952, who had died after a long illness in October 1955.

EDA's efforts to form a coalition with non-Communist
parties were assisted by the electoral system itself. The new
Electoral Act provided for the majority system in certain con-

---

[12] *Report* by Kostas Koliyiannis to the Eighth Congress of the KKE, September
1961.

stituencies and the proportional system in others. Karamanlis' opponents decried this arrangement as a transparent attempt to falsify public feeling and assure an electoral victory for Karamanlis' party, the National Radical Union'(ERE). This, together with the realization that ERE would win a substantial majority if the candidates of the centre parties had to compete with both ERE and EDA, led many anti-Communist leaders, less than seven years after the end of the Communist rebellion that had ravaged Greece, to form an electoral coalition with the representatives of the Communist Party. This electoral coalition, known as the 'Democratic Union', received 48·15 per cent. of the popular vote in the elections of 19 February 1956, while Karamanlis' ERE received 47·38 per cent. Yet the intricacies of the electoral system favoured ERE, which in the end emerged with 165 deputies against 132 for the 'Democratic Union'. Of these 132 only eighteen deputies belonged to EDA.

That this popular-front type of coalition was merely a 'marriage of convenience' became obvious soon after the opening of the new Parliament. The coalition broke up and the parties resumed their independent courses. The whole affair left a bitter taste. True, the parties which had joined forces within the 'Democratic Union' had succeeded in winning a respectable number of seats in Parliament, plus a majority of the popular vote. But as the number of EDA deputies in Parliament clearly showed, the non-Communist members of the coalition could have attained in large measure much the same result by simply forming an electoral coalition without the Communist front-organization. As it was, EDA proved in the end to be the true beneficiary. After a long period of political isolation it had finally succeeded in breaking into the realm of political respectability.

There were—and still are—many opportunities for political agitation by EDA, particularly among the ill-paid workers, the groping intellectuals, the uncertain youth who remember the war years only as a dim childhood memory. In spite of a remarkable recovery, Greece still faces a host of economic and social problems which play into the hands of pro-Communist agitation. The income of large segments of the population remains quite low, particularly in agriculture, while wealth is concentrated in the hands of a relatively narrow economic élite. American economic aid has helped to improve the infrastructure of the economy but, directed as it was towards defence and long-range development projects, has been rather slow in finding direct reflection in the personal incomes of the lower strata of the population. Taxation falls heavily on the shoulders of the lower income groups as, even today, 78 per cent. of the state revenue comes from indirect taxes.[13] On the other hand, between 1952 and 1963 Greece has enjoyed an unusually long period of political stability. First under Marshal Papagos and then, after his death in October 1955, under Constantine Karamanlis, inflation has been to a large extent arrested, electrification has made spectacular progress, the tourist traffic has more than quadrupled, while since November 1962 Greece has been an associate member of the European Economic Community. These achievements are reflected in the nation's income. Since 1955 the national income increased by 69·8 per cent., from $1,973,000,000 in 1955 to approximately $3,350,000,000 in 1962. During the same period the cost-of-living index showed a real increase of only 13 per cent. Yet behind the glittering façade—mirrored in the interminable rows of sumptuous apartment buildings in Athens—Greece faces a host of economic and social problems; there is still a long way to go in bridging the gap which separates the small minority of the wealthy from a multitude of near-paupers.

In 1956 these social and economic cleavages were even more pronounced than they are today. After the election of February 1956 EDA, freed of its self-imposed isolation, proceeded vigorously with the adroit exploitation of economic and social grievances. Its efforts were greatly aided by another issue of major emotional force at the time, the Greek–Cypriot demand for Enosis (Union) with Greece. This was the one issue which commanded the unswerving support of the overwhelming majority of the Greek people. In the early days of the dispute (1953–6), especially before the downfall of Zachariades, the Communist slogan, faithfully echoed by EDA, was 'a free Cyprus united with a free Greece', the word 'free' meaning Communist-dominated. As most Greeks were unreservedly in favour of Enosis, the Communist slogan merely deprived EDA of any political gains it might have obtained from a more vigorous exploitation of this highly emotional issue.

---

[13] *Budget Report* by Spyros Theotokis, Minister of Economics, to the Greek Parliament, 31 January 1963.

With the removal of Zachariades from the leadership of the KKE in March 1956, the class-oriented slogan was replaced by more or less straightforward support for Enosis. Even without any social overtones, the Cypriot issue blended nicely with the larger Communist policy of 'anti-colonialism', offering vast opportunities for agitation against Greece's NATO allies. The policies of Britain, and after September 1955 those of Turkey, blocking Enosis, together with the indecisive attitude of the American Government, were in effect tailor-made for Communist exploitation. Needless to say, with the Greek people in such a highly-charged emotional state, the Communist agitation, unhindered by any considerations of allied unity, and prudently clothed in purely patriotic phraseology, was of wide appeal.

Following the XX Congress of the CPSU and the 6th Plenum of the KKE's Central Committee, which in March 1956 wrested the leadership from Zachariades, the party adopted a more moderate line on Greece's international affiliations, which definitely eased the task of the EDA spokesmen. I. Passalides and Efraimides, two of the leading EDA deputies in Parliament, spoke on 23 and 24 May 1956 and, to the astonishment of many of their listeners, suggested that NATO membership was not incompatible, for the time being, with closer relations with the Communist bloc. Krushchev's policy of relaxation in world tensions was thus finding its way into EDA's political pronouncements. The two EDA spokesmen added that Greece should establish closer economic relations with the countries of Eastern Europe and with the Soviet Union, which had offered to absorb some of the best Greek agricultural products. Moderation and flexibility opened up new opportunities for expanding EDA's political influence; these opportunities were exploited with vigour and imagination.

Strangely enough, the fact that the KKE remained outlawed eased EDA's path. While in effect pursuing pro-Communist policies, the leaders of EDA have been able to claim that their party is an independent political organization, unburdened by the objectionable record of the KKE. Because of this, thoughtful observers question the wisdom of keeping the KKE outlawed. They say that a return of the Communist Party to the political scene would lead either to the absorption of EDA by the KKE or to a fight between the leaders of EDA, faced with the prospect of giving up their positions and the returning KKE leaders, bound to claim their due. In either case, they say, the Greek electorate would finally have to deal directly with the Communist Party without the distracting smoke-screen of confusing labels. It seems to this writer that this line of reasoning merits careful consideration. A 'legalization' of the KKE would add few new dangers, as the party today carries on its subversive activities through its illegal apparatus, and its propaganda and agitation through EDA.[14] It may be objected that the influx of ten or twenty thousand expatriates—the rank and file now behind the Iron Curtain—will pose a serious challenge to the security and orderly political life of Greece.[15] This danger appears to be rather exaggerated. The Communists among them—known as they will be to the authorities—will find it fairly difficult to engage in subversive activities. Needless to say, many of these expatriates now in the Communist countries—particularly the abducted children, now young adults—may show an understandable reluctance to return to a country of which they remember very little, and in which they will have to start their life anew under somewhat unfavourable conditions. It is also to be expected that some among those returning from the Communist world will be disillusioned with the system and inclined to stay away from any active involvement in party activities.

The first major test of the flexible and expedient policies adopted by the KKE and EDA since 1956 came in the parliamentary election of May 1958. The KKE, from abroad, advised a policy of 'United Front from below and from above', even at the price of substantial concessions to the parties of the Centre. Apostolos Grozos, party chairman after the removal of Zachariades, even suggested in a broadcast from abroad that the KKE should not pose 'at this time as a condition for co-

---

[14] As an illustration it may be noted that in a three-month period—November 1960 to January 1961—EDA and its publishing agencies issued 111 volumes of various pro-Communist books with a total of 100,000 pages. In addition there are seven daily and weekly newspapers, and nine periodicals, circulating freely within the country. Moreover, they are in effect subsidized by the Greek Government, which provides all newspapers with newsprint at a substantial discount (*Sovietologia*, February 1961).

[15] There are reportedly at present 60,400 political refugees from Greece in the Soviet Union and other Eastern European countries, of whom 30,000 are children and old, disabled people. Of these, 5,690 are young adults of 17–21 years of age who have grown up in the Communist countries.

operation Greece's withdrawal from NATO'.[16] EDA's leaders felt that they were in a better position to evaluate the political realities in Greece and their own party's increasing influence. In their talks with the leaders of the Centre parties they insisted on a common platform, to include a declaration of opposition to the installation of missile sites in Greece, while they refused to agree to a statement that Greece would maintain its alliance with the West. On domestic issues, EDA followed without deviation the general directives of the KKE, concentrating on such unrealistic proposals as a 30 per cent. increase in salaries and wages and a 50 per cent. increase of all pensions. They added, of course, the familiar demands for an amnesty for all political prisoners and exiles, meaning in effect the return of Communists from abroad and the legalization of the KKE. The talks broke up, and EDA, co-operating only with some 'democratic personalities', went to the polls on its own. The Electoral Act for the elections of May 1958 gave added advantages to the party or coalition of parties winning the second largest portion of the national vote above a certain percentage. This provision was expected to improve the chances of the Centre parties. To everyone's surprise, EDA came second with 24·42 per cent. of the vote, thus capturing 79 seats in the 300-seat Parliament. Although its voting strength had increased by only 15 per cent. compared to the elections of 1956, its representation in the Greek Parliament had scored a more than 300 per cent. increase. This significant expansion of EDA's political influence did not mean, of course, that a sizeable block of the Greek electorate, particularly in the largest Greek cities, had suddenly become pro-Communist. It did indicate that many people were no longer content with the familiar excuses for unsatisfactory conditions and were willing to register their protest by voting for the EDA candidates.

ERE, the governing party, remained the strongest political organization, with 41·16 per cent. of the vote and 171 deputies in Parliament assuring a comfortable majority for governmental stability. EDA, thrust into the role of the 'leading opposition party' in the Legislature, found itself in a politically uncomfortable position. To remain true to its political and ideological concepts, EDA could not but reject all proposed legislation and denounce as inadequate and deceptive even

[16] *Avgi*, 11 April 1958.

those governmental proposals which were necessary to meet pressing economic and social problems. In the end, its opposition degenerated into sterile obstructionism.

Shortly before the elections of 29 October 1961, EDA, following in this specific instructions from the Eighth Congress of the KKE, made another attempt to form an electoral coalition with the parties of the Centre. The effort failed. Lefteris Apostolou, a former leading member of the KKE who has left the party, attributed the failure to two reasons.

The parties of the Centre [he wrote in *Eleutheria*] (*a*) fear that this co-operation will not be politically honest on the part of EDA, and (*b*) they suspect that behind this call for co-operation lies EDA's real objective of reaching power through this co-operation and, once in power, abolishing the democratic system as well as every democratic right of all those who do not accept its leadership.[17]

Apostolou implied that these fears were fully justified, and so they are. EDA has never made any serious effort to disassociate itself from the KKE or even mildly criticize its past policies. One can scan in vain the record of EDA's Second Congress, which convened in Athens in December 1962, to find any traces of independent thinking.[18] Throughout its history EDA has echoed the Communist line, whether it emanated from Zachariades or, after 1956, from his successors.

The parties of the Centre had another reason in October 1961 for shunning EDA's overtures. They were confident that this time, united in a coalition of their own, they had a strong chance of winning a majority in Parliament. These hopes were not borne out. The Union of the Centre received 34·3 per cent. of the vote and 107 seats, while ERE emerged with 49·6 per cent. and 169 seats. EDA, without the advantage of such emotional issues as the Cypriot question or the missile scare, fell to 15·1 per cent., with 24 seats. The parties of the Centre, astonished by the outcome, alleged that the results were rigged, and launched a stubborn campaign for new elections. EDA was only too happy to second the charges, which provided a convenient explanation for its substantial loss of voting strength.

The Centre parties were justified in their complaints, but not

[17] *Eleutheria*, 17 October 1961.
[18] *Avgi*, 9, 11, 12–18 December 1962.

the EDA. That this pro-Communist party was indeed losing ground as conditions in Greece improved became all too evident in the election of 3 November 1963, and even more so in the election of 16 February 1964. In this last parliamentary election EDA's candidates received only 14·3 per cent. of the total vote.

There is some evidence at the present time that certain elements in the KKE find the Soviet brand of Marxism–Leninism too mild and feel that the Chinese version is more in tune with their revolutionary aspirations. Living, however, in Eastern Europe and in the Soviet Union, most of them have to contain their revolutionary fervour. Officially, the KKE leadership is siding with Moscow in its quarrel with Peking.

Insiders also contend that there is another hidden conflict in progress. The leaders of the KKE, they say, suspect that EDA would like to become the sole representative in Greece of the so-called international Communist movement (at least of that part directed by Moscow), tacitly relegating the KKE and all its past follies to the scrap-heap of history. As long as the KKE remains outlawed the conflict need not come to a head. The KKE leaders have been away for more than fourteen years now. Potential followers of Communist ideology in Greece are bound to gravitate to the ranks of EDA. The effect of this is not hard to see. EDA, untainted by the KKE's sorry record, is a relatively better vehicle for the promotion of Communist objectives, especially in this period of peaceful coexistence. The KKE may remain outlawed on paper for ever, but Marxism–Leninism is not deprived of spokesmen in Greece. One need only read the published statements made at EDA's Second Congress.

Foretelling the future is admittedly a hazardous undertaking. Yet one may suggest that, with an acceleration of economic development in Greece, conditions will eventually emerge which will allow the Greek political leadership to deal more effectively with the appeal of revolutionary Marxism–Leninism. If the national leadership tackles with realism and consistency the major problem of a more equitable—and economically more productive—distribution of the increasing national wealth, the agitation for an 'anti-imperialist, democratic revolution' will find even less response among the public

288 *Revolution and Defeat*

than it does today. After all, as the record of the KKE expounded in this volume amply shows, the Greek people never followed the Communist lead except in desperation exploited through deceit.

Biographical Notes

1. Nikos Zachariades was born in 1902, at Nicomedia, in Asia Minor. Between 1922 and 1925 he studied in the Soviet Union at the Communist school KUTV. After graduating from the KUTV he came to Greece and became a leading member of the Salonika party organization. In 1926 he was prosecuted and convicted for his agitation in favour of a Macedonian state. Released from prison, he left again for the Soviet Union, where he remained from 1928 to 1931. In that year he was installed by the Comintern as the party's leader. In 1934 he became Secretary General of the KKE. Elected a parliamentary deputy in January 1936, he was arrested shortly after the establishment of the Metaxas dictatorship. He remained in prison till 1942, when he was transferred by the German occupation authorities to Dachau concentration camp. He was liberated by the Allies and returned to Greece in May 1945. After the collapse of the 1947 revolt he fled behind the Iron Curtain. Denounced in 1956 as a 'traitor' by the present leadership of the KKE, he was ultimately expelled from the party. According to certain reports, he is at present living somewhere near Moscow, working in a Soviet factory.

2. George Siantos was born in Karthitsa in 1890, son of a poor family of tobacco growers. His formal education did not go beyond fourth grade. He worked from the age of thirteen as a tobacco worker in Karthitsa. At the age of fifteen he became a member of the Tobacco Workers' Union and soon began to take an active part in strikes, demonstrations, and riots. He served in the Greek Army from 1911 to 1920, reaching the rank of sergeant. He joined the party in 1920, and was leading participant in the 'struggle without principles', 1929–31. In 1934 he became secretary of the Piraeus party organization, and proved particularly successful in the recruitment of new members. He was arrested in August 1936 and was exiled to the island of Anaphi. He escaped in 1937, but was again arrested in October 1939 and imprisoned in Corfu, where he remained till September 1941. He escaped while being transferred to Athens to stand trial. Elected Secretary of the Central Committee in January 1942, he became the leading figure of the party throughout the Occupation. He remained Secretary of the Central Committee and a member of the Politbureau after the return of Zachariades, till his mysterious death on 20 May 1947. In October

1950 he was denounced by Zachariades as a 'traitor' and 'an agent of the class enemy'.

3. D. Gyftodimos or Kostas Karayiorgis was born in 1906 in Khalkis, the son of a judge. He studied medicine in Athens, Berlin, and Paris (1927–34). A party member since 1927, he acted as correspondent to *Rizospastis* while studying abroad. He was arrested and exiled in 1936. He escaped in 1941 and became a member of the Central Committee of EAM, and later, in 1943, *Kapetanios* of the 16th ELAS Division in Thessaly. He served as editor-in-chief of *Rizospastis* after November 1944. He participated in the 1947–9 revolt and became Minister of War Supplies in the Temporary Democratic Government in April 1949, and also a member of its War Council. He was denounced by Zachariades in 1953. Karayiorgis died in 1958 somewhere in Eastern Europe.

4. Yiannis Ioannides, a barber by profession, was born in Volos, in 1901. A party member since 1923, he went to the Soviet Union in 1928 for medical treatment as a consumptive. He returned to Greece in 1931 after three years as a student at the KUTV. Arrested in 1936, he remained in prison till September 1942, when he was liberated by a guerrilla band from a medical centre at Moni Petras, where he had been sent for treatment. He was, with Siantos, one of the two most powerful individuals in the party's Central Committee and in EAM/ELAS during the Occupation. Ioannides became Minister of War in the Temporary Democratic Government during the 1947–9 rebellion. In 1953 he was denounced by Zachariades.

5. Markos Vafiades, or Markos, was born in 1906 at the village of Tosia in Asia Minor, one of seven children. His father, a teacher and minor public official, died in poverty in 1917, his mother in 1920. His formal education did not go beyond fourth grade. He started working as a labourer at the age of twelve. In 1923 he went as a refugee first to Constantinople and then to Salonika. In 1924 he moved to Kavalla, where he became a tobacco worker. In 1927 he joined the KKE and worked as a leading member of OKNE, the Communist youth organization. He was jailed for a year and a half in May 1932. Arrested again in July 1936, he escaped in September from the island of Ai Stratis. Arrested in November 1938 in Piraeus, he was exiled first to the island of Aegina, then to Acronauplia, and finally to Gavdos. He escaped in May 1941 after the collapse of Greece. During the Occupation he became *Kapetanios* of the 10th ELAS Division in Macedonia. In 1947 he became the military

commander of the Democratic Revolutionary Army (DSE) and in December 1947 Premier and Minister of War in the Temporary Democratic Government. In January 1949 he was relieved of all his posts as a result of his dispute with Zachariades. In October 1950 he was denounced by Zachariades as 'a Trotskyist, adventurer, and defeatist, who has never been a true Communist'. Restored briefly to Central Committee membership by the Grozos–Koliyiannis group, he was finally expelled from the party in 1961. According to some reports he now lives in Poland.

Bibliography

BOOKS

Anastasoff, Ch. *The Tragic Peninsula*. St. Louis, Blackwell Wieland, 1938.

Axioti, Melpo. *Apantisi se 5 Erotimata* (A Reply to Five Questions). Athens, Maris Press, 1945.

Barker, Elizabeth. *Macedonia: Its Place in Balkan Power Politics*. London, Royal Institute of International Affairs, 1950.

Bartzotas, Vassilis. *I Politiki Stelekhon tou KKE sta Teleutaia Dheka Khronia* (The Cadres Policy of the KKE in the Last Ten Years). Central Committee of the KKE, 1950.

Blueprint for World Conquest. Washington, Human Events, 1946.

Bolshaya Sovetskaya Entsiklopedya. Moscow, 2nd Edition, 1954.

Borkenau, Franz. *World Communism; a History of the Communist International*. New York, W. W. Norton, 1939.

— *European Communism*. London, Faber and Faber, 1953.

Capell, Richard. *Simiomata; a Greek Note Book, 1944–1945*. London, Macdonald, 1946.

Dafnis, Gr. *I Ellas metaxy thyo Polemon, 1923–1940* (Greece between Two Wars, 1923–1940). Athens, Ikaros, 1955.

Dheka Khronia Agones, 1935–1945 (Ten Years of Struggle, 1935–1945). Central Committee of the KKE, 1946.

Dhrakoulis, Maximos. *Ta Ikogeniaka tou KKE* (The Family Affairs of the KKE). Athens, 1949.

Djilas, Milovan. *Conversations with Stalin*. New York, Harcourt, Brace and World, 1962.

Eastman, Max. *Marx, Lenin, and the Science of Revolution*. London, George Allen and Unwin, 1926.

Glynos, Dimitrios. *Ti inai kai ti theli to Ethniko Apeleutherotiko Metopo* (The National Liberation Front, what it is and what it wants). Athens, 1944.

Houtas, Stelios. *I Ethniki Antistasis ton Ellinon* (The National Resistance of the Greeks). Athens, 1961.

I Enantion tis Ellados Epivouli (The Plot against Greece). Athens, Ministry of Press and Information, 1947.

I Nea Katastasi kai ta Kathikonta mas (The New Situation and our Duties). Central Committee of the KKE, 1950.

Kabaktsiev, Ch. *Balkanskaya Kommunisticheskaya Federatsia* (Balkan Communist Federation). Moscow, Gosizdat RSFSR, 1930.

Kabaktsiev, C., Boshkovits, B., and Vates, D. *Kommunisticheskiye Partii Balkanskikh Stran* (The Communist Parties of the Balkan Countries). Moscow, Gosizdat RSFSR, 1930.

Karayiorgis, Kostas. *Gyro apo to Dekemvri* (On the December Revolution). Athens, 'Ta Nea Vivlia', 1945.

Kommunisticheskii Internatsional pered VI Vsemirnim Kongressom (The Communist International on the Eve of the Sixth World Congress). Moscow, Partizdat, 1928.

Kommunisticheskii Internatsional pered VII Vsemirnim Kongressom (The Communist International on the Eve of the Seventh World Congress). Moscow, Partizdat, 1935.

Kousoulas, D. G. *The Price of Freedom; Greece in World Affairs, 1939–1953.* Syracuse, Syracuse University Press, 1953.

Lenin, V. I. *Selected Works.* New York, International Publishers, 1943–6.

Malainos, Miltiades. *I Tetarti Avgoustou; pos kai thiati Epevlithi* (The Fourth of August; How and Why it was established). Athens, 1946.

Myers, E. C. W. *Greek Entanglement.* London, Rupert Hart-Davis, 1955.

Nefeloudis, Vassilis. *Ellines Polemistes sti Messi Anatoli* (Greek Warriors in the Middle East). Athens, 'O Rigas', 1945.

Nenoff, Dragomir. *The Communist Party of Bulgaria.* MS. in the Library of Congress, Washington, D.C.

Outline History of the USSR. Moscow, Foreign Languages Publishing House, 1960.

Papakonstantinou, Th. *I Anatomia tis Epanastaseos* (The Anatomy of Revolution). Athens, 1952.

Papandreou, G. *I Apeleutherosis tis Ellados* (The Liberation of Greece). Athens, Elliniki Ekthotiki Etairia, 1945.

Petsopoulos, Yiannis. *Ta Ethnika Zitimata kai i Ellines Kommounistes* (The National Questions and the Greek Communists). Athens, 1946.

— *Ta Aitia tis Dhiagraphis mou apo to KKE* (The Reasons for my Expulsion from the KKE). Athens, 1946.

Pinson, K. S. *Modern Germany.* New York, Macmillan, 1954.

Postanovleniya IV Vsemirnovo Kongressa Kommunisticheskovo Internatsionala (Resolutions of the IV World Congress of the Communist International). Petrograd, Izdatelstvo K.I., 1923.

Pros tin III Synthiaskepsi tou KKE (Towards the III Conference of the KKE). Central Committee of the KKE, 1950.

Report; the Secretariat of the ECCI to the Fifth World Congress. Moscow, 5 May 1924.

Report; the Town Committee of KOA to the 6th Conference. Athens, KKE, 1945.

Rothschild, Joseph. *The Communist Party of Bulgaria*. New York, Columbia University Press, 1959.

Saraphis, Stefanos. *ELAS*. Athens, 1946.

Scott, Andrew M. *The Anatomy of Communism*. New York, The Rand Corporation, 1952.

Seventh Congress; Resolutions and Decisions. Moscow, Co-operative Publishing Society of Foreign Workers in the USSR, 1935.

Shmelev, N. C. *Shto meshaet razresheniyu gretskoi problemi* (What hinders the Solution of the Greek Problems). Moscow, Izdatel-stvo 'Pravda', 1949.

Stalin, J. V. *Problems of Leninism*. Moscow, Foreign Languages Publishing House, 1947.

Stavrides, El. *Ta Paraskinia tou KKE* (The KKE; Behind the Scenes). Athens, 1953.

Stratigiki kai Taktiki tis proletariakis Epanastasis (Strategy and Tactics of Proletarian Revolution). Central Committee of the KKE, 1946.

Sweet-Escott, B. *Greece: A Political and Economic Survey, 1939–53*. London, Royal Institute of International Affairs, 1954.

Swire, J. *Bulgarian Conspiracy*. London, Robert Hale, 1939.

Tezisi, Resolyutsii i Postanovleniya XI Plenuma IKKI (Theses, Resolutions, and Decisions of the XI Plenum of the ECCI). Moscow, Ogiz Moskovskii Rabochii, 1931.

Theses and Resolutions; adopted by the Third Congress of the Communist International. New York, Contemporary Publishing Association, 1921.

Theses and Resolutions of the Fourth Congress of the Communist International. Published by the CP of Great Britain for the Comintern, 1922.

The 22nd Congress of the CPSU; Proceedings, 1961 (mimeographed).

The New Party Programme of the CPSU, 1961 (mimeographed).

To 7o Synethrio tou KKE (The Seventh Congress of the KKE). Central Committee of the KKE, 1945.

To 8o Synethrio tou KKE; Proceedings, 1961 (mimeographed).

To Programma tis Kommounistikis Thiethnous (The Programme of the Communist International). Athens, Laiko Vivliopolio, 1932.

'To Programma tou Kommounistikou Kommatos Ellados' (The [new, 1961] Programme of the Greek Communist Party), approved by the Eighth Party Congress, October 1961; mimeographed copy.

Thirteen Plenum of the ECCI; Theses, Reports and Speeches.

Tsakalotos, T. I. *40 Khronia Stratiotis tis Ellados* (Forty Years a Soldier of Greece). Athens, Akropolis, 1960.

Tsatsos, T. D. *Ai Paramonai tis Apeleutheroseos* (On the Eve of the Liberation). Athens, 1949.

Tsouderos, E. I. *Ellinikes Anomalies sti Messi Anatoli* (Greek Conflicts in the Middle East). Athens, Aetos A.E., 1945.

Twelfth Plenum: Theses and Resolutions. New York: Workers Library Publishers, 1932.

Vasiki Kanones Epagrypnisis (Basic Rules of Vigilance). Athens, Komep, 1947.

Voithimata gia tin istoria tou KKE (Material for the History of the KKE). [Somewhere in Eastern Europe], Central Committee of the KKE, 1952.

Vouros, G. *Panagis Tsaldaris.* Athens, Elliniki Ekthotiki Etairia, 1955.

Vukmanovic, S. *How and Why the People's Liberation Struggle of Greece met with Defeat.* London, 1950.

Woodhouse, C. M. *Apple of Discord.* London, Hutchinson, 1951.

Ypsilon, *Pattern for World Revolution.* Chicago, Ziff-Davis, 1947.

Zachariades, N. *Dheka Khronia Palis* (Ten Years of Struggle). Central Committee of the KKE, 1950.

— *Kenourghia Katastasi, Kenourghia Kathikonta* (New Situation, New Tasks). Nicosia, Cypriot Edition, 1950.

— *O Kommounistis, Laikos Agonistis, Melos tou KKE* (The Communist, People's Fighter, Member of the KKE). KKE.

— *Provlimata Kathothigisis* (Problems of Leadership), mimeographed copy, 1950.

— *Theses gia tin Istoria tou KKE* (Theses for the History of the KKE). Athens, Central Committee of the KKE, 1945.

Zevgos, G. *I Laiki Antistasi tou Dekemvri* (The People's Resistance in December). Athens, 'O Rigas', 1945.

Zinoviev, G. *Mezhdunarodniye Perspektivi i Bolshevizatsia* (International Perspectives and Bolshevization). Leningrad, 1925.

OTHER PUBLICATIONS

Arkhio Ethnikis Antistasis (Archives of National Resistance); collection of EAM documents.

Avgi; the daily organ of EDA.

Dheltion; organ of the Central Committee of the KKE (1925–6).

Efimeris ton Sizitiseon tis Voulis; official record of parliamentary debates.

Ergatikos Agon; a Communist daily in Salonika.

International Press Correspondence; organ of the Comintern.

Kommounistiki Epitheorisi (Communist Review); the KKE's theoretical organ.

Praktika ton Sizitiseon; minutes of parliamentary debates.

Rizospastis; the daily organ of the KKE.

Collections of documents used by special permission.

Index

---

[1] Meetings not specifically mentioned in the text are listed here to complete the record.